Individuals, relationships & culture

Both biologists and social scientists have much to say about human behaviour. Yet attempts to combine their approaches to provide a deeper understanding of human nature have not so far been generally successful. This book offers a new and original way of bridging the gap between them.

The key to bringing the two approaches together is, Professor Hinde suggests, to recognise crucial distinctions between levels of social complexity (individuals, interactions, relationships and groups), whilst at the same time bearing in mind that all are processes in dialectical relations with each other and with the socio-cultural structure of institutions, beliefs, values, and so on. Professor Hinde argues that principles derived from ethology are essential for understanding some aspects of behaviour at the lower levels of social complexity, but has severe limitations at higher ones. This innovative approach will interest research workers, lecturers and students of psychology, biology, anthropology and sociology, as well as other readers seeking a comprehensive understanding of the nature of human social behaviour.

Themes in the Social Sciences

Editors: John Dunn, Jack Goody, Eugene A. Hammel, Geoffrey Hawthorn, Charles Tilly

Edmund Leach: *Culture and Communication: The logic by which symbols are connected: an introduction to the use of structuralist analysis in social anthropology*

Anthony Heath: *Rational Choice and Social Exchange: A critique of exchange theory*

P. Abrams and A. McCulloch: *Communes, Sociology and Society*

Jack Goody: *The Domestication of the Savage Mind*

Jean-Louis Flandrin: *Families in Former Times: Kinship, household and sexuality*

John Dunn: *Political Theory in the Face of the Future*

David Thomas: *Naturalism and Social Science: A post-empiricist philosophy of social science*

Claude Meillassoux: *Maidens, Meal and Money: Capitalism and the domestic community*

David Lane: *Leninism: A sociological interpretation*

Anthony D. Smith: *The Ethnic Revival*

Jack Goody: *Cooking, Cuisine and Class: A study in comparative sociology*

Roy Ellen: *Environment, Subsistence and System: The ecology of small-scale formations*

S. N. Eisenstadt and L. Roniger: *Patrons, Clients and Friends: Interpersonal relations and the structure of trust in society*

John Dunn: *The Politics of Socialism: An essay in political theory*

Martine Segalen: *Historical Anthropology of the Family*

Tim Ingold: *Evolution and Social Life*

David Levine: *Reproducing Families: The political economy of English population history*

Individuals, relationships & culture

Links between ethology and the social sciences

ROBERT A. HINDE

Royal Society Research Professor
in the University of Cambridge

CAMBRIDGE UNIVERSITY PRESS

Cambridge

New York   New Rochelle   Melbourne   Sydney

Published by the Press Syndicate of the University of Cambridge
The Pitt Building, Trumpington Street, Cambridge, CB2 1RP
32 East 57th Street, New York, NY 10022, USA
10 Stamford Road, Oakleigh, Melbourne 3166, Australia

First published 1987

Printed in Great Britain by Bath Press, Bath, Avon

British Library cataloguing in publication data

Hinde, Robert A.
Individuals, relationships & culture:
links between ethology and the social sciences.
– (Themes in the social sciences).
1. Sociobiology.
I. Title. II. Series.
304.5 GN365.9

Library of Congress cataloging in publication data

Hinde, Robert A.
Individuals, relationships & culture.
(Themes in the social sciences)
Bibliography.
Includes index.
1. Human behavior. 2. Sociobiology.
3. Human biology – Social aspects. I. Title.
II. Title: Individuals, relationships, and culture.
III. Series. IV. Title: Ethology and the social sciences.
HM106.H55 1987 304.5 87-5220

ISBN 0 521 34359 3 hard covers
ISBN 0 521 34844 7 paperback

CE

Contents

Preface

The current division between the biological and social sciences has the unfortunate consequence of implying a clear distinction between the biological and social sides of human nature. Yet attempts to understand the relations between biological and social factors in human behaviour, attempts that go back at least to Darwin (1871, 1872), have certainly not met with general acceptance. Indeed, as knowledge accumulated and opinions became entrenched, for a long while it seemed increasingly improbable that any general agreement could be reached. Recently, however, the possibilities for progress have appeared brighter. This book is intended as a further step, or rather two simultaneous and inter-related steps, towards that distant goal.

One involves the recognition that the study of social behaviour requires distinctions between successive levels of social complexity – interactions, relationships, and group and socio-cultural structure – and at the same time a willingness to see them not as entities but as processes, with dynamic and dialectical relations between them. There is now a growing sub-discipline involving the study of interpersonal relationships which is helping to close the hiatus that social scientists had left between their studies of individual attitudes, etc., and those concerned with group dynamics. It is becoming apparent that a 'relationships' approach is crucial for many issues in the social sciences, including the understanding of how individuals affect and are affected by the societies in which they live. This approach is even more important for attempts to build bridges between the biological and social sciences. Whilst it would certainly be unfair to caricature biologists as talking about individual behaviour and culture-wide religious beliefs in the same breath, as if they were equally 'close' to their biological determinants, there would be an element of truth in it. Any attempt to apply biological principles to human social behaviour must respect the dialectical relations between successive layers of social complexity.

That brings us to the second step. To discover new territory scientists must set out from a known home base. Partly for that reason, biologists are prone to focus on biological factors affecting human behaviour, whilst many social scientists point to the social ones. Both are one-sided views, and the emphasis here is on the two-way influences between them acting through the successive levels of social complexity.

There is a related reason why biologists and social scientists tend to look at the same phenomena from different directions. Many biologists become interested in what is general about human behaviour, and particularly in how it differs from that of other species, whilst many social scientists are concerned with differences between individuals, groups or cultures. Perhaps, then, liaison can be established through the study of 'human universals'? 'Oh no', says the social scientist, 'there are no human universals, at least only at a very simple level that does not greatly interest us.' But, as we shall see, resolution of that issue brings us again to the dialectical relations between individual behaviour and the successive levels of social complexity.

Biologists interested in human behaviur are not concerned only with its evolution, but they do tend to see the theory of evolution by natural selection as one of their most powerful integrating tools. This has led to a heated controversy; and whilst this book is not about the sociobiology debate, it inevitably obtrudes. In brief, whilst I agree with Wilson (e.g. 1978, 1984) that an evolutionary perspective provides important insights, I agree also with Gould and Lewontin (1979) that such an approach is easily over-used, and that it readily lends itself to after-dinner flights of fancy. The crucial task is to define the limits of its usefulness. In brief, I suggest that it may be valuable when applied to basic human propensities, that it can be revealing when applied to relationships, but is of much more limited value when applied to the sociocultural structure.

Discussion of human behaviour in terms of biological evolution is often criticized because it is open to political interpretation or misinterpretation: it is implied that we should not discuss issues if misinterpretation of the discussion might have socially undesirable consequences. This is a view with which I disagree. If a given perspective has social implications we must pursue it: if there are biological factors mitigating against our building the sort of world we would like to build, it is urgent for us to know about them, understand them and learn how to circumvent them. We must bear the paucity of the evidence constantly in mind, and at the same time be continuously ready to grapple with the possibilities that are revealed.

Since I am hoping to make only a few specific points about links between biological and social sciences, I have not attempted to provide a comprehensive review of relevant material: the discussion covers rather a wide span, and it seemed preferable to illustrate each issue with just one or two examples.

In coming to terms with the determinants of human behaviour, biologists maintain that the study of animal behaviour can be of some use. This question is discussed in Chapter 1, where it is argued that direct comparisons between animal and human behaviour are dangerous, but principles drawn from the study of animals can be valuable. This does not mean that studies of animals play a major part in what follows: I have drawn also on developmental and social psychology, anthropology and psychiatry. But because principles derived from studies of animals are sometimes dismissed out of hand by social scientists, the matter merits special consideration.

The relationships approach, and the levels of social complexity, are introduced in Chapter 2. Some principles throwing light on the causation and development of social behaviour are discussed in Chapters 3, 4 and 5: many of the principles discussed are drawn from studies of animals, but emphasis is placed on the social and culture-specific environmental influences affecting human development. Chapters 6 and 7 take up the question of so-called human universals at the levels of individual behaviour and inter-individual relationships respectively: the examples are selected to show the value of integrating the approaches of the biologist and the social scientist. Some aspects of the higher levels of social complexity are discussed in Chapter 8, where an attempt is made to show that understanding of phenomena at each level requires an appreciation of the dialectics between levels. Finally, the extent to which the biologist's functional approach can and cannot be useful at the higher levels of social complexity is discussed in Chapter 9.

The description of this book as involving but two steps towards a distant goal was a deliberate one. There would be no difficulty in pointing to tasks yet to be tackled. But a better description would have been two faltering steps. As an erstwhile biologist and aspiring social scientist, I am conscious of shortcomings on both sides of the gap I am trying to bridge. Furthermore, in trying to write for two groups of readers, I am only too aware that much of what I have written will seem like naïve truisms to one or other. Any attempt to build a bridge requires firm foundations and my debt to a number of other authors will be abundantly apparent in the text. Beyond that, whilst all deficiences are my own, I have been helped by the critical and constructive comments of Patrick Bateson, Monique Borgerhoff-Mulder, Tim Caro, Jack Goody and Joan Stevenson-Hinde.

Finally, some of the material in Chapter 6 has been amended and updated from *Biological Bases of Human Social Behaviour* (1974, McGraw-Hill); and some of that in Chapter 7 from articles in *Frontiers of Infant Psychiatry*, Vol. 2, eds. J. D. Call, E. Galenson & R. L. Tyson, M. D. (Copyright © 1985 by Basic Books Inc., Publishers. Reprinted by permission of the publishers) and in *Journal of Social and Personal Relationships*, Vol. 1 (1984, Sage).

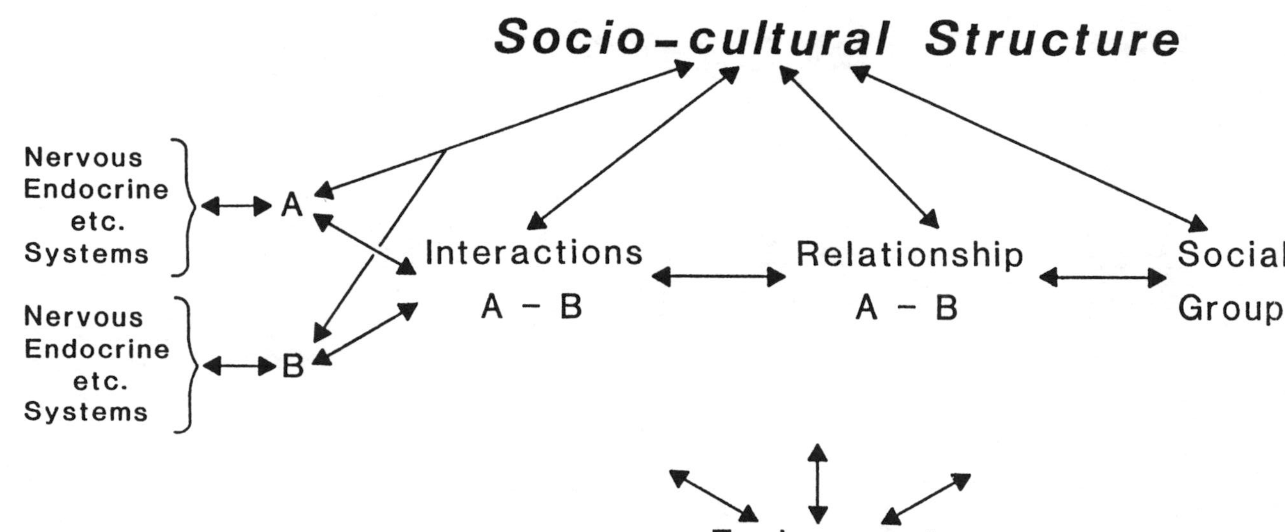

Fig. 1 The dialectics between successive levels of social complexity

1

The biological perspective

ANIMALS AND HUMANS

The two principle themes in this book are closely inter-related. One involves the view that full understanding of human nature requires the judicious use of a biological perspective, though this is not to be understood as one involving direct comparisons between man and animals, or as one concerned merely with the evolution[1] of behaviour. The second is that the integration of biological with more conventional approaches requires clearer understanding of the relations between successive levels of human social complexity than have been apparent in the writings of biologists, or indeed of many social scientists, in the past. This chapter introduces the first of these themes.

Many social scientists are, with some justice, resistant to the view that studies of animals can contribute to the understanding of human behaviour. Much of this book is concerned, not with proving them wrong, but with showing that they are only partially correct, and with specifying the sorts of contributions that ethology can make, in certain limited but important ways, to the human social sciences. Indeed it goes further than that, for the argument implies that a view of mankind that neglects the biological perspective is necessarily not merely impoverished but also inaccurate. It should be taken as a plea for what is (at any rate in the author's opinion) a balanced view, a view that rejects on the one hand biological determinism, and on the other the insistence by some social scientists that we are above biology.

Although parts of this book apply principles derived from an animal-based ethology to our own species, for most readers it will be unnecessary to emphasize that human behaviour is much more complex than, and in some ways fundamentally different from, that of any animal. However,

[1] In this book the term 'evolution' is used in a biological sense, and implies genetic changes. Social scientists often use it more broadly to refer to any form of directed change.

misunderstandings do arise, and it seems worthwhile to devote part of this first chapter to considering some limitations of ethology, which has its roots in the study of animal behaviour, for the understanding of human behaviour. Much of the rest of the book is concerned with the contributions it can make.

(i) *Differences in cognitive abilities*

The first and obvious issue is that human cognitive abilities are very much superior to those of any animal. The increased brain size and longer period of development permits greater phenotypic (including behavioural) variability, and thus more capacity to adapt to circumstances (Changeux, 1983). More importantly, every human group has a spoken language much more complex than the signal system of any animal, and this in itself sets humans apart from all other species. The capacity for language has further consequences for cognition, permitting the individual to manipulate symbols in a manner that would not be possible without language. Indeed it is a reasonable assumption that, in adult humans, all behaviour is in some sense social, since it depends upon internalized previous social experience. Furthermore language permits communication with other individuals about events distant in space and time and, perhaps even more important, about their own thoughts and feelings (Humphrey, 1986; Burling, 1986). This last capacity provides further opportunities for cognitive development through understanding of the difficulties experienced or solutions achieved by others.

No animals show behaviour approaching this complexity. Of course all animal species are capable of inter-individual communication, and it may be that the higher apes are capable of a degree of symbolic communication that approaches in some limited respects human language. Chimpanzees have been taught a sign language in which words are represented by gestures of the hand and arm, and are able to combine signs into 2–5 word sequences (e.g. Fouts, 1975). A chimpanzee has learned to use 120 plastic shapes to represent words (Premack, 1978) and another has learned an artificial grammar through a computer keyboard which displayed word symbols on a screen (Rumbaugh, 1977). However their abilities are limited, especially in the capacity to coin new phrases (e.g. Terrace, 1979), and there is no evidence that any animal has a linguistic ability comparable to our own. Although research continues to reveal new subtleties in the behaviour of many species, and it is clear that some operate at a much more complex cognitive level than has been suspected hitherto (e.g. de Waal, 1982; Kummer, 1982; Goodall, 1986), yet none comes near the human level.

This difference in cognitive level means not only that men and women do things that animals cannot do, but also that apparent similarities between human and animal behaviour can be deceptive. For example, parallels have been drawn over the effects of crowding. High densities can bring a deterioration of behaviour, and inter-individual aggression, in both rats and humans. However, the extent to which an individual human is affected by crowded conditions is markedly influenced by how much sense he can make of the situation. In an ingenious experiment Chandler (1985) placed children armed with rulers in a small room and asked them to arrange themselves in order of height. The groups contained children at different stages of cognitive development. Some had as yet no notion of relative size. Others could order by magnitude objects that could be directly compared, and successfully seriate by height things that could be stood back to back. Yet others were capable of unit measurement, being able to use rulers to assess the relative size of objects that could not be compared directly. The experiment was conducted under two conditions – namely with a flat floor and with a floor with a number of irregular steps in it so that it was at several levels. The children were more disturbed (as assessed by a variety of psychological and physiological measures) in the latter situation than in the former. But how disturbed they were was related also to their level of cognitive development. Children experiencing an irregular floor who lacked unit measurement skills failed in their efforts to find or recognize their place in the emerging social organization, and experienced the room as crowded. In brief, experience of crowding was related to how much sense they could make of the situation. Now making sense of the situation may be important also to rats, but the issue has been totally neglected in animal experiments, perhaps because the sort of sense rats can or do make of such a situation is likely to be very different from the children's, and in any case there is no clear way for us to find out about it. Thus simple comparisons are likely to be misleading.

(ii) *Culture*

The second issue, closely related to the last and indeed depending on the capacity for language, is the possession of discrete 'cultures'. The precise definition of culture is notoriously difficult (see note 2). When we talk about human cultures, we refer to differences between societies in such matters as the tools and other artefacts made, their knowledge of and beliefs about nature, their cosmology, customs, values, laws and so on. These are matters that, by or large, do not apply to animals, and we can thus speak of the possession of 'culture' as being a uniquely human attribute. Of course this does not imply that 'culture' is uniform across human groups: indeed it is better regarded as a convenient label for many of the diverse ways in which human practices and beliefs *differ between groups*.

Biologists sometimes claim a sort of proto-culture for animal species on the grounds that they have traditions, concerning for instance methods of obtaining food, that are passed on from individual to individual. A frequently cited example is the troop of Japanese monkeys in which one individual 'invented' a technique for washing sand off potatoes, and another technique for separating grain from sand by throwing it onto the surface of the sea and allowing the sand to sink: these techniques spread through the troop and are being handed down to successive generations (Kawamura, 1963). Again, the making of tools, formerly regarded as a specifically human ability, is well-known in chimpanzees and other species (Goodall, 1986). Furthermore tool use requires a great deal of practice (Schiller, 1957) and chimpanzee groups differ in the sorts of tools that they make and use: for instance the use of hammer and anvil to open palm nuts, widespread in parts of West Africa, is unknown at the Gombe Stream in Tanzania (McGrew, 1985). But the existence of these traditions (see also Mainardi, 1980) does not imply culture in the sense in which human societies have cultures.[2]

[2] A terminological note is necessary. Culture is used in this book to refer to those ways in which human social groups (or sub-groups) (see footnote p. 24) differ that are communicated between individuals. For instance the capacity for a spoken language is not a cultural phenomenon, but differences between languages are. It is acknowledged that there is a potential difficulty in putting the emphasis on differences because, by this definition, a characteristic possessed by all groups except one would be a cultural characteristic, whilst a characteristic possessed by every single group would not. However this purely theoretical difficulty is of minor importance compared with those that arise from ascribing a particular mechanism (such as learning) to the acquisition of cultural characteristics. For instance, if there were common features of all languages that owed their existence to the fact that gravity acts 'downwards', or that causes precede effects (in so far as that is not a matter of definition), these features of languages would not be aspects of culture even though learning were involved in their acquisition.

'Culture' can be used in a descriptive sense, to refer to the artefacts, customs, institutions, myths etc. as described by an outsider (or indeed by a member of the society). Such a description, however, tends to imply a static whole external to individuals. In practice culture is best viewed as existing in the minds (separately or collectively) of the individuals of a society and as in a continuous process of creation through the activities of individuals in their relationships. Of course individuals differ somewhat in their perceptions of the customs and so on of their society,and those differences can be an important source of creative change (cf Goody, in press: Barth, in press). Whilst 'culture' often refers to features common to all (or most) individuals, it must not be forgotten that aspects of the culture may be the special responsibility of particular categories of individuals. With this admittedly mentalistic view, the actual artefacts, institutions, myths etc. are seen as expressions of the culture. Of course they may in turn act back upon and influence culture in the minds of individuals.

The customs, institutions, myths etc. of a society are inter-related in diverse ways (see Chapters 8 & 9). Thus here the whole – the parts and relations between them – are referred to as the 'Sociocultural structure'. Again, the sociocultural structure can be described, but it is not an entity and exists only in the minds of individuals (at least in non-literate societies: the

Thus the human language-based capacity for culture has consequences much more fundamental than those of these animal traditions, affecting virtually all aspects of our behaviour and experience. The manner in which we perceive the world depends upon acculturation within the society in which grew up. The particular language used in that society plays a major role in the manner in which we group our percepts into categories. Language-based culture permits the members of each group to share linguistic symbols that impose order on the world, and that classify natural phenomena in ways that are more or less specific to that group, and different from those found in other groups. Language-based culture permits the concepts thus formed to be manipulated to make higher-order concepts, including deities and fictitious creatures and myths that have no direct correspondence with the real world. Furthermore the belief systems that unite these concepts and relate them to behaviour in the real world are adjusted to minimize contradictions – at least within each of the several domains of life (cf Goodenough, 1963). (But, to anticipate later chapters, nothing that is being said justifies a view of 'culture' as a force uniquely *determining* the nature of concepts, beliefs, etc.).

Perhaps most important of all, the language-based capacity for culture permits the labelling of relationships between individuals, and the classification of such relationships into types. This permits the existence of a limited set of roles, involving specified rights and duties, within institutions within each society. Thus 'husband' and 'wife' are roles, each with its specified rights and duties (some obligatory and some merely expected, and differing between societies), within the institution of marriage. In British society Prime Minister and Member of Parliament are roles in the institution of Parliament. Non-human species have no such roles or institutions. The term 'role' has sometimes been applied to non-human species to refer to individuals who perform a particular function with respect to the group as a whole – for instance, the 'leadership role' or the 'lookout role' (e.g. Gartlan, 1968). However in the human case 'roles' are internalized as goals and thus causes of behaviour ('He tried to play the role of good husband') as well as referring to the consequences. This implies an ability to conceptualize the role, and there is as yet no substantial evidence that such an ability is shared by

advent of literacy is likely to be an important issue here (Goody, 1968)). Real-life relationships within the group may or may not have counterparts in the socio-cultural structure, and idealised relationships in the socio-cultural structure may be realised to only a limited extent in actuality. The socio-cultural structure as perceived in the consciousness of individuals has a regulatory function. Thus the socio-cultural structure affects group structure, relationships and individuals. However, as we have noted, at the same time it is to be seen as continuously being created by the activities of individuals in their relationships.

non-human species. Of course pairs are formed in non-human species, and in some cases their maintenance may be affected by their reproductive success, but this does not imply an institution of marriage with its constituent roles, each with their attendant rights and duties. Apparent similarities can be misleading, and thus great care is necessary in specifying where parallels can validly be drawn.

This problem arose in an acute form in the study of non-verbal communication. Human spoken language is accompanied by a variety of non-verbal signals that augment or qualify its meaning. Thus we may raise or lower our voice, accentuate certain words, gesticulate, raise our eyebrows and so on. In addition, we use non-vocal signals in the absence of words. We smile, frown and so on. Indeed we may use the two in association: the doctor who welcomes his patient with a smile and by rubbing his hands together as he says 'Well, what can I do for you?' is both making a genuine enquiry and conveying the message 'I'm a very competent doctor and you can trust yourself in my hands.' Now biologists have also been interested in non-verbal communication, for animals use postures, vocalizations and other signals in situations of aggression, courtship and so on. Inevitably, parallels were drawn between the non-verbal signals used by animals and humans. These parallels were reinforced by the finding that some human non-verbal signals, such as smiling and crying, develop normally in children born deaf and blind, so that imitation and most forms of learning cannot be essential to their development. Although most biologists were careful in their claims, acknowledging that 'Many of the expressive movements in man are certainly passed on by tradition' (Eibl Eibesfeldt, 1972), others overstated the role of genetic factors and as a result some anthropologists fiercely resisted the view that there could be anything in common between animal and human signals. Thus Leach (1972) wrote "'Qui dit homme, dit langage, et qui dit langage, dit société' (Lévi Strauss 1955; 421). This is a viewpoint which I share, and which leads me to an extreme scepticism about the alleged similarities between the communicative processes of men and other animals" (Leach 1972, p. 317).

Partial resolution came through a classification of human non-verbal signals by Ekman and Friesen (1969) which emphasized that some were pan-cultural, and developed independently of specific experience, in these respects resembling many (but not all) animal signals, whilst others were culture-specific or even idiosyncratic, and acquired by individual learning. Beyond that, even those that are pan-cultural may be modified by learning and all may carry culture-specific subtleties of meaning of a sort as yet unknown in animals (see pp. 87–98). Indeed many (and some would say all) human activities that at first sight appear to have merely practical significance also carry a symbolic meaning which can often be understood only in relation to the social experience of the individual and to the structure of the society. This means in turn that the analysis of behaviour in man is very much more complicated than in any animal: only rarely can behaviour in a social situation be interpreted in terms of a specific motivation.

Such issues are of particular importance in later chapters. We shall see that many of the misunderstandings between biologists and social scientists have been due to inadequate attention to the dialectical relations between characteristics of individuals, and especially their pan-cultural propensities, and the successive levels of social complexity.

(iii) *The problem of diversity*

The third limitation on the utility of animal/human comparisons arises from the very diversity of animal species and human cultures. There is a very large number of species of animals, each with a behavioural repertoire adapted to its own peculiar way of life. There is also a not inconsiderable number of human cultures. It is thus not too difficult to find parallels between animal and human data that will support practically any thesis. Straight comparisons between particular aspects of animal behaviour and particular human characteristics are almost bound to be misleading.

Indeed there is diversity to reckon with even within the species. Aggressive behaviour is a case in point. Some biologists have been happy to draw lessons about our own species from the study of animals. They forget that there is a variety of types of aggressive behaviour on both sides. Let us define as aggressive behaviour those behaviours directed towards causing harm to another individual. Most vertebrate species show aggressive behaviour in a variety of contexts – for instance in defence of territory, food, young, mates etc. The aggressive behaviour shown in each case may differ in a number of ways – in the eliciting situation, the motivating conditions, the motor patterns used, and so on (Moyer, 1968). Man also shows a variety of kinds of aggression. Amongst children, at least four types have been recognized: instrumental aggression, directed towards securing some object or situation; hostile or teasing aggression, with no such objective; defensive aggression appearing in response to an attack; and games aggression, escalating out of rough-and-tumble play. Again these differ in a variety of ways – the motivating circumstances, the methods used, their association with other types of behaviour in the individual, their ontogenetic course, and so on (Feshbach, 1970). In adults aggressive behaviour is even more diverse:

indeed the diversity is so great that there is no general agreement as to how it should be categorized. One system for subdividing the use of violence by adults includes: instrumental or planned aggression; emotional aggression; felonious aggression, committed in the course of another crime; bizarre or psychopathic violence; and dyssocial violence, approved of by the reference group (Tinklenberg & Ochberg, 1981).

In view of this diversity, even if the differences in cognitive level are taken into account (see above), it is clear that generalizations between human and animal aggression must be treated with great caution. This is especially the case with discussions involving modern warfare. Aggressive disputes between groups of individuals are extremely rare in animals, though cases are known – some, indeed, in the higher primates (Goodall, 1986). Whether useful parallels can be drawn between these and war between non-industrialized human groups is at least problematic – though Durham (1976) has argued that the incidence of war in small stateless societies is compatible with the view that individuals maximize their survival and reproduction by participating in collective aggression when access to scarce resources is at stake. But parallels between war amongst such groups and war as now conceived in the western world would be totally erroneous. Aggressive disputes between neighbouring non-industrialized societies usually involve relatively small numbers of individuals, confronting each other face to face, with leaders often actively involved in the fray, and with the combatants on the two sides often personally known and even related to each other. A variety of mechanisms operate, though of course not invariably with full success, to minimize the number of casualties. Modern industrialized warfare, by contrast, is concerned with access to resources or to matters of national prestige or power that are only very distantly related to the life goals or to the immediate motivation of the individuals who do the fighting. It involves massive numbers of individuals, with participants on the two sides usually miles apart, and with their leaders occupying relatively safe positions far removed from the conflict. The brakes on killing that operate in hand to hand conflict, the inhibition produced by signs of surrender or suffering, are not present (Lorenz, 1966; see Chapter 8).

Of course, nothing that has been said here denies the existence of some common features in the different types of aggression shown by an animal species, or in the aggressive behaviour of different animal species, or indeed in some aspects of animal aggression and some aspects of human aggression. For instance, aggressive behaviour is often associated with fear, and is less subject to inhibitions when directed towards strangers, in many cases both animal and human. The point being made is that slick comparisons between animal and man may be misleading.

(iv) *The problem of level of analysis*

A final issue concerns the difficulty of knowing the level of analysis at which to search for parallels between animal and human species. Thus some have sought for parallels at a global level, comparing for instance the human propensity to seek for exclusive group or individual rights over a particular area with animal territoriality, whilst others work at a lower level of analysis, for instance searching for animal models of the mechanisms of depression. In either case it is important to remember that superficial similarities in behavioural/psychological characteristics do *not necessarily* imply similar underlying mechanisms or similar functional significance. The converse, of course, is also true.

In yet other cases, the problem is to find the right level for making comparisons. An example is provided by some experiments on the effects of separating rhesus monkey infants from their mothers. These experiments were initiated at a time when children who had to go into hospital often saw little or nothing of their mothers for days or weeks at a time. It was suspected that such separations could have long-term adverse effects on psychological development, but the only evidence was retrospective: some teenagers with behaviour problems were found to have had separation experiences early in life. In view of the importance of the issue, an experimental attempt to demonstrate a causal link between early experience and subsequent behavioural disturbance seemed justified. In the initial experiments, mothers of 20–30 week rhesus monkey infants were removed from the groups in which they had been living for 6 days, and then returned. Although the infants continued to live in the same physical and social situation as before, apart from the absence of their mothers, some were severely affected. They went through phases of 'protest' (with much calling) and 'despair' (with lowered activity, sitting around in a hunched 'depressed' posture) comparable to those seen in human children. When the mother was returned, the mother-infant relationship returned only slowly and erratically to its previous course. Some consequences of the separation experience could be detected a year later. However, not all infants were affected equally: those with the more rejecting mothers suffered the more adverse consequences.

In later experiments the separation was performed the other way round, the infant being removed from the group to spend six days on his/her own, the mother staying with the group. In this case 'protest' lasted much longer, and 'despair' was delayed. Furthermore, on reunion the mother–infant relationship soon returned to its previous course.

Now although there are no precise data, this last finding is exactly the opposite from that which would be expected in the human case. A child left by his or her mother in familiar home surroundings with other family members would surely be less upset than a child taken out of its family and sent to a strange hospital (eg. Robertson, 1970). The monkey and human data seem to agree in showing that there could be long-term sequelae, but to disagree in the variables that are important.

However, the data can be reconciled at a different level of analysis. When the mother monkey was removed and then returned, she had to re-establish her relationships with her group companions as well as to cope with the demands of her infant. Because she had to devote herself to this additional task, the mother–infant relationship was re-established only slowly, and was sometimes permanently affected. When it was the infant that was removed, the mother had no such task and was much more prepared to devote herself to the demands of her infant when it was returned. Thus the greater effect on the infant in the former case can be ascribed to the greater disturbance to the mother–infant relationship. This is also in harmony with the individual differences within the 'mother-removed' group of monkeys: with the more rejecting mothers the mother–infant relationship was re-established with greater difficulty after reunion. Thus in the monkey case the re-establishment of the mother–infant relationship is a crucial variable (Hinde & McGinnis, 1977).

With human children, the child in hospital is (or was, with the hospital practices then current) largely deprived of relationships with adults previously familiar to him, whilst this is not true for most children who remain at home whilst their mothers go to hospital. Thus in so far as it is in fact the case that the effects of a mother leaving her child at home for a spell are less than those of sending a child to a strange place for a similar period (see Robertson, 1970), it is probably because important relationships are disrupted less. This would also be in harmony with the finding that a period of separation produces long-term effects only in psychosocially disadvantaged families (Rutter, 1972). Thus monkey and human data seem to disagree over the type of separation that produces the greater effect, but agree in that in both the most severe outcome is produced by those conditions of separation that most severely disrupt the mother–infant relationship. The monkey data highlight the importance of the mother's emotional availability to the infant after reunion.

To summarize the argument so far, there are at least four issues that seem to make it improbable that studies of animals can contribute much to the understanding of human behaviour – man's incomparably superior cognitive abilities, his possession of cultures specific to groups of individuals, the diversity of both animal species and human groups, and the difficulty of finding the appropriate level of analysis. These matters indicate that direct comparisons between animal and human behaviour can be misleading. But this does not mean that animal models are always useless. Evidence drawn from monkey studies in a number of laboratories did help to change hospital practices with regard to children being visited by their parents (Bowlby, 1969), and animal studies have helped in the understanding of human expressive movements (Smith, 1977). But it is not easy to know in advance which parallels between animal and human behaviour are likely to be useful, and which will be merely misleading.

Indeed comparisons that depend as much on the differences as on the similarities between animal and man may be useful. The relative simplicity of the animal case facilitates the refining of concepts and the elaboration of principles whose applicability to the human case can then be judiciously assessed. The very fact that animals lack verbal language and culture comparable in complexity to our own can be turned to good advantage, because our ability to understand the impact of language and culture on man's cognitive abilities, or on human personal relationships, can be enhanced by comparison with non-man, where their influences are absent or minimal. And the diversity of animal species can be turned to good advantage if we compare pan-cultural human characteristics with a range of animal species to see where man 'fits'. This is a technique well known to the anatomists – for instance the teeth of every animal species are adapted to the sorts of foods it eats (and/or vice versa, see pp. 63–4), and by comparing human teeth with those of animals we can make deductions about the sort of diet that our ancestors took.

Too often the conclusion that direct parallels between aspects of animal behaviour and aspects of human behaviour can be dangerous is taken to imply that ethology has nothing to contribute to the understanding of human behaviour. I hope that the rest of this book will show that an ethological approach, if applied with humility, has much to contribute. Perhaps the most important contribution of all is the extent to which the orienting attitudes of ethology prompt new perspectives on human behaviour. The nature of these orienting attitudes form the subject of the next section.

THE NATURE OF ETHOLOGY

Most -ologies refer to an area of knowledge. The term ethology, as used nowadays, refers in the first instance to the study of behaviour, and especially animal behaviour. However it was earlier used to refer to a particular approach to the study of animal behaviour, an approach pioneered by biologists and differing in a number of respects from that then used by comparative psychologists. The distinction between ethologists and comparative psychologists has now largely disappeared – though there remain extremists on either side still flying the banners of their respective former camps. However it is worth emphasizing the earlier distinctions, because the orienting attitudes of the early ethologists, such as Tinbergen and Lorenz, are highly relevant to the issues discussed in subsequent chapters. Four of these orienting attitudes may be mentioned.

(i) *Description and classification*

Modern biology depends on the work of generations of taxonomists and systematists who described and classified living organisms. Ethologists likewise have emphasized the importance of an initial descriptive phase – not as an end in itself, but as providing a base from which analysis can proceed. However the task of describing behaviour is far from easy. Total description is neither possible nor desirable. Decisions must be made as to the level of analysis at which behaviour is to be described, and the degree of precision to be used, and all such decisions may be influenced by the implicit theories of the research worker. An especially important decision concerns whether to use 'physical description' or 'description by consequence'. The former refers ultimately to the strength, duration and patterning of muscular contractions, though it is usually limited to patterns of limb or body movement. Terms such as 'knee jerk', 'eye-blink' or 'breast stroke' are shorthand terms for such descriptions. Physical description is suitable for the stereotyped action patterns of animals, but for relatively few aspects of human behaviour. 'Descriptions by consequence' do not refer to particular patterns of movement, but cover all patterns that lead, or could lead, to the result specified: 'going home', 'making love', 'seeking for food' are examples. Description by consequence calls attention to important aspects of the behaviour that would otherwise be missed, for instance the responsiveness to particular stimuli that is implied by 'seeking for food'. But it also has dangers: we may not be sure whether the individual is seeking for food or something else, and a description by consequence can imply that all types of behaviour that would lead to the specified end result are equally available to the individual concerned. The type of description used may have profound consequences for the subsequent analysis: whether we describe an individual as 'escaping from enemies' or 'running home' will prejudice the future course of enquiry into his behaviour.

(ii) *Analysis and resynthesis*

The initial data of ethology concerned the behaviour of whole animals in nature. Understanding required first the description and analysis of behaviour, perhaps in experimental conditions, and then analysis of the mechanisms underlying the behaviour. But analysis is not enough. It must be accompanied by resynthesis, or at any rate by a comparison between the properties of the initial whole and those of its parts. The whole is likely to have properties which may be explicable in terms of the properties of its parts but yet not to have been predictable from them. Furthermore there is a continuing dialectic between parts and whole: the parts contribute to the functioning of the whole, and the whole controls the functioning of the parts. We shall return continuously to this issue in considering the importance of distinguishing successive levels of social complexity.

(iii) *The four questions*

In studying the anatomy of animals, biologists have striven to answer four distinct yet interrelated questions. First, 'How does it work?' or 'What causes it to operate in the way in which it does?' Second 'How does it develop in the individual?' Third, 'What use is it?' or more specifically 'What are the consequences of possessing this structure upon which natural selection acts to maintain it in its present form?' And finally 'How did it evolve?' and/or 'What was its evolutionary origin?' Thus we can answer the question 'Why does the thumb move in a different way from the other fingers?' in terms of the actions of the bones, muscles, ligaments and nerves involved (causation), in terms of the different courses of development taken by the finger rudiments (ontogeny), in terms of the ways in which the thumb is useful for picking things up or holding onto objects (function) or in terms of the relation of our opposable thumb to those of our monkey-like ancestors (evolution).

In the same way the ethologist asks about the control, development, function and evolution of behaviour, and many ethologists would insist that the same questions must be asked about much human behaviour. Later we shall see that, although questions about function and evolution can usefully be asked about human behaviour, to apply them indiscriminately to all aspects may involve a neglect of the complications introduced by the dialectics between successive levels of social complexity and by historical factors. Be that as it may, we shall also see that these four questions, though logically distinct, are also inter-fertile: for instance knowing what a certain type of behaviour is for can help us in our search for the factors involved in its causation.

Since problems of function and evolution (in a biological sense) are perhaps less familiar to the social scientist, a few further words of explanation are in order.

Questions about the biological functions of behaviour normally concern the ways in which variations in behaviour between individuals or groups are or are not associated with differences in reproductive success in current circumstances. As we shall see later, reproductive success[3] refers not only to that of the individual concerned, but also to that of his kin (p. 10). Let us discuss one example from animals, based on data comparable to that available for many cases in our own species. Patterson (1965; Tinbergen, Impekoven and Franck, 1967) studied the breeding success of colony-breeding gulls. Competition for territories in the centre of the colony is often severe, and some birds of necessity breed on the periphery or even in outlying situations. The latter are less successful in rearing young. There is thus a correlation between nesting in the centre and reproductive success. Such correlations are often taken as proof of a biological function, though of course correlation does not prove causation: it could be that birds are successful in obtaining a central site and in rearing young because they are healthier. However if it is observed that ground predators often take chicks from the periphery of the colony but are driven away from the centre by the concerted action of the birds nesting there, the evidence becomes much stronger. We might then reasonably suggest not only that the behaviour of competing for a central site had a function, but also that it was an adaptation[4] to the presence of ground predators. Further evidence in this direction would be provided if we were to find that the birds did not compete for central sites on islands where ground predators were absent.

Given such data, we could reasonably propose that natural selection acts through predation by ground predators to maintain the behaviour in question. (However, without further evidence we could not say whether natural selection had promoted central nesting as such but had been relaxed on the islands, or whether it had promoted central nesting only as

[3] This is a frequent source of misunderstanding between biologists and social scientists. Many of the latter would insist that success must refer not just to number of offspring but to 'quality of life' defined in some way. The more extreme sociobiologist might then ask whether a better 'quality of life' was or was not associated with more descendants (see Chapters 6–9).

[4] Adaptation is another term used somewhat differently by biologists and social scientists. The latter often use it in a sense similar to the physiologists' 'accommodation' or even 'acclimatization'. For instance a society is said to be adapted (i.e. accommodated) to its environment, with the implication that the structure has changed, perhaps over one or a few generations, to adjust to changed circumstances. Biological adaptation refers to a structure or pattern of behaviour that enhances inclusive fitness (see p. 101) in the environment in question, with the implication that the character has evolved under the influence of natural selection. It is also used to refer to the process whereby that occurs.

a response to predator proximity. In the latter case the island nesting birds would be expected to revert to colony nesting if transported to the mainland.)

In most cases, the effects of behaviour on breeding success are more difficult to measure, and the functions of behaviour are often of necessity assessed in terms of its shorter-term consequences, themselves in turn presumably affecting reproductive success. For instance experimental evidence has shown that display leads to territorial acquisition in gulls, territorial behaviour leads to the spacing out of nests, this makes the eggs more difficult for predators to find, and thus enhances reproductive success (Tinbergen *et al.*, 1967).

Although 'function' can only be operationally assessed in terms of differences, it is sometimes useful to talk about the functions of features that are equally present in all members of the species. For instance, we can say that the function of the heart is to pump blood round the body. We shall use this sort of language in talking about universal human psychological characteristics in later chapters, but it must be remembered that it is a loose use of the term function, for two inter-related reasons. First it implies comparison with a hypothetical individual lacking the characteristic in question but identical in every other respect. Second, since the characters of an individual are inter-related (see pp. 110–11), absence of any one would be likely to have widespread repercussions. For both reasons such a postulated function would be impossible to prove.

In discussing function or adaptation, many biologists make a further distinction which is important in the present context. Any given character may be 'a good thing' in innumerable different ways. Thus the immediate beneficial consequences of territorial defence for a male song bird may include privacy for mating, prevention of cuckoldry, availability of a nest-site, food for the young, refuges from predators and so on. However one of these may be critical: the costs incurred in territorial defence may be determined by the gain in one of these consequences, the others being adequately served if the crucial one is attained (Hinde, 1975). In discussing the functions of pan-cultural human behavioural characteristics in later chapters we shall at best be able to point to probable beneficial consequences of the behaviour, and not to any particular consequence that is (or was) of crucial importance.

One other theoretical issue must be mentioned. At one time, discussions about the operation of natural selection often implied that selection operated for the good of the species or group. For instance, in some seabirds breeding is delayed for several seasons. It was formerly suggested that this is an adaptation to prevent over-population: if young individuals delay breeding the reproductive rate of the population would be reduced, and all individuals would have better access to resources. However any individual who 'cheated' by breeding early would be at an advantage and leave more offspring that its peers. If the tendency to breed early were also inherited, it would spread through the population (Lack, 1966; Williams, 1966). On grounds such as these it is now generally accepted that, in most species and except in rather exceptional circumstances, selection acts primarily on individuals and at most rarely to favour one group rather than another.

There is a possible exception here. Some animal and human activities depend on co-operation between individuals. Co-operation in warfare with a neighbouring group is a possible human example. It is possible that, in some circumstances, one group might survive and reproduce better as a group because the individuals within it co-operated as a group. In such cases, the character on which selection (not necessarily natural selection) acts involves more than one individual doing it and a form of 'mutualism' or of group selection could operate (Alexander & Borgia, 1978; Bateson, 1986). Although group selection could operate there is no clear proof that it does so. A few cases in which it seems to provide the most plausible explanation of some human characteristics will be mentioned later.

Nothing that has been said here implies that all aspects of behaviour promote reproductive success. Biologists would hold that natural selection would tend to eliminate any characteristic that markedly diminished reproductive success, but characteristics may be effectively neutral so far as natural selection is concerned. Indeed behaviour with effectively neutral consequences may be the result of natural selection if the behaviour had beneficial effects in the past, or if the genetic factors on which it depends are linked to others with beneficial consequences, or themselves have other beneficial consequences that are selected for (Gould and Lewontin, 1979). Whilst any one aspect of behaviour may have many consequences, or different consequences in different contexts, natural selection may act through only one of them, the others being 'carried' by the effect of natural selection on that one. There may be some contexts in which, or some individuals for whom, a normally functional characteristic has deleterious consequences: natural selection can promote a characteristic that enhances biological success for some individuals but not for all, or for some individuals at the expense of others. Indeed, whether or not a given type of behaviour has functional consequences may depend on what others do. Finally the genetic structure of a (small) population may be in part a matter of chance. These issues, important in studies of animal behaviour, become especially so when functional questions are applied to human behaviour.

To the biologist, questions of function and of evolutionary history are clearly separable: the former concern how aspects of behaviour influence events that succeed it in time, the latter concern the behaviour of ancestral generations. However the environment of the human species has changed dramatically in a period that is relatively short by standards of evolutionary time. Thus when we ask 'What is this behaviour for?' we could often more appropriately ask 'What *was* this behaviour for?' in our 'environment of evolutionary adaptedness' (Bowlby, 1969) – that is, in the environment to which characteristics of our species became adapted. The supposition is that in the meanwhile our environment may have changed more rapidly than our behaviour (though see Chapter 6), and that at least some of our behavioural predispositions may have been acquired when our physical and social environments were different from, and perhaps less heterogeneous than, the present ones (Fox, 1980).

Questions about the function that a particular aspect of behaviour may have had in the remote past are of course legitimate questions, even though they can never be answered with certainty (Gould, 1980). Strictly speaking, it would be necessary to establish at least two other things first (Caro & Borgerhoff Mulder, in press). One is that the character actually occurred then and is transgenerationally stable. The evidence for this is often comparative, based on the occurrence of the behaviour in related species, and such evidence is of course fallible. The second is that the character is now either selectively neutral or is selected for on the basis of the same beneficial consequences as it was in the past. But we know for certain neither the details of the past environment of any species, nor the selective pressures to which it was subjected, and we certainly cannot demonstrate selective advantages in the past. Indeed the character in question could be a mere by-product of genetic factors that control other characteristics through which natural selection has acted or acts now (see eg. Tinbergen, 1963; Hinde, 1975; Gould and Lewontin, 1979; Caro, 1985). We must therefore fall back on an 'argument from design': the behaviour must have served such and such a function because it is so admirably well fitted to do so. This also carries a number of dangers, including especially the difficulty of identifying precisely the function of a given type of behaviour. For example, we do not know how far the selective forces affecting a bird's foraging behaviour act through the energy intake, or through the amount of some particular nutrient obtained, or through some other aspect of the intake; nor do we know how far maintaining a look-out for predators is involved, and so on. Whilst acknowledging such difficulties, the questions with which we are concerned are scientifically interesting and in some cases socially important: we shall therefore use the argument from design where other sources of evidence are not available. But it must be remembered that hypotheses about past functions can never be proven.

To demonstrate the limitations of the argument, consider the case of stranger anxiety in a one-year old. Postulation that this was once adaptive involves the implication that, in our environment of evolutionary adaptedness, infants varied in their tendency to show stranger anxiety and some variants were better able to survive and reproduce. It also involves the assumption of some degree of stability in the behaviour over successive generations. However there is no suggestion that the degree of stranger anxiety shown to-day would have been appropriate in our environment of evolutionary adaptiveness. The conditions under which children are raised has changed, and the child's relationships with others are likely to affect the degree to which it shows stranger anxiety. There is also no necessary suggestion that the degree of stranger anxiety shown to-day is adaptive. It could be that natural selection is still acting sufficiently strongly to adjust stranger anxiety to present day conditions, or alternatively it could be a relic, like our appendix.

In spite of these problems, in specific cases discussion of the functions of behaviour in our environment of evolutionary adaptedness can call on a number of mutually supporting lines of evidence. In later chapters it is suggested that, provided we are constantly aware of the limitations of our evidence and recognize that we cannot prove all our hypotheses as rigidly as we would like, it can help to give us an understanding of our nature. However the aim is solely to indicate where this approach is and is not likely to be useful: more comprehensive treatments stressing primarily the merits (Lumsden & Wilson, 1981; Lopreato, 1984) and deficiencies (Kitcher, 1985) are available elsewhere.

(iv) *Humility in the face of diversity*

The early biologists were trained in a tradition that emphasized the diversity of nature. They were interested, for instance, in the amazing diversity of ways in which amphibians, although laying shell-less eggs liable to dessication, manage to breed away from water; in the miraculous diversity of insect mouth parts which, although all based on three pairs of appendages, are used for biting, chewing, piercing, sucking, licking and so on in different species; and in the many mechanisms used by fish to propel themselves through the water – tail, body, dorsal fins, pectoral fins and so on. The training of biologists at that time played on their sense of wonder, and inculcated a feeling of humility in the face of the diversity of nature (Wilson, 1984). Whilst the over-arching theory of evolution by natural selection was and still is of course crucial, most ethologists did not seek for general theories of causation. In this they differed especially from the learning theorists of the thirties, forties and fifties, who attempted to elaborate theoretical schemes that would embrace all, or at least most, learning phenomena. Rather the ethologists sought for concepts and generalizations with a limited range of validity, coupling their generalizations with statements about the limitations of that validity. This attitude implies in the present context that the concepts and generalizations of ethology can have only a limited applicability to the human case, and that one task must be to specify what the limits are.

For the purposes of the present book, perhaps more important than any of these four orienting attitudes is that the ethologist sees us as a species, doing some things less well than our non-human relatives and some things very much better, and with potentials which, though perhaps expanding with every generation, are nevertheless limited by virtue of our biological nature. This means that the ethologist's contribution to the understanding of human social behaviour involves an emphasis on its biological aspects. Of course the ethologist must remember that he cannot solve all the problems of human behaviour on his own, but I believe that, armed with humility, his approach can make a considerable contribution and perhaps help to set right a balance which has been awry for too long.

The facilitation of that process is one aim of this book. In pursuing that aim it is less concerned with ethological data than with where and how the ethological approach to the study of human social behaviour can be married with more traditional ones. And the emphasis on the ethological contribution does not imply lack of appreciation of other approaches, or any presumption that ethologists have all the answers – only that they can contribute.

There is, however, a second aim. Social scientists have long recognised that the behaviour of individuals in groups poses special problems that merit study in their own right. More recently both ethologists and social psychologists have focussed on the special problems posed by dyadic and triadic relationships. As a result, it is now apparent that the understanding of social behaviour demands not only distinctions between levels of social complexity, but also an appreciation of the dialectical relations between them. This in turn will help us to specify where the biologist has something useful to contribute to understanding human behaviour, and where the limitations of a biological approach lie. This relationships approach is the subject of the next chapter.

SUMMARY

In the first part of this chapter we have discussed four of the issues likely to pose difficulties when attempts are made to draw lessons about human behaviour from that of animals – the differences in cognitive abilities, the human capacity for language and culture, the diversity of both animal species and human cultures providing evidence for almost any hypothesis, and the problem of the level of analysis at which parallels should be drawn.

Nevertheless it is argued that the orienting attitudes of ethology can provide important new perspectives on human behaviour. These orienting attitudes include the emphasis on description, the importance of synthesizing the results of analysis and moving between levels of complexity, the emphasis placed on questions of function and evolution as well as those of development and causation, and the sense of humility engendered by the diversity of nature. But there is no suggestion that a biological approach is ubiquitously useful for understanding human behaviour; a major task is to specify just where it is and where it is not.

2

The relationships perspective

LEVELS OF SOCIAL COMPLEXITY

This chapter introduces the second main theme of this book – the need to come to terms with successive levels of social complexity and the dialectical relations between them. Whilst this is an issue well appreciated by most social scientists (in principle, if not always in practice), and will be discussed mostly in relation to human behaviour, it is also clearly illustrated by recent work on non-human primates.

Studies of man's closer non-human relatives really took off in the 1950s. For heuristic purposes, it is useful to contrast two approaches. In the Western world, biologists, and psychologists turned primatologists, focussed first on the behaviour of individuals. They described the stereotyped movement patterns that were characteristic of the species and the vocalizations and other signals used in communication. They noted how individuals interacted with each other, but did little to relate this to the size and composition of the groups, the habitats they preferred and so on. The importance of sex as a cohesive force, at first over-emphasized as a consequence of studies of captive animals, was replaced by a preoccupation with aggression and dominance between individuals as structuring factors within the group. Another group, anthropologists turned primatologists in Japan, initially having little influence in the West, tended to focus first on the group as a whole. They contrasted the properties of the different groups observed and attempted to explain the differences found in terms of differences between the individuals or types of individuals who played particular roles within each group, such as the leader male or the adult females. Of course this distinction between two approaches does scant justice to many of the individuals involved, especially to some of the western anthropologists whose approach was in some ways intermediate. But it serves to emphasize how the phenomena with which we are concerned can be approached from two directions, the first starting with

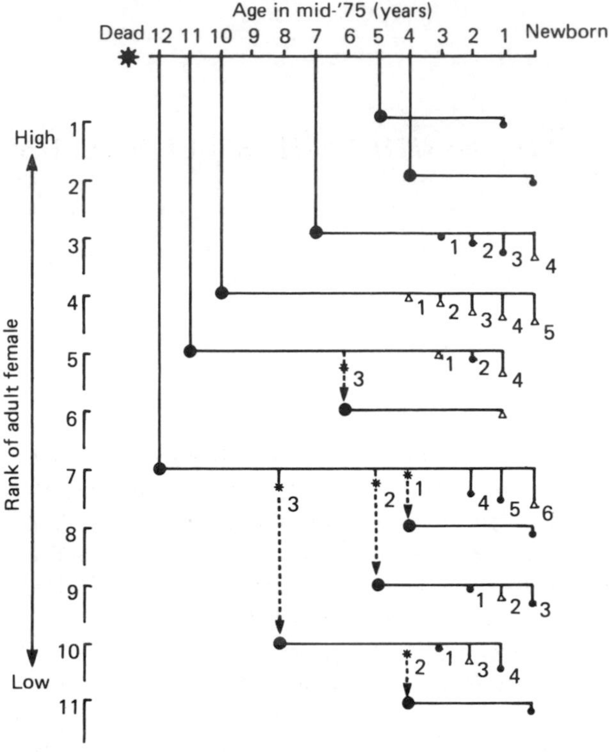

Fig. 2 Social structure of rhesus macaques: the rank relationships within one matriline. Each group may contain several matrilines. Age reads horizontally, the eldest individuals being to the left of the figure. Rank reads vertically. The female from whom the matriline orginated is shown at the top left hand corner but was dead at the time to which the figure refers. The numbers indicate the rank relationships between siblings within families. The broken arrows lead from the rankings of a particular adult female among her maternal siblings to her ranking among the adult females. The solid and vertical lines indicate descent.
• = non-adult female; △ = non-adult male; ● = adult female; ★ = the position of a female, now adult, among her maternal siblings (the same individual female is connected by a broken arrow to her position as an adult female with respect to other adult females). (After Datta, 1981).

individuals and building up falteringly towards the group, the other starting with the group and analysing downwards.

As a result of these endeavours it has been shown that many non-human primates live in groups of surprising complexity. As one example, Fig. 2 represents two aspects of the structure of one matriline of rhesus macaques, namely the dominance and biological kinship relations between the females. The group consisted of three matrilines, all animals in the top matriline being dominant to those in the second and those in the second to those in the third. Within each matriline mothers were dominant to their daughters but young females usually rose in rank above their elder sisters when a few years old. Thus dominance relations between sisters tended to be in inverse order of age.

But Fig. 2 does not do justice to the full complexity that exists in a natural troop. First, the males are not shown. Whereas the females stay for life in the troop into which they were born, males leave their natal troop when a few years old and join another. There is a hierarchy of adult males in each troop, dominance bringing increased access to food, and probably to females and other resources. Other less dominant males often occupy a position on the periphery of the troop. Second, many interactions involve more than two individuals, and one female normally subordinate to another may yet defeat her with the aid of a colleague. Indeed, although the fully adult males are normally dominant to all individual females, a male may be defeated by a coalition of females. And many relationships of other types are not shown – 'friendships' involving mutual support, play partners amongst juveniles, etc.

Our understanding of the complexity of monkey social groups has come about from recognition of the fact that how an individual behaves depends in part on whom he or she is with. This has demanded a change in focus from how individuals behave in general to the nature of their relationships, and of how those relationships contribute to the structure of the group. Indeed, it is essential not only to distinguish several levels of social complexity, but also to be constantly aware of the mutual influences betwen them. The issues here are not different from those in the human case, and are implicit in much work in the social sciences, but they were cast into relief by the *relative* simplicity of non-human primates (Hinde, 1983). Here, in keeping with the aims of this book, let us consider them as they apply to our own species. To begin with we will concentrate our attention on overt behaviour.

Many of the data about social behaviour concern interactions between two or more individuals. An interaction involves a series of interchanges over a limited span of time, and for present purposes the behaviour involved can be described in terms of the content of the interchanges (Are they fighting, talking, kissing etc.?) and their quality (Are they shouting or whispering, kissing passionately or dutifully, etc.?). The course of the interaction will be influenced by both participants.

When two individuals interact, each will bring preconceptions about the likely behaviour of the other or about the behaviour appropriate to the situation. In addition, if two individuals have a series of interactions over time, the course of each interaction may be influenced by experience in the preceding ones. We then speak of them as having a relationship – a relationship involves a series of interactions over time between two individuals known to each other. The distinction between an interaction and a relationship is not of course absolute, for a prolonged interaction takes on some properties of a relationship, but this definitional issue does not affect the argument. So far as behaviour goes, we can describe a relationship in terms of the content and quality of the constituent interactions, and of how they are patterned. Of course in neither the case of interactions nor of relationships is behaviour the only issue. The attitudes, hopes, expectations, emotions (whether expressed or concealed) and so on of the participants are of crucial importance. Furthermore, to a greater or lesser extent, each enters into or has some awareness of, the attitudes, hopes, intentions, etc., of the other. And through its subjective concomitants a relationship can continue for long periods in the absence of interactions.

Relationships are virtually always placed within a network of other relationships. We customarily describe networks of relationships with terms such as family, relatives, the local drama club, the faculty of the college, and so on – networks which may overlap extensively or may be quite separate and behave as distinct (e.g. competing or cooperating) groups[1] with respect to each other.

[1] A terminological note is necessary here. When individuals come together under the influence of a common attractant, as moths to a flame, the result is termed an aggregation. Aggregations are of little concern to us here.

When individuals come together because they are attracted to each other, the result may be termed 'a social group'. A social group need involve no inter-individual relationships: thus a shoal of fish is a group. Usually, however, relationships are involved, and in this book the term is used to refer to a network of relationships which may either be more or less distinct from, or share members with, other groups. In the former case, a given individual may have a number of different roles (see p. 5) in the group. In the latter case, an individual may have relationships (and roles) in more than one group. The term 'social group' can thus be applied to non-human primates. The group persists over time, and the individuals maintain boundaries between their own and other groups. In the human social sciences, however, application of the term 'group' usually requires the additional criterion of its being recognised by the participants – i.e. given a name.

The surface structure of a group can be described in terms of the content, quality and patterning of the constituent relationships. Such a description can refer only to an arbitrarily isolated span of time: in reality, of course, structure is a dynamic process in time. Shared properties of a number of groups can be referred to as their (common) social structure. The constancies observed are not of course to be perceived as regulatory, but primatologists are beginning to analyse the observed social structure in terms of 'principles of organisation' and to deduce a generative 'deep structure' which, using concepts not found in the data language of description, 'explains' the structure (Hinde, 1976).

The term 'society' usually refers to one or more groups, in which the individuals share certain institutions etc., perceive each other as similar and have some understanding of the whole. Although it is often applied to groups of lower species, such as ants, this would be inappropriate given the sense in which the term is used here.

Finally, each group influences and is influenced by other groups with which it overlaps or is juxtaposed, and each group affects and is affected by the physical and biological environment in which it lives.

We must thus recognize a number of distinct levels of complexity in social behaviour – interactions, relationships and social structure, the latter leading on to yet further levels of complexity concerned with the interrelations between groups. Each of these levels has properties that are simply not relevant to the levels below. Thus the behaviour of two individuals interacting, but not that of a single individual, can be described as synchronous or well-meshed. Some properties of relationships (see pp. 35–7) like commitment, or intimacy, are hardly if at all applicable to isolated interactions. Indeed, as implied above, properties concerned with the temporal patterning of interactions, or with their relative frequency, can apply only to relationships (see p. 36). And within a group the relationships may be arranged hierarchically, centrifocally and in many more complex ways – issues not applicable to the individual relationships.

THE DIALECTICS BETWEEN LEVELS OF SOCIAL COMPLEXITY

Whilst it is crucial to distinguish these levels of complexity, it is equally important to remember the two-way relations between them (see Fig. 1). The nature of an interaction or relationship depends on both participants. At the same time, the behaviour the participants show in each interaction depends on the nature of the relationship: what an individual does on each occasion depends on his assessment of and expectations about the interaction in which he is involved, or of the relationship of which it forms part. Indeed, in the long run, the behaviour an individual *can* show is affected by the relationships he has experienced in the past. At the next level, the participants' views of the relationship affect the nature of interactions within it, and the nature of the relationship is determined by its constituent interactions. And at the group level the relationship between A and B is affected by A's relationship with C, and thus by the nexus of relationships in which it is embedded, but conversely the properties of the group are determined by those of its constituent dyadic (and higher order) relationships. Furthermore how individuals behave in any interactional context is influenced by the social norms current in the group, and by the rights and duties appropriate to persons in the role (see p. 5) they are currently occupying. These roles, and the institutions of which they form part, together with the beliefs, customs and capacities shared by the members of the group, and the inter-relations between them, are referred to here as the socio-cultural structure of the group (see note pp. 4–5). The socio-cultural structure can be regarded as a further level of social complexity, though the relations between it and group structure differ in kind from those between group structure and the constituent relationships, or between relationships and their constituent interactions. Nevertheless group structure, relationships and interactions affect, and are affected by, the socio-cultural structure.

Finally, at each level there are dialectical relations with the environment. Although technological progress encourages the view that humans are set against nature because it has increased our power to change our environment, humans are part of nature. Their propensities were evolved in association with a limited range of environments, whilst currently their development and behaviour is affected by and affects their environment.

There is of course nothing novel in distinguishing between levels of social complexity. For instance Harris (1979) distinguishes infrastructure (infant care, work patterns, etc.), structure (division of labour, class structure, etc.) and superstructure (art, music, rituals etc.), levels which are comparable with those used here but in my view less likely to lead to an understanding of process. Others have attacked such an approach: for example, for Geertz (1970) it involves the successive superposition of the findings of Anthropology, Sociology, Psychology and Biology – though this implies an over-simplistic view of the inter-relations at each level and between levels. The important issue in the present approach is the emphasis on the dialectics between levels. Whilst most biologists lay the primary emphasis on influences from the individual to society, only a few social scientists (e.g. Marx and Engels, 1976), have recognized the importance of such 'biological' factors, and most emphasize the dominating significance of influences of society on the individual (see Fig. 1). Thus Benedict (1961, p. 236), recognizing the great span of human potential, emphasized the role of institutions in moulding human personality 'even to extremes of which the observer, deep-dyed in the culture of which he is part, can have no intimation'. Real understanding, however, must embrace the influences within each lifetime both by the individual as he is at any point in time on his relationships and on the socio-cultural structure, and by the group and socio-cultural structure on relationships and the individual. Indeed the various levels of social complexity we have distinguished are in part heuristic devices: they are not entities but complexes of inter-related processes in continuous creation through the dialectical relations between levels. This implies that individuals have no separate 'biological' and 'cultural' characteristics: rather as development proceeds the processes of socialization (becoming a person, able to perceive others as comparable persons) and acculturation (acquiring the beliefs, values etc. of the society) proceed simultaneously (see Chapter 5).

The individual's development depends crucially on relationships with others whose influences are internalized and affect his/her behaviour. The values and norms and other aspects of the socio-cultural structure become parts of the minds of individuals (see footnote pp. 4–5).

These dialectical relations between levels of social complexity are crucial for understanding the relations between the biologist's and the social scientist's approach to human social behaviour. They imply not only that cultural forces affect the natures of individuals, but also that the natures of individuals affect the cultural forces that impinge on them. Neither the crude view of some popularizers of ethology that men and women are little more than naked apes (e.g. Morris, 1967), nor the view of some extremists amongst social scientists that culture is all that really matters (e.g. Sahlins, 1976), with the implication that every individual comes into the world as a *tabula rasa* to be moulded by social forces, is adequate. All human psychological characteristics depend on these dialectics. Nor can we say that relationships are fashioned either by individuals or by social pressures: all relationships are a product of both. Social events cannot be understood solely in terms of social events (e.g. Durkheim, 1912), and it is not the case that causation flows solely from culture to the individual (e.g. Sahlins, 1976; Geertz, 1973). But neither is it the case that the principles of social psychology and sociology are to be understood solely in terms of the non-social behaviour of individuals (e.g. Homans, 1961), nor that cultural phenomena can be related directly to particular biological needs (Malinowski, 1929). A search for direct links between particular human dispositions and human social practices, institutions or beliefs is unlikely to be rewarding. Rather understanding requires us to cross and re-cross the levels of social complexity, and to comprehend the inter-relations at each level and the two-way relations between levels.

Although the necessity for such a systems approach (von Bertalanffy, 1952) is widely recognized, the requirements of in-depth research also necessitate specialization. But whilst many branches of the social sciences seem to be concerned with only one or two of these levels of social complexity, in fact the dialectics always obtrude. Indeed failure to recognize this has often been a brake on progress. Whilst post hoc wisdom is easy to produce, it may be salutary to mention one or two examples.

Personality theorists twenty years ago attempted to explain the behaviour of individuals in terms of traits. However the cross-situational consistency of the traits proved to be only moderate. Whilst some of the weakness in the correlations was due to measurement error, and could be overcome by aggregating measures (Block, 1981; Rushton, Brainerd & Pressley, 1983), it became apparent that individuals differed also in the extent to which their behaviour varied across situations, and in the extent to which different types of behaviour were affected (Mischel, 1973; Endler & Magnusson, 1976; Bem & Funder, 1978; Kenrick & Stringfield, 1980). The most important situational factors are the relationship or social ones.

Developmental psychologists, also, have come to recognise that what seem to be properties of the child may in fact be properties of its relationships, and that the understanding of many aspects of child development can be fully understood only when the child is seen as a contributing member of a network of relationships (Bowlby, 1969; Sullivan, 1938). A recent example is provided by data from the 'Ainsworth strange situation' (Ainsworth *et al.*, 1978). As this technique was first used, a 12–18 month old child was brought into a laboratory playroom with its mother, and observed through a number of episodes, each of a maximum of 3 minutes duration. In the first, the mother was present, then a stranger entered as well, then the mother left, and then the mother returned and the stranger left, and so on. On the basis of behaviour in these episodes, the children were classified as 'securely attached', 'avoidantly attached' and 'ambivalently attached'. For instance a securely attached child may go straight to the mother when she returns, and then get on with playing with the toys; an avoidantly attached child may play with the toys whilst avoiding the mother, and an ambivalently attached child mingles proximity seeking with angry resistant behaviour. The early data indicated that children's categorizations were highly stable from 12–18 months. However those earlier studies involved middle class families: later studies with more socially disadvantaged children showed that the categorization fluctuated with the families' fortunes, securely attached children ceasing to be so if misfortune struck the family (Vaughn et al., 1979). Furthermore, it was found that children were classified differently if tested with their fathers rather than their mothers (Grossmann, et al., 1981; Main & Weston, 1981): thus the Ainsworth classification is a means for categorizing not children but an aspect of the child's relationship with each parent.

Furthermore the child's network of relationships is in dialectical relation to a sociocultural structure, so that the processes of development, socialization and acculturation proceed hand-in-hand. Whilst there are many cross-cultural similarities in child-rearing practices, there are also differences that are believed to affect personality development (e.g. Ainsworth, 1967; Whiting & Whiting 1975), and Mead (1950) has emphasized the close correspondence between the nature of a culture and the patterns of child-rearing in that culture. Even cultural artefacts affect the course of cognitive development. For instance in the laboratory infants find it easier to find objects when they are hidden in an upright cup than when they are concealed beneath an inverted one, presumably because of their experience with cups in the world outside (Freeman, Lloyd & Sinha, 1980). At the same time, cultural artefacts reflect to some degree the cognitive and other propensities of individuals.

Cognitive psychologists have shown that much cognitive development largely depends on interpersonal relationships (e.g. Vygotsky, 1934; Doise & Mugny, 1984; Perret-Clermont and Brossard, 1985), and that the cognitive operations an individual uses to solve a given problem may vary with the social context (Donaldson, 1978; Carraher & Carraher & Schliemann, 1985). Furthermore assessments of cognitive ability may depend crucially on the social context. For instance Donaldson (1978) showed that Piagetian tests for capacities such as number constancy could be seriously affected by the child's relationship with the experimenter. In one such test, a child is asked to compare two rows of identical counters placed side by side, and usually judges them to be equal. The experimenter then changes one row by increasing or decreasing the distances between the counters. The child is then asked to compare the rows again. Many children then report that they are not equal, usually saying that there are more counters in the longer row. Donaldson showed that this was due to the child's seeing an important and imposing adult arrange a situation, ask a question about it, change it, and then ask the same question again. Of course they were disposed to give a different answer! (McGarrigle & Donaldson, 1974; Samuel & Bryant, 1984; Light & Perret-Clermont, 1986)). Whilst such data show an influence of relationships on cognitive processes, we must beware of speaking of cognition and relationships as separate entities. In fact, as we shall see, cognitive models, expectancies, hopes and so forth form part of all relationships, and an individual's relationships may be incorporated in the cognitive models used in other situations.

Social psychologists are constantly confronted with the ways in which individuals are affected by their group environment, and with how the properties of groups are affected by the individuals within them. Amongst students of relationships, the symbolic interactionists describe individuals as having a number of role identities which come into play in different relationships (Goffman, 1959; McGall, 1974), and the exchange and interdependence theorists emphasize that interactions within a relationship depend on the participants' perceptions of its past and their expectations about its future (Kelley, 1979).

The influences of the individual on his/her relationships and of relationships on the individual are central for the psychotherapist. And anthropologists, concerned with the sociocultural structure, must seek to understand not only the ways in which beliefs, myths and legends affect the lives of individuals but also reciprocally of how those beliefs reflect the natures, desires, wishes and frustrations of individuals (Herdt, 1981; Keesing, 1982).

In its emphasis on the dialectical relations between social relationships, group structure and the extra-group physical and social environment, the present approach is not incompatible with many aspects of functionalism (in an anthropological sense), though emphasizing the importance of human needs and the properties of the human mind in shaping the dialectics. But the need for compatability between the social forms and the sociocultural structure, and the logic of the sociocultural structure itself, are seen not only to depend upon, but also to fashion, the human mind (see e.g. Geertz, 1973). In its insistence on the role of the individual mind in determining social forms this approach is also not incompatible with structuralism, though it would advocate a search for the bases of deep structure in the forces of natural selection which have created minds capable themselves of being moulded by and moulding cultural forms. Whilst acknowledging the ubiquitous importance of cultural forces, the present approach emphasizes also the role of human biological characteristics in shaping social phenomena.

GENERALIZING FROM INTERACTIONAL DATA

Social behaviour implies a social context: what the individual does depends in part on that context. Often the data of the social psychologist concern interactions between two (or more) participants: what happens depends on the present and past behaviour of both. Neglect of this fact can cause errors of interpretation. How quickly a mother goes to a crying baby is not solely a reflection of her maternal responsiveness, but depends also on how often the baby has already cried that night, and how often the baby cries depends in part on how quickly the mother goes to it. Such facts imply that the manner in which data on social behaviour are analysed can be a matter of crucial importance.

For the moment we may focus on behaviour: we shall return to its subjective concomitants shortly. As we have seen, data about social behaviour concern interactions. From data on interactions there are two principle routes to generalizations (Hinde & Stevenson-Hinde, 1987). These are illustrated in Fig. 3 which concerns data on two-parent, one-child families. In that Figure, rectangles 1, 2 & 3 represent specific instances of three types of interaction between a particular mother and her infant – say mother inhibits and child complies, mother inhibits and child ignores, and mother speaks affectionately. Such are the basic data. From them we can make generalizations about the incidence (in terms of means, medians, ranges etc.) of these three types of interaction in that mother–infant dyad (4, 5 & 6). The rectangles behind 4 represent comparable data on maternal inhibitions with child compliance for other mother–infant

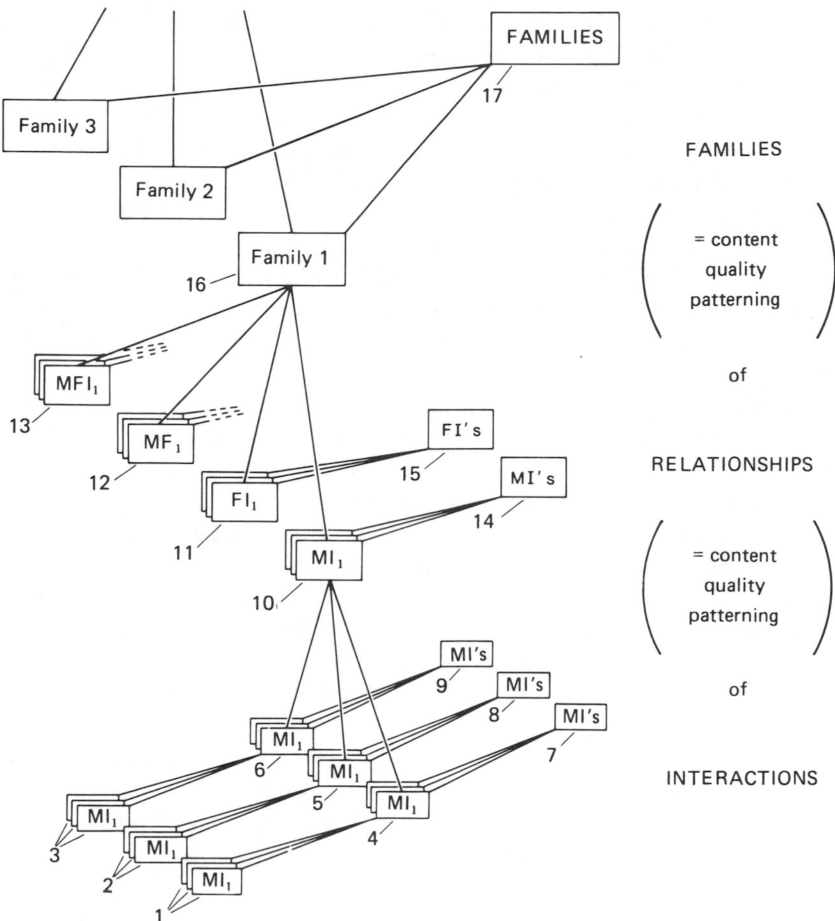

Fig. 3 The relations between interactions, relationships and families, illustrating the two routes for generalizations from data on interactions (modified from Hinde & Stevenson-Hinde, 1987).

dyads, those behind 5 for maternal inhibition without compliance and those behind 6 for maternal affection. The procedure then usually adopted involves remaining at the same level of social complexity, and seeking for generalizations about *each type* of interaction *across dyads*, as at 7, 8 and 9. This is the route followed in most studies of the relations between particular independent variables (e.g. sex or age of child) and particular dependent variables (e.g. maternal affection).

Comparable procedures could be followed for interactions between father and infant, between mother and father, and for triadic interactions.

A second route involves proceeding upwards to the relationship level of social complexity, examining the incidence of and relations between *different types* of interaction in the *same dyad*. Thus 10 in Fig. 3 represents aspects of this particular mother–infant relationship (and the rectangles behind it comparable aspects of other mother–infant relationships). These will include not only the frequencies of the different types of interactions, but also their relative frequencies (e.g. were expressions of affection more or less common than maternal inhibitions?), the sequential relations between different types of interaction (e.g. were maternal inhibitions accompanied by expressions of affection, or were these two maternal modes always separated in time?), and other properties (see below).

Comparable procedures permit generalizations about other relationships in that family, e.g. father–infant (11), mother–infant (12) and their triadic relationship (13), and in other families.

From here we can again remain at the same level, seeking generalizations about mother–infant relationships for a number of dyads (14), father–infant relationships (15) etc.; or we can proceed to the group level, in this case examining the nature and structure of that particular family (16). The latter would include the relations between the intra-familial relationships. This could lead in turn either to generalizations about families (17) or to descriptions of higher order groups within which the families were located (not shown).

Although Fig. 3 portrays the task of description as proceeding from interactions to relationships and family structure, it can sometimes proceed in the opposite direction: that is, descriptions of relationships can permit deductions about the nature of interactions. More importantly, as discussed later, cause–effect relations proceed in both directions (Fig. 1).

The diagram emphasizes that attempts to obtain generalizations about relationships (14, 15) from generalizations about specific interactions (7, 8 & 9) would lose information about some of the most important properties of relationships, especially those that depend upon the relative frequency and patterning of different types of interactions. The number of maternal inhibitions provides different information about the mother–child relationship from the proportions of inhibitions complied with; and a given number of commands from a mother who also often expresses affection is likely to have a meaning for the child very different from that of the same number of commands from a mother who never expresses affection. Such properties of the mother–child relationship would be lost if we examined merely the absolute frequencies of different types of interactions.

Similarly attempts to obtain generalizations about families (17) from generalizations about relationships (14, 15) would lose important information about how relationships affect each other within families. A mother–child relationship involving frequent inhibitions might have quite different impacts on the child depending on whether or not the father–child relationship was also inhibitory. Furthermore the properties of the mother–child relationship may affect the father–child relationship, and the manner in which it does so may depend on the nature of the parental relationship. Such issues would be lost if we merely examined the properties of the several relationships.

Of course, which of the approaches represented in Fig. 3 is more appropriate depends upon the problem. Studies of the effects of given independent variables upon particular types of behaviour often involve generalizations across dyads (7–9). Where dyadic differences are important or are the focus of study, and one type of interaction is salient, it may be adequate to use differences at the interaction level (e.g. 4, 5 or 6) as an index of the relationship. But interaction measures (e.g. frequency of maternal controls) may be less revealing than the relations between interactions (e.g. proportion of maternal controls that are successful, proportion of interactions that are positive). And where the relations between different types of interaction within the relationship are important, the comparisons are at the relationship level (e.g. 10). For instance the distinctions between authoritarian, authoritative and permissive parents depend upon assessments of several types of interaction concerned with parental control and acceptance (Baumrind, 1971). This type of approach (reviewed Maccoby & Martin, 1983) has been more successful than those involving simple aspects of parent–child interaction.

It is apparent that relationships can never be adequately assessed along a single scale. Of course the same is true of interactions: aggression must be assessed not only in terms of frequency, but also of quality, context dependence, and so on. But the problem is much more severe with relationships. Relationships are measurable along many dimensions, and some of the most important may involve ratio measures (Hinde & Herrmann, 1977). The proportion of occasions on which a baby cries in which the mother picks it up tells us something different about their relationship from the absolute frequencies of crying or picking up. Since relationships involve so many possible dimensions, the best we can do is to categorize them according to where they stand along a limited number of dimensions that we deem to be important.

DESCRIPTION OF RELATIONSHIPS

At each level of complexity, we need a descriptive framework in order to systematize the knowledge gained. Only when we can describe interactions, relationships, groups, etc., categorizing each according to its properties, can we transform our knowledge into generalizations whose range of validity can be specified. There can be no hope of building up adequate social *sciences*, and science is used here in the sense of an ordered body of knowledge, where description is inadequate. Indeed adequate description is rendered even the more necessary by the multitudinous interacting variables – biological, physiological, psychological, environmental, cultural – which influence social behaviour. Interactions between variables are ubiquitous, and we must remember their potential when making generalizations about our observations and experiments. If we are to specify the limits of our generalizations, a descriptive base is essential. Of course description is only the first step, but it is the basis on which theories and generalizations must rest.

Description must be selective, and suited to the task in hand. Its initial aim must be to facilitate the identification of differences. The difficulty is that, for many problems, we do not yet know which are the important dimensions. We do not even know at what level of analysis we should attempt to describe the phenomena in which we are interested. In the case of interpersonal relationships, for instance, should we focus on details of the behaviour exchanged, the winks and nods and eyebrow flashes? Or should we use more global properties, like the competitiveness of the relationship, the intimacy of the partners, or who wears the trousers? Description is inevitably affected by our implicit theories about process, and it has been suggested elsewhere (Hinde, 1979a) that it is quite reasonable not to discard as preliminary guidelines the qualities we notice in everyday life – for instance, what sorts of things people do together, who takes the initiatives, whether they are committed to each other, and so on. Such a course has a special appeal to an ethologist, for it is likely that we have been shaped during development to notice (though not necessarily consciously) the sorts of things that we do notice because they help us to be good prognosticians about relationships (Humphrey, 1976).

Sometimes, the judgements we make have too global a character to be useful for scientific enquiry, but it is then usually possible to specify the criteria on which we base those judgements. For instance, we are more likely to say two people have an affectionate relationship if they like doing things together, try to make each other happy, are reasonably intimate with each other, and organize their behaviour each in relation to that of the other. If we try to find dimensions at this sort of level, it is always open to us to analyse more finely, if that seems necessary for an understanding of dynamics, or to amalgamate dimensions if we are interested in higher level properties.

But even if we settle on an intermediate level at which to make our description, there are still an almost infinite number of dimensions that might be used. However, we can achieve some sort of order if we categorize those dimensions according to the sorts of issues with which they are concerned. Thus the dimensions important for describing relationships can be grouped into eight categories, as follows. The categories move from those concerned primarily with what the individuals do together, and with the properties of individual interactions, to more global properties involving subjective aspects of the relationship as a whole.

The *Content* of the relationship refers to what the individuals do together. Whether we are concerned with differences between major categories of relationships (e.g. mother–child vs teacher–child) or with differences within a category (e.g. between mothers who play with their children and mothers who do not), content dimensions provide an initial basis for differentiating among relationships. We know, for instance, that the content of the mother–child relationship may differ from that of the father–child relationship, and that children may do different things with friends and non-friends. What we do not know is whether it matters how interactions of different types are 'parcelled up' into relationships. For instance, in two-parent families fathers are more often involved in physical play with the baby than mothers, and mothers tend to provide more solicitude than fathers. If, in a one-parent family, the mother attempted to provide the same amount of physical play, would the fact that the rumbunctious play now came from the same individual who provided tender loving care make any difference?

The *Diversity* of the interactions refers to the number of different things the participants in the relationship do together. It depends in part on the level of analysis involved: thus a mother–child relationship could be described as uniplex, involving only maternal–filial responses, or multiplex, involving nursing, playing, protecting and so on. In any case, the more diverse the interactions within a relationship, the more opportunities for interactions of one type to be influenced by those of another and the more diverse the experiences shared by the two partners.

The *Quality* of the interactions within a relationship are one of its most crucial properties, and yet at the same time amongst the hardest to evaluate. What matters in a marriage is not just what the partners do together, but how they do it. If a mother responds sensitively to her child's needs (Ainsworth, *et al.*, 1978) or shows herself to enjoy physical contact (Main & Stadtman, 1981), the relationship may take a course quite different from that which it would take if the mother were insensitive or resistant to physical contact. Quality is important in relationships of all types, including everyday formal relationships and close personal ones.

The qualities of a relationship, as opposed to those of its constituent interactions, may depend on the *Relative Frequency and Patterning* of those interactions. Several different issues arise here. First, if a number of different types of interaction have similar qualities, the participants (and outsiders) may be more prone to apply certain global labels to the relationship: thus a relationship is described as 'warm' or 'loving' on the basis of interactions in many social contexts, not one. This is important to the participants because individuals evaluate their relationships, and their assessments influence its future course. Another issue concerns the *relative* frequencies of interactions – what matters about a relationship may be not how often A comforts B, but how often A comforts B relative to how often B needs to be comforted. Yet another issue concerns properties of relationships that are consequent upon interactions of quite different sorts. For instance, a mother who was always ready to play with her child might be seen as indulgent, but one who sometimes refused and at other times insisted on playing might be seen as controlling.

Another important set of dimensions concern the *Reciprocity vs Complementarity* of the interactions comprising the relationship. Reciprocal interactions are those in which the participants each do the same thing (e.g. one chases the other and then the other chases the one), whilst in complementary interactions they do different but complementary things (one bosses and the other is bossed). Power and dominance constitute one type, but by no means the only type, of complementarity. Parent–child or teacher–pupil relationships involve mainly complementary interactions, whilst some friendships involve more reciprocity. Most close personal relationships involve an idiosyncratic interweaving of reciprocal and complementary interactions.

Intimacy, the extent to which the participants in a relationship reveal all aspects – experiential, emotional and physical – of themselves to each other, is a crucial dimension of many relationships. Casual observation indicates that intimacy in the more limited sense of sharing secrets, is a matter of some significance to six year olds, and perhaps to younger children. Intimacy in the sense of the extent to which the individual is prepared to reveal him or herself to others could be said to appear even earlier. In adults not only the extent but the location of areas of intimacy and privacy are crucial characteristics of relationships. Whilst we usually deem a relationship to be closer, the more the participants reveal themselves to each other, areas of maintained privacy may be important for the relationship as well as for the individual participant.

Interpersonal Perception involves a number of dimensions differing in their requirements for cognitive complexity – whether A sees B as B 'really' is; whether A sees B as B sees B (i.e. Does A understand B?); whether B feels that A sees B as B sees B (i.e. Does B feel understood?), and so on. The issues here, of course, relate to those of empathy and role-taking, but nevertheless require study in their own right. To see B as B 'really' is or as 'B sees B' involves much more than sharing another's emotional state, for it is necessary to comprehend B even when B's thoughts and feelings are different from one's own. The study of interpersonal perception may thus be of crucial importance for understanding the development of the self-concept, of self esteem, and thus of many aspects of personality. However abilities are not all: adults who are capable of understanding another's point of view do not always do so, so it is necessary to specify not just whether two individuals are capable of mutual understanding, but the extent to which it actually influences the course of their relationship.

Finally, *Commitment* usually refers to the extent to which the partners accept their relationship as continuing indefinitely or direct their behaviour towards ensuring its continuance or towards optimizing its properties. It may be imposed from outside, as in an arranged marriage, or it may arise endogenously as a relationship develops. In either case it maybe facilitated by a private or public pledge. As important as commitment itself is belief in the partner's commitment: in many relationships it is that belief which forms the basis of trust. Commitment may depend more on what an individual sees him or herself as putting into a relationship than on what he or she gets out of it (Lund, 1985).

It is suggested that these categories will provide convenient pigeonholes for ordering descriptive data on interpersonal relationships (Hinde, 1979a). Not all will be relevant to any one problem: complete description of a relationship is impracticable and unnecessary. For many purposes they would be supplemented by additional categories concerned for instance with the institutional context or the relationship's history: here these are regarded as relevant to an understanding of process (see below). In this scheme, the categories are concerned with dimensions seen as important in everyday life. Although in large part based on data referring to a finer level of analysis (e.g. interactions, perceptions), they involve also higher level properties emergent from their patterning (Hinde, 1979a). Another approach, of Kelley *et al.* (1983), rests more exclusively on the interaction level of analysis. Picturing a relationship as the interconnections between the temporal chains of two individuals' affect, thought and action, they suggest analysis of relationships in terms of (i) the kinds of events in each chain that are interconnected and the (ii) pattern, (iii) strength, (iv) frequency, and (v) diversity of interconnections; (vi) the extent to which the interconnections facilitate or interfere with the chains of action etc., (vii) their symmetry vs asymmetry (i.e. whether the effects of each chain on the other are similar or different); and (viii) the duration of interactions and/or the relationship.

These two approaches to description are not incompatible: that of Kelley *et al.* attempts to specify the events upon which some of the more global properties, described in the first approach, depend. Discussion at the interaction level may often be necessary to explain the dynamic importance of some of the more global properties of relationships. However the interaction level cannot be sufficient by itself because, apart from anything else, we evaluate relationships in terms of global properties and the evaluations of the participants affect their relationship's future course.

In whatever way it is described, it must be remembered that a relationship is not a static entity but a process in continuous creation through time. Thus any description must refer to a limited span of time, and we must not forget that the future course of a relationship may be affected by events before the period in which it was studied. Indeed *changes* in dimensions may be as important for prognosis as the dimensions themselves.

So far, we have considered only the description of relationships. With the approach outlined above, this involves in essence the description of the interactions (content and quality), description of properties arising from the relative frequency and patterning of interaction within the relationship, and description of certain properties that are more or less common to some or all of the interactions within the relationship. Description is not an end in itself, but a means for understanding process. The study of relationships involves a further search for principles to aid understanding of the ways in which interactions are patterned within relationships. A number of such principles are available, stemming from the study of extra-dyadic social influences, dissonance and balance theories, learning paradigms, exchange and inter-dependence theories, etc. (see e.g. Hinde, 1979a; Kelley *et al.*, 1983; Duck and Gilmour, 1981).

In the same way description of a group will include reference to the nature of the constituent relationships, to the principle ways in which those relationships are patterned (e.g. centrifocal, hierarchical), and to properties of the group as a whole (e.g. whether the relationships are closely or loosely integrated) (Hinde, 1979b). This in turn will provide substance for a search for principles to aid understanding of the ways in which relationships are patterned in the group.

SUMMARY

This chapter introduces a relationships approach to the study of human behaviour. Emphasis is placed on the necessity to consider successive levels of social complexity, with dialectical relations between them. Whilst many problems in the social sciences seem to be concerned with one level, in fact the dialectics nearly always obtrude. Since the different interactions within a relationship may affect each other, it is necessary to attempt to base generalizations on relationships instead of (or as well as) on interactions. Finally, some categories suitable for the description of relationships are outlined.

3

The study of immediate causation – some implications of a relationships approach

A major theme throughout this book concerns the dialectics between successive levels of social complexity, illustrated in Fig. 1, and, more particularly, the importance of the level of dyadic relationships between those of the individual and the group. In this chapter we discuss some consequences of a relationships approach for understanding the behaviour of individuals.

THE COURSE OF INTERACTIONS – CONFLICT

The early ethologists gained considerable understanding of interactions between individuals by analysing them as stimulus–response sequences. Each response of one individual was interpreted as a response to the preceding response of the other, and as providing a stimulus for its next move. However it soon became apparent that each response of one partner might elicit several possible alternatives from the other. Thus in the courtship of the fish *Badis badis* each possible male activity may be followed by one of several possible female ones, and vice versa (Fig. 4) (Barlow, 1962).

Such interactions between rivals, or between potential mates, usually involve a great deal of posturing and display by both participants. The posture shown by each individual at any particular point in time predicts approximately, but not precisely, what it will do next. An example is shown in Table 3.1 (Stokes, 1962). The posture of the displaying bird was recorded in terms of 5 components, and its immediately following behaviour categorized as approach, stay or flee. Two points may be noted. First, no combination of components predicted accurately what the displaying bird would do next. This could, of course, be due to inadequate or inaccurate observation. However another possibility is suggested by the second point, namely that fleeing was predicted more accurately than approach. Since these postures occur in conflict situations and are usually

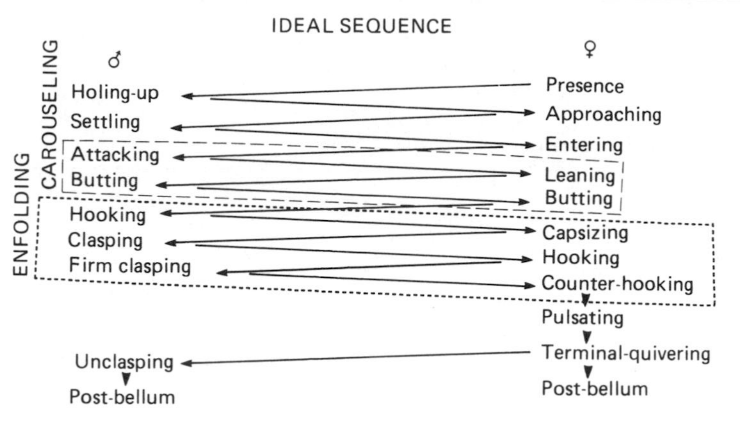

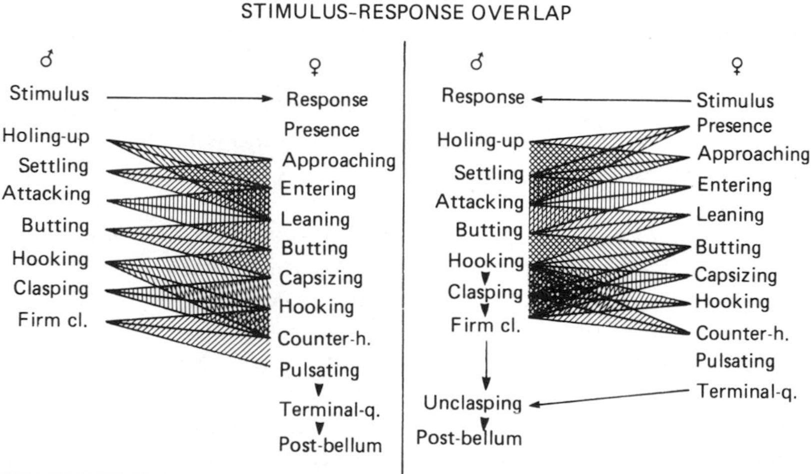

Fig. 4 The courtship behaviour of the fish *Badis badis* (after Barlow, 1962). Upper diagram: a hypothetical scheme in which the sequence of behaviour shown by male and female is shown as a chain response. Lower diagram: the actual stimulus-response relations that occur.

described as threat postures, it is a little surprising to find that they predict fleeing by the posturing bird more accurately than attack. Similar data are available for other species. However the data do make sense if we interpret the posturing as a form of negotiation, with each participant's postures signifying not sequelae with fixed probabilities but rather 'I want to do X, but if you do Y I will do Z.' If the posture indicates 'I want to stay here, but if you approach, I will flee', the rival would be likely to approach

Table 3.1 *The use of five behaviour elements to predict outcome of encounter between two Blue Tits at a feeding station* (Stokes, 1962)

Initial behaviour elements					Subsequent action (per cent of total occurrences)			Total occur-
Crest erect	Nape erect	Facing rival	Body horizontal	Wings raised	Attack	Escape	Stay	rences
+	–	+	–	–	0	94	6	34
+	–	–	–	–	0	89	11	83
–	–	–	–	+	7	14	79	14
–	–	–	–	–	0	35	66	240
–	+	+	+	+	28	16	56	25
–	+	+	+	–	48	10	42	48
–	–	+	+	+	44	20	37	46
–	–	+	+	–	43	21	36	89
Best single indicator of outcome								
Body horizontal					40			
Crest erect						90		
Crest normal							52	

and such postures would frequently be followed by fleeing. If the posture indicated 'I want to stay here, but if you approach, I will attack, the other individual would be less likely to approach and attack would follow less frequently.

That negotiation is a reasonable way of describing many animal conflicts is illustrated by data on interactions between males of the Siamese fighting fish (*Betta splendens*). When two males are put together the intensity of the posturing often increases gradually, each partner escalating the intensity of its threats in line with that of the other until one individual actually bites the other and/or one capitulates (Simpson, 1968). In such cases the interaction can be described as involving negotiation, each participant 'raising his bid' in accordance with his expectations about the behaviour of the other.

An interesting series of observations on European Jays (*Garrulus garrulus*) provides clear support for the view that the behaviour of each individual in such a situation depends on the probable behaviour of the other. Bossema & Burgler (1980) identified two signals made by a dominant bird on a feeder when approached by another – monocular and binocular fixation combined with particular postures (Fig. 5). They showed that:

1 Attack by the dominant bird was more likely to follow binocular than monocular fixation, and was more probable if the subordinate bird were near than if it were distant. The four situations Binocular/short distance, Monocular/short distance, Binocular/long distance, Monocular/long distance involve a decreasing probability of attack by the dominant bird.

Fig. 5 Upper: communicator on feeder monocularly looking at recipient (the latter is binocularly looking at the communicator). Lower: communicator on feeder binocularly looking at recipient (recipient is hopping around the feeder). (Bossema & Burgler, 1980)

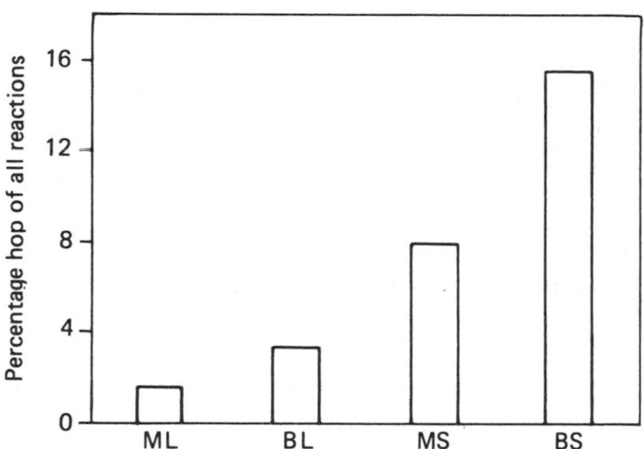

Fig. 6 Going backwards with one hop expressed as a percentage of all reactions shown by recipients for each of the four signal situations. ML vs BL, ML vs MS, ML vs BS, BL vs MS, BL vs BS and MS vs BS significant at the 0.01 level (X^2-tests) (Bossema & Burgler, 1980)

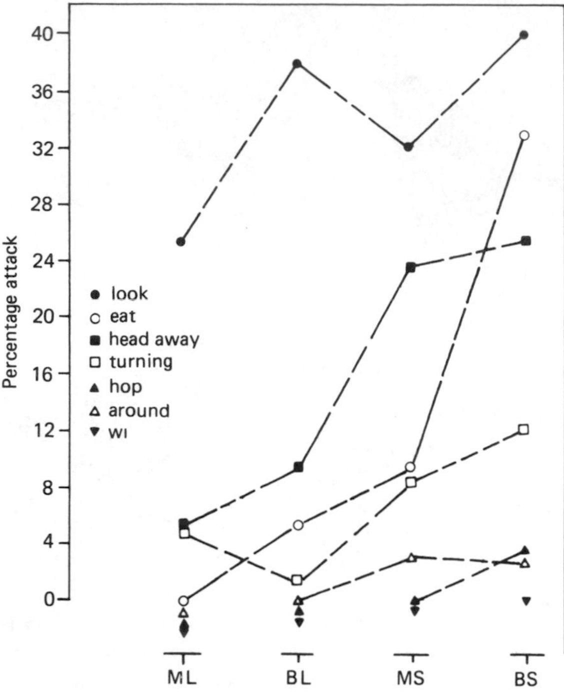

Fig. 7 The probability the communicator attacks after signalling in each of the four signal situations in relation to the type of reaction shown by recipients (wi = withdrawal) (Bossema & Burgler, 1980)

2 The subordinate bird was more likely to hop away when the dominant bird gave a signal likely to be followed by attack (e.g. Binocular/short) than one relatively unlikely to be followed by attack (Monocular/long) (Fig. 6).

3 After signalling, the probability of attack by the dominant bird was highest if the subordinate showed behaviour indicating approach to the feeder and lowest if it retreated (Fig. 7).

Thus the behaviour of each individual can be interpreted on the assumption that it was behaving in accord with the probable or expected behaviour of the other.

The same sort of thing happens in human conflicts. Muhammed Ali was credited with one of the fastest left jabs in the history of heavy-weight boxing. Stern (1977) was able to show that 53% of those in one contest were of shorter duration than the generally agreed fastest reaction time of 180 milliseconds. However very few of them connected. Since a fighter of that calibre does not signal his moves in advance, one must presume that his opponent had the ability to decode his behavioural sequences over a longer time span and anticipate his next move. In detailed studies of human mother–infant interaction Stern has shown that similar principles apply. And a similar conclusion must apply to interactions in general. Each action by either participant in a dyadic social situation depends on his/her expectations about the response of the other, expectations based in part on how the other has responded on previous occasions. In the case of interactions within long-term relationships the signalling may become much attenuated because negotiation is unnecessary: the relations between the displays of blue tits and subsequent behaviour change with the season, and threats become rare in well-established groups of monkeys. Such conclusions, painstakingly reached by ethologists, are indeed a commonplace to the social psychologist, and especially to symbolic interactionists (Goffman, 1959; McCall, 1974). Whilst much of this book is concerned with lessons from ethology that might be useful to the social psychologist, here the boot is on the other foot. However the issue has further implications.

THE NATURE OF EXPLANATORY CONCEPTS

Because the behaviour of each participant in an interaction is influenced by the current and expected behaviour of the other, measurements of the behaviour of an individual in a social situation may reflect not characteristics of that individual, but of the relationship between the interactants or of the social situation as a whole. We have already seen (pp. 27–8) that this has implications for trait theories of personality: the relatively low cross-situational consistency of the supposed traits can be understood, at least in part, in terms of the social situation.

A specific example, arising from studies using the Ainsworth Strange Situation, was discussed in Chapter 2 (p. 28). As another example, developmental psychologists often group a number of dimensions, mostly referring to the style rather than the content of behaviour, under the rubric of 'temperamental characteristics' (e.g. Thomas & Chess, 1980). Temperament assessments are usually based upon questionnaire or interview data on the child's behaviour in particular situations – for instance when going to bed, or at breakfast time. The correlations obtained between assessments based on data from fathers and mothers, or from teachers and observers (reviewed Bates, in press) are usually only moderate. Whilst the shortfall could be due to error, it could also reflect differences between (e.g.) the father–child and mother–child relationships. These might include differences in what father and mother do with the child, the quality of their interactions, the extent to which their

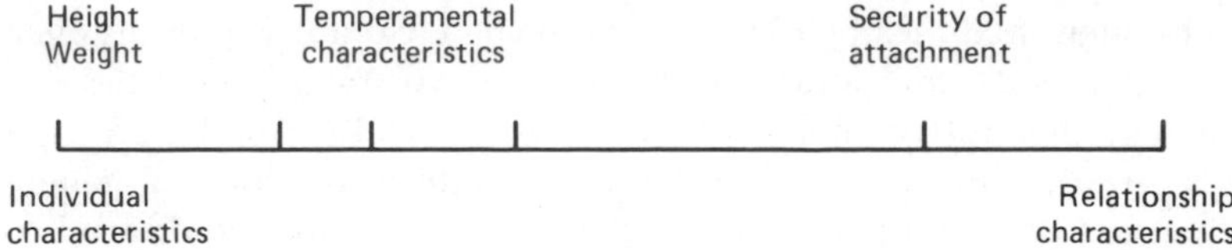

Fig. 8 Characteristics of individuals and characteristics of relationships (After Stevenson-Hinde, 1987).

relationships with the child are nurturant/succorant, authoritarian/permissive, etc., their differing intimacy with the child, the differences in their perceptions of the child and in those of the child of them, in each case as assessed against the expectations and values of the perceiver, and so on (see pp. 35–7).

Indeed Stevenson-Hinde (1987) has suggested that it is useful to regard measures of supposed individual characteristics as arranged along a continuum from pure individual characteristics at one end to relationship characteristics at the other. Height and weight, but only a few psychological characteristics, would lie right at the individual end, attachment categories (see p. 28) nearer the relationship end (Fig. 8). The several temperament characteristics would lie near, but at different distances from, the individual end. This of course does not mean that relationship characteristics such as attachment may not affect characteristics lying closer to the individual end in the longer term.

THE DYNAMICS OF CONSISTENCY/INCONSISTENCY: UNDERSTANDING PROCESS

If measures of behaviour, or of characteristics such as temperament, differ with the social situation, two courses are open to the investigator of inter-subject differences. One possibility is to aggregate measures across situations. This can help in two ways. First, every measure is inevitably subject to error, and aggregation is likely to give a more stable and representative estimator than any simple measurement. The validity of this principle has been demonstrated in diverse areas of psychology: low correlations are often improved by aggregating measures (Rushton, Brainerd & Pressley, 1983). Second, aggregation may provide an index of a more basic mediating variable that would predict inter-subject differences (e.g. Block, 1981). This would be more appropriate, the more the measure reflected an individual characteristic rather than a relationship one. Even then, however, such a variable would not necessarily predict behaviour in particular situations accurately: that might or might not be a matter of concern, according to the aims of the investigator.

A second possible course is to attempt to understand the psychological processes underlying cross-situational differences in behaviour. This, of course, is what clinicians are attempting to do all the time: they seek to explain neurotic symptoms appearing in particular situations in terms of more general psychological processes. However social and developmental psychologists, in part because they tend to focus on group data rather than on the idiosyncracies of individuals, are often content with recording the nature and extent of cross-situational consistency or inconsistency. The way forward may lie not in aggregating measures but rather in looking in greater detail at more measures to understand the dynamics of what is going on. The supposition is that, whilst behaviour may not be consistent across contexts, it differs in a meaningful way between contexts, with the differences at least partly understandable in terms of underlying propensities or cognitions that are expressed differently in the different social contexts.

For example, in a study of the behaviour of preschool age children at school and at home, correlations between similar measures in the two situations were seldom significant. Children who interacted much with their mothers did not necessarily interact much with teachers or peers, and children whose interactions with their mothers were often positive did not necessarily tend to have positive interactions in school. Cross-situational consistency was thus low. However there were meaningful patterns of correlations between the two situations: for instance infrequent warm intercourse with the mother was correlated with greater overall sociability in school, but the interactions tended to be negative in character, involving hostile and controlling behaviour to adults and peers (Hinde & Tamplin, 1983). A possible clue towards an interpretation of these correlations comes from data on the children's temperamental characteristics. These were assessed from maternal descriptions of the child's behaviour at home. Children high on the temperamental characteristics Active and Moody tended to have few positive interactions with their mothers at home, but Moody children tended to have frequent interactions with peers in school, and Active children to have a high proportion involving hostility. It is a reasonable supposition that the lack of positive interactions at home was a consequence of a tensionful mother–child relationship induced in part by the child's characteristics, and that these characteristics were expressed in a different way in school.

A more interesting example involving both a cross-situational difference and coherence over time is provided by the study of Sroufe, Jacobvitz, Mangelsdorf, De Angelo and Ward (1985) of mothers showing a 'seductive' pattern with their two year old sons. 'Seductive' is used here to refer not to behaviour intended to lead to frank sexual contact, but to behaviour involving physical contact, sensual teasing or promises of affection that were motivated by the mother's needs rather than being responsive to the needs of the child. Mothers showing this pattern to their sons tended to show hostility (in the form of derision) to their daughters. Thus although the seductive pattern could be identified from 24 to at least 42 months, and was thus a stable aspect of the mother's behaviour, it could not be viewed in maternal trait terms, but only as depending critically on the relationship.

However the mother–son/mother–daughter difference was understandable in terms of psychological processes in the mothers. It was related to a history of emotional exploitation by their own fathers. Sroufe *et al.* suggest that the mothers behaved seductively to their sons because their own needs for nurturance had not been met and because they had learned in childhood that parents may attempt to meet their own emotional needs through their children. However the mothers' childhoods were reflected in a different way in relationships with daughters. The distance these mothers had felt from their own mothers led to feelings of self depreciation and, Sroufe suggests, in depreciating their daughters they reconstructed a relationship pattern with which they were already familiar.

These studies show that the behaviour of individuals may be affected by their relationships, past and present, and thus that relationships may affect each other within a family. This, of course, is the basis of family therapeutic techniques (Minuchin, 1974). Another example, including also sociological variables, is provided by a study of child abuse. Elaborating an earlier model suggested by Gelles (1973), Engfer & Schneewind (1981) obtained the data shown in Fig. 9 from a study of 285 West German families. The immediate antecedents of harsh punishment were psychological variables – a 'problem child' (i.e. showing a variety of behaviour problems), maternal anger-proneness and rigid power assertion, and family conflicts. Anger-proneness was related to the mother's childhood relationships indirectly both via maternal personality characteristics (irritability) and via the incidence of family conflict. The latter was related also to the social and economic situation of the family, which itself was related to maternal (rigid-authoritarian) personality factors and educational goals. The two latter variables were related to the rigidity of power assertion, and thereby to the incidence of harsh punishment. Although this study is based on cross-sectional data, it illustrates the complexity of the factors related to the use of harsh punishment, and the importance, for understanding the behaviour of one individual, of considering not only her or his present (marital) and past (family of origin) relationships, but also the sociological situation of the family.

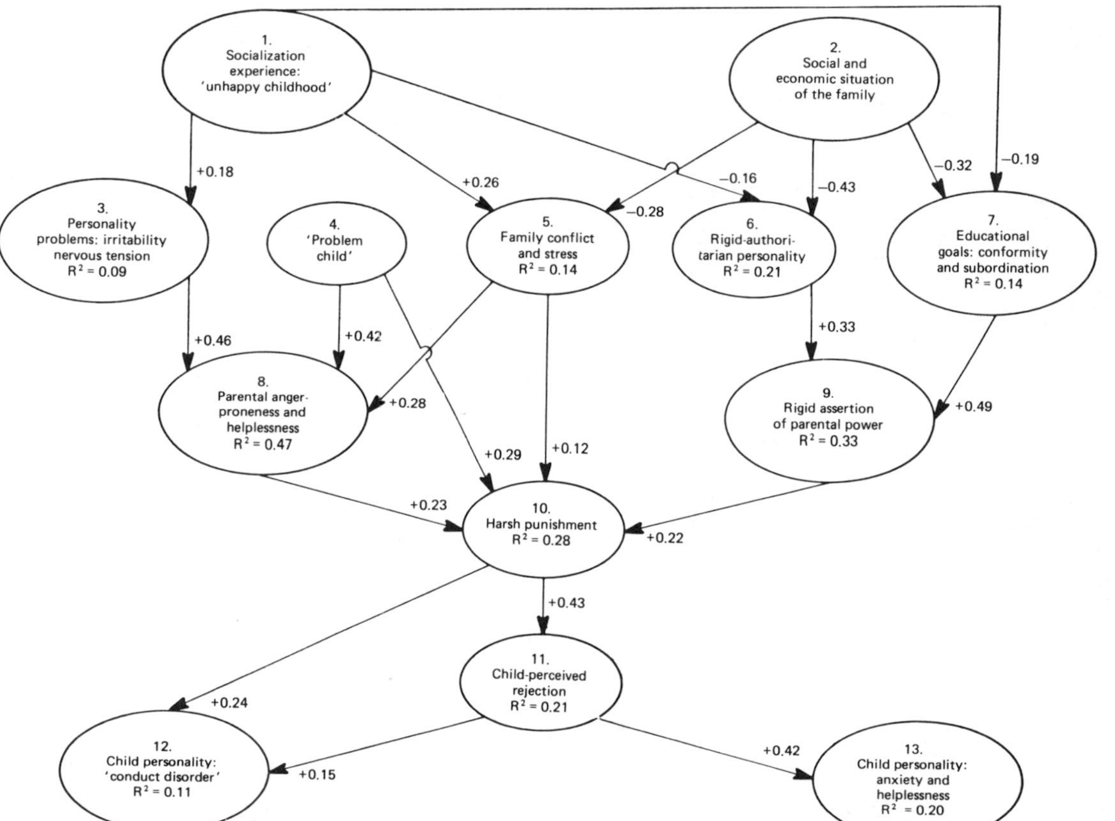

Fig. 9 Empirical model of the causes of harsh maternal punishment of boys. The small figures indicate the path coefficients and R^2 the variance accounted for. (From Engfer & Schneewind, 1982)

Thus to uncover the dynamics of the processes by which individuals affect the characteristics of relationships, or to understand why individuals behave differently in different situations, we must be prepared to cross the levels of social complexity (Fig. 1 and Fig. 3). In addition, the multiplicity of the causal factors affecting social behaviour in turn raises the possibility that any one factor will have different effects on social behaviour according to the incidence of others. For example, authoritarian parental control can have different effects on a child's development according to the child's nature. Such issues suggest that there is a need to substitute, for the more traditional linear correlational approaches, analytic methods that make more allowance for the differing impacts of a given variable on different individuals (Hinde & Dennis, 1986).

WHO DETERMINES WHAT?

The analysis of behaviour within an interaction usually requires recording techniques such that the successive moves of the two partners can be dissected. Often, however, our initial data concern whole interactions or even relationships, and we need to tease apart the relative roles of the participants.

Just because at least two individuals participate in every interaction or relationship, and each is continuously influencing the other, simple answers to questions of the type 'Who is influencing whom?' are seldom meaningful. Many of the flaws in attempts to answer such questions have been reviewed by Maccoby & Martin (1983). In addition, behaviour within a relationship usually involves long sequences of interactions, so that specifying the initiation may be arbitrary.

One approach to this problem involves assessing the influence of measures of the relationship during one time period on the same or different measures at a later time period. Suppose that two aspects of a relationship (P & Q) are measured at two points in time (1 & 2). The four measurements will generate 6 correlation coefficients, two of which will concern synchronous measurements (P1 vs Q1, P2 vs Q2), two autocorrelations of the same dimension at different points in time (P1 vs P2, Q1 vs Q2), and 2 cross-lagged coefficients (P1 vs Q2 and Q1 vs P2). The difference between the two latter is called the cross-lagged differential. The synchronous and autocorrelations are used to reject the trivial explanation that a correlation between P1 and Q2 is due to correlations between variables within each time period and consistency in one of them between time periods, and to assess stationarity, i.e. that there is no change in the relations between the variables over time. If the cross-lagged

Table 3.2 *Changes in the behavioural tendencies of mother or infant rhesus monkey, and consequent changes in the two measures of the relationship. Successive rows indicate Mother more possessive, Mother more rejecting, Infant more demanding, Infant more independent*

	Time on Mother	*Frequency of rejections*
$\underset{\rightarrow}{M} - I$	+	–
$\underset{\leftarrow}{M} - I$	–	+
$M - \underset{\leftarrow}{I}$	+	+
$M - \underset{\rightarrow}{I}$	–	–

differential is positive it suggests that P causes Q, but if negative, that Q causes P. Equality would indicate that any relation between P & Q was due to an unmeasured third variable. There are, however, many difficulties in the interpretation of the pattern of correlations, and the procedure has been much criticized (Kenny, 1975; Rogosa, 1980). Furthermore it has been used with the implication that P & Q assessed aspects of the two partners independently, when in fact they referred to aspects of the relationship at each point in time.

A second method, so far used only with non-human species, also depends on the use of correlations between measures to tease apart the direction of effects. The measures that are correlated are such that an alteration in one measure due to a change in one partner would be associated with a change in the second measure in one direction, whilst a change in the first measure due to a change in the other partner would be associated with a change in the opposite direction in the second measure. Take for instance the time a rhesus monkey infant spends attached to its mother, and the frequency with which the mother rejects the infant. If the mother becomes more possessive, she will reject the infant less and (other things being equal) the infant will spend more time in contact with its mother. Similarly, other changes in mother or infant in the tendency to make contact will produce the changes shown in Table 3.2. It will be noted that changes in the mother cause these two measures to move in opposite directions, while changes in the infant cause them to move in the same direction. Thus the direction of correlation between the two measures indicates whether a given change in the relationship is due more to a change in one or the other partner.

This approach demonstrates very clearly the crucial importance of specifying questions about the direction of effects very precisely. Thus it can be used to answer questions such as 'Are changes in the mother or changes in the infant primarily responsible for the increase in the time the infant spends off the mother with age?'; 'Are differences between mothers or differences between infants primarily responsible for differences between mother–infant dyads at any one age?'; 'Is the effect of a given experimental treatment on the relationship due more to an effect on the mother or on the infant?'; and so on. The answer to any one of the questions is not necessarily predictable from another. This method also implies a degree of stationarity: its application has been discussed in more detail elsewhere (Hinde 1979a).

A more usual route towards teasing apart the roles of the two partners is to study the extent to which differences between relationships are associated with differences in the characteristics of one or other of the participating individuals. This is the usual method used in developmental psychology – for instance in comparison between mother–child and father–child relationships (Lamb, 1981), or between depressed mother–child and non-depressed mother–child relationships (Pound, 1982; Zahn-Waxler *et al.*, 1984), and in adult psychiatry – for instance between the marital relationships in which the husband was a psychiatric outpatient and controls (Collins *et al.*, 1971).

Such an approach can demonstrate changes in the determinants of a relationship characteristic over time. For instance Engfer (1986) asked whether differences between mothers or differences between their babies were primarily responsible for differences in an aspect of their relationship (perceived child difficultness) at a later point in time. Difficultness at 4 months and at 18 months was associated with lack of maternal sensitivity, as observed on the maternity ward and at 8 months, more closely than with any of the infant characteristics measured. Difficultness at 43 months, however, was more closely associated with lack of child co-operativeness in another situation at 33 months than with any maternal characteristics. On the basis of these and other data Engfer suggested that lack of maternal sensitivity early on made the babies seem more difficult, but later on these babies developed characteristics that substantiated the maternal perceptions.

An important consequence of such an approach is that it can show up interactions between the effects of different characteristics of one or both partners on the relationship. For instance in a study of preschool children there were few differences between boys and girls in measures of mother–child interactions, or in shyness. However the relation between shyness and the mother–child relationship differed with the sex of the child. By a variety of observational and interview measures, shy girls were found to have less tensionful relationships with their mothers than non-shy girls, but shy boys had more tensionful ones. The difference appeared to stem from the parental value systems – in the interviews several mothers made remarks implying that they considered it alright for little girls to be shy, but not for little boys (Simpson & Stevenson-Hinde 1985). This exemplifies the way in which understanding how an individual behaves often requires us to cross the levels of social complexity, considering in this case both the parent–child relationship and the norms of the sociocultural structure.

This approach also demonstrates the importance of thinking in terms of relationships, rather than in terms of independent interactions, in another way. In the study of preschoolers referred to in the preceding paragraph, the structure of mother–son relationships differed from that of mother–daughter ones in an important respect. Although there was no overall difference in the extent to which mothers used strong controls with sons and with daughters, in sons they were used primarily in relationships that were generally tensionful, whereas in daughters their prevalence was more independent of other aspects of the relationship. Thus a possibly important difference between mother–son and mother–daughter relationship lies not in the absolute frequencies of particular interactions, but in their relative frequencies, that is, in the structure of the relationship.

SUMMARY

The issues discussed in this (and the preceding chapter) emphasize that (i) the behaviour of each partner in an interaction may depend on the past, present and/or expected behaviour of the other; (ii) the behaviour observed in an interaction depends on both participants; (iii) the different types of interaction within a relationship may affect each other; (iv) related to the above, an individual may behave differently in different relationships, and it is necessary to attempt to understand the psychological consistencies underlying the apparent behavioural inconsistency; (v) in considering who determines what in a relationship, it is necessary to phrase the questions asked very precisely; and (vi) in attempting to understand the dynamics of an interaction or relationship, or for that matter of a group, it is necessary to take account of the participants' value systems and, in general, to move between successive levels of social complexity in both directions.

4

Development – organism and environment

It is convenient to separate questions of development from those of causation, though the distinction is not absolute. Questions of immediate causation are concerned with the factors that cause an individual to behave in a particular fashion at a particular time, given that he/she is what he/she is. Questions of development are concerned with the factors that led to the individual being what he or she is at the time in question. However both are concerned with antecedent events, and thus often merge. For example, the 'causes' of mob violence may be sought in the conditions of deprivation in which the individuals grew up, in the recent long hot summer, in the current conditions of unemployment and frustration, or in the desire of individuals to outshine their peers in bombast and daring. Which are developmental issues and which issues of current causation is to some extent arbitrary.

Discussion of the whole range of principles found useful by ethologists for understanding individual development would be out of place here (see e.g. Bateson & Martin, in press). Instead, the focus of this and the following chapter involves selected issues emerging from ethology or from a relationships approach that are relevant to the social scientist. But one orienting attitude of the ethologist should be emphasized from the start. The psychologist often tends to see development as involving a series of stages that lead towards a more mature or adult condition. To the biologist, development need take no such direct route: subsidiary goals must be reached if the final one is to be achieved. Thus if it is to grow up into a butterfly, a caterpillar must be a good caterpillar, finding and metabolising food efficiently, protecting itself from predators, and so on (Tinbergen 1963). In the same way the stages of childhood must be seen not just as way-stations on the route to adulthood, but as delicate adjustments to enable an organism of that degree of development to survive and progress further to best advantage. Some of the behavioural characteristics of children are to be seen as temporary devices for the job of growing up, to be subsequently discarded as adult functions emerge.

THE MISLEADING NATURE OF DICHOTOMIES OF BEHAVIOUR

It is necessary first to review some old ground. At one time most of the questions asked about the development of behaviour were in the form of dichotomies – is a given aspect of behaviour 'innate' or 'learned', 'instinctive' or 'intelligent', 'biological' or 'cultural'? For three principle reasons, ethologists have long recognized that such dichotomies are both false and sterile (Hinde, 1968; Lehrman, 1953, 1970).

(i) Such dichotomies were often taken to imply that the factors influencing the development of behaviour were of two types only – genetic, and those associated with learning. In practice, environmental factors can influence behaviour in many ways, many of which do not come within any generally accepted definition of learning. To take an extreme example, a given genetic strain of the fruitfly *Drosophila melanogaster* may be capable of full normal flight, or erratic flight, or of no flight at all, depending on the temperature during development. Similarly, learning abilities can be influenced by nutrition whilst the organism is growing up.

(ii) Such dichotomies usually involve a definition of 'innate behaviour' in negative terms: a response is said to be 'innate' or 'unlearned' just so long as no learning process (or other environmental influence) has been identified in its development. The difficulty here is not merely the theoretical one of proving the null hypothesis, but arises from the fact that all development depends on both nature and nurture. There are limits to the environmental conditions under which any pattern of behaviour will develop – limits of temperature and humidity and of many other physical variables as well as limits of various types of social stimulation: in some cases the limits may be coincident with those in which life itself is possible, in others they may be quite narrow. For this reason, it is sometimes useful to characterize aspects of behaviour according to their stability or lability under environmental influences. Some are stable under a wide range of environmental (including social) conditions, whilst the appearance or nature of others is clearly determined by experiential factors. 'Stable' behavioural characters include those for which the relevant environmental factors are ubiquitously present for all members of the species: these are often called 'species-typical' characteristics, but this does not imply an absence of environmental influences on their development. However it must still be remembered that development may be stable up to the first appearance of the behaviour in question and subsequently labile, or labile up to the time of first performance and subsequently stable.

(iii) Such dichotomies concern items of behaviour, rather than the factors or processes involved in their development. Since all development depends on both nature and nuture, attempts to assign aspects of behaviour to one or other source are doomed to failure. If attention is focussed on processes, rather than on items of behaviour, it is sometimes convenient to distinguish the consequences of 'maturation' from those of 'experience'. However this is useful only if we remember that it is only a convenient abstraction, and depends on the universe being considered. Processes of maturation occur in the intraorganismic environment: they are not influenced by extraorganismic factors only in so far as the environment relevant to them is maintained constant by homeostatic mechanisms. In any case, the consequences of tissue differentiation may depend on experience: the functioning of the visual system depends on exposure to patterned light.

IDENTIFYING THE BASES OF DIFFERENCES

Thus attempts to dichotomize behaviour into that which is innate and that which is learned are not a fruitful way to study development (see Oyama, 1985, for a recent critical and stimulating survey of these issues). Development involves a nexus of causal relations, with action, reaction and interaction, both within the organism and between the organism and environment, at every stage. Somehow ways to tease apart these complicated processes must be found. A route often profitable is first to focus on differences in behaviour, seeking to distinguish whether they can be traced to genetic or to environmental differences.

With animals, experiments are possible. If two genetic strains are bred under identical conditions, differences between them can safely be assigned to the genetic difference between the strains. If two genetically identical animals or groups of animals are bred under different conditions, any difference can safely be ascribed to experiential factors. Of course in both cases there are limitations to the conclusions that can be drawn. A genetically based difference appearing under one set of conditions may not appear under another (see p. 55), and an environmental factor important for the development of a particular aspect of behaviour in one genotype may not be so in another. However this method of differences is an extremely powerful tool. Whilst its rigid application demands fairly precise experimental control, it can also be applied to natural situations with the aid of very reasonable assumptions – for instance, that groups of individuals within one interbreeding population are (statistically) genetically similar; or that when a phenotypic difference is not affected by environmental factors likely to be relevant to it, differing genetic influences are probable (e.g. racial differences in skin colour); or that when a reversible phenotypic difference tracks environmental influences it is likely to have powerful environmental determinants (differences in skin colour among Caucasians).

Stemming from the logic of the method of differences, 'heritability' estimates purport to measure the magnitude of the genetic contribution to a given trait. These involve dividing the total *variation* of the trait into genetic and environmental components, and a component representing their interaction. Heritability is defined as the proportion of the trait's variance due purely to genetic variance. This can be a useful concept if its limitations are recognized, but unfortunately they are not always spelled out. First, since it is assessed from variation in the character within a species, it is irrelevant to characters that are equally present in all individuals. We shall see later that this poses a problem with human universals. Second, the range of environmental variation studied is clearly crucial. In a constant environment all variation must have a genetic basis and heritability will be 100%: as environmental diversity increases, heritability is likely to decrease. For this reason, heritability measured in one range of environments does not necessarily apply to another. Third, calculation of heritability assumes that the genetic and environmental influences are additive – an improbable assumption especially if genetic or environmental variation is large. Too often the data are processed to get rid of non-additive interactions, and the ratio becomes meaningless (see e.g. Scarr & Kidd, 1983; Bateson, 1987).

In the human case, an experimental approach is not possible, but substantial progress can be made by making use of 'natural' experiments. Here extreme caution is necessary. For example Chisholm (1983) found a marked difference in irritability between Navajo Indian babies and white (English and American) babies. A genetic explanation is clearly tempting. However newborn irritability is associated with maternal blood pressure during pregnancy, and this could be affected by a number of non-genetic factors such as diet, exercise and psycho-social stress. A genetic explanation in this case is thus at least unproven. However over other issues reliable progress can be made by comparing the differences in behaviour between identical twins with that between non-identical twins and siblings, in each case when brought up in the same family or apart. This is discussed further below.

ORGANISM–ENVIRONMENT INTERACTION

The method of differences permits us to specify whether genetic or experiential factors or both are responsible for a given difference in behaviour and, with the reservations specified above, how far the variance in a given character within a population can be accounted for by genetic or by environmental variance. It is appropriate now to stress the intricacy of the ways in which the effects of internal (e.g. genetic) factors and external (environmental) factors may be interwoven. We shall consider some examples.

Young great tits (*Parus major*) beg noisily for food when in the nest. However they cease to do so the moment that they hear the parental alarm call. This inhibitory response is found in all individuals and does not require previous exposure to the call. Nevertheless experience can affect the effectiveness of the call. If the call is heard frequently just before parental feeding, it loses much of its effectiveness. On the other hand, exposure to the call in neutral or aversive circumstances enhances its effectiveness. Furthermore prolonged exposure to artificial sounds resembling the parental alarm decreases the effectiveness of the latter. This raises the possibility that the effectiveness of the alarm call depends in part on its acoustic contrast with the predominant sounds of the nestling's auditory environment (Ryden, 1978).

Similar principles apply to some aspects of human social behaviour, for instance to some of the movements used in non-verbal communication. We have already seen that smiling, laughter, crying and some other expressive movements appear in deaf and blind-born children, suggesting that their development does not require imitation or learning from others (Eibl Eibesfeldt, 1972). Furthermore, some of the situations that elicit them are effective without training or the operation of any obvious form of reinforcement. However there are marked cultural differences in the situations that elicit these movements, in the extent to which they are enhanced or concealed, and in the responses they elicit, indicating that their subsequent use is much affected by experience (Ekman & Friesen, 1969). Of course other communicatory gestures are culture-specific or even idiosyncratic, and heavily influenced by experience (see pp. 86–98).

Another example of complex interaction between motivational and experiential factors, and one which we may consider in more detail as it has obvious implications for the human case, concerns the development of gender differences in behaviour. In rhesus monkeys young males show more rough play, threat, aggression and sexual mounting than do females. These differences depend in part on pre-natal hormones: genetic females exposed whilst *in utero* to exogenous male hormones show the above patterns almost as frequently as do males (Goy, 1978). However these sex differences are affected also by the social conditions of rearing. For example:

1 Male rhesus reared in restricted environments show deficiencies in mounting behaviour that last into adulthood;

2 Infants reared by the mother subsequently show competent sex behaviour and low levels of aggression, but infants reared in peer groups tend to be aggressive;
3 The mounting frequency of males is higher in mother-reared heterosexual groups (i.e. containing both young males and females) than in isosexual ones (i.e. containing individuals all of the same sex), whilst the opposite is true for females;
4 Males reared in heterosexual groups show more aggressive behaviour and less peer behaviour than those reared in isosexual groups: this is probably because the males occupy only the dominant positions in the former case, whilst in isosexual groups they are both dominant and subordinate;
5 Females show less rough play in heterosexual groups than do males, but even less in isosexual groups: this sex difference in heterosexual groups therefore does not depend on suppression by dominant males (Goldfoot & Wallen, 1978).

These results show clearly that, in monkeys, sexual behaviour that is dimorphic in one situation may not be so in another. Social experience clearly contributes to the acquisition of sex-typical behaviour.

In humans the determinants of gender-role are, of course, much more complex, and great caution must be exercised in generalizing from monkeys (e.g. Adkins, 1980). But, as in monkeys, there are in the first place genetically based differences operating at least in part through pre-natal hormonal factors and influencing both structural characters and behavioural propensities (Money & Ehrhardt, 1972; Meyer-Bahlburg *et al.*, 1984). (In some cases it is possible that these pre-natal hormones produce their effects through parental treatment consequent upon knowledge of the hormonal abnormality, or through an influence of physical abnormality on the child's self concept, rather than by affecting brain mechanisms directly (Hines, 1982).) Social experience, however, again plays a crucial part, but in a more complex way than monkeys (e.g. Adkins, 1980). There are differences not only in the ways others treat boys and girls (e.g. Condry & Ross, 1985), but also and as a consequence, in the ideas boys and girls acquire about behaviour appropriate for the gender they conceive of themselves as having (review by Smith, 1986; Archer and Lloyd, 1985; Deaux, 1985). Indeed, in individuals who, through hormonal abnormalities or hormonal treatment, have ambiguous sex, the only factor that reliably predicts gender identity is the sex assigned to the child by those who reared it (Money & Ehrhardt, 1972). During the last 3 decades a large number of studies have documented the existence and crucial effectiveness of social stereotypes in determining gender role (e.g. Block,

1983), many having considerable cross-cultural generality (e.g. Williams & Best, 1982). Thus in humans it seems that the pre-natal and hormonal influences on gender role differences are of lesser importance compared with the experiential effects of the treatment received from others and the self-image acquired as a result of that treatment. In later chapters we shall see how social stereotypes can induce major differences in behaviour and personality by magnifying small sex differences in basic propensities. The origin of such stereotypes poses further problems to which we shall also return later (pp. 142–4).

Yet another way in which organismic and experiential factors interact in development stems from the fact that the environment individuals select for themselves, and the environment individuals provide for their offspring, are affected by the (genetically influenced) natures of the individuals themselves. Thus heredity and environment are not fully independent. In fact genotype–environment correlations may arise in several ways. First, children actively select and create their own environments from that which is provided, and how they do so will be affected by their genetic constitution. This has been termed 'active' genotype–environment correlation. Second, parents may not only pass on genes conducive to a particular characteristic, but also be themselves predisposed genetically to give their children an environment that augments the characteristic in question: for instance parents who are shy might not only pass on genes predisposing towards shyness but also provide an environment in which the children saw few strangers and thus never got used to them (passive correlation). Third, parents and others may react differently to children of different genotypes (reactive correlation) (Jaspars & Leeuw, 1980; Plomin & de Fries, 1983; Scarr & McCartney, 1983). The further complexities that may arise are exemplified by the fact that twins reared apart may be more similar than those reared together (Shields, 1962) – presumably because the proximity of the other causes each to seek environments different from those occupied by the other.

SENSITIVE PERIODS

We have seen that development involves a continuing interaction between a changing organism and a changing environment. The changes in the latter may be objective, involving for instance changes in the frequency and nature of interactions with others, or they may lie in the perceived or effective environment. What matters to a one month old baby differs from what matters at a year, and comparable changes continue throughout life. Since progressive changes in the individual may involve changes in susceptibility to environmental influences, it is not surprising that some aspects of behaviour can be influenced by environmental events more readily at one stage than either earlier or later.

A classic case concerns the 'imprinting' of the behaviour used by birds such as ducks, geese and chickens in maintaining proximity to their parent. The young of these species will follow a moving object as they would normally follow a parent, provided that the object is presented within a period starting a few hours after birth and finishing a few hours or days later. There are probably good adaptive reasons why the period for learning the characteristics of the parent is limited in this way. As we shall see later, it is to the parent's evolutionary advantage to look after its own offspring, but to reject those of others. It is thus important for the chick to follow and address its filial responses to its own parent, and not other adults who would reject it. The adult nearby when it first starts to walk is most likely to be its own parent. However an adult looks very different from different points of view, and the newly hatched bird probably lacks the ability to classify together different views of the parent as coming from the same object. Hence the need to learn its characteristics rapidly (Hinde, 1961; see also Bateson, 1979).

Somewhat later in life, as they are moulting into adult plumage, they learn the characteristics of their siblings. In this case the adaptive significance appears to lie in the avoidance of inbreeding or excessive outbreeding: in adulthood they mate preferentially with individuals slightly different from their own siblings (Bateson, 1983).

Lorenz (1935) regarded the time during which the parental characteristics were learned as immutable, and referred to it as a critical period. However it soon became clear that the limits of the period were not irrevocably fixed, and the term 'sensitive period' was seen as more appropriate. This implies merely that a given experience produces an effect on behaviour more readily during a certain period than either earlier or later. It does not imply that the period is absolutely tied to chronological age, or that comparable effects cannot be produced, though perhaps with more difficulty, at other times.

Unfortunately the persisting use of the earlier 'critical period' concept by some psychologists has led to considerable controversy over whether the concept of sensitive periods is useful in the study of human development (e.g. Clarke & Clarke, 1976). However in some cases the evidence is considerable. For instance children subjected to multiple stressful separations from their mothers in the first few years, but not later, have an increased risk of emotional or behavioural disturbance in late childhood or adolescence (Douglas 1975; Quinton & Rutter, 1976), and some environmental influences seem to have a greater effect on cognitive development during the preschool period than earlier or later (McCall, 1981).

Just why, in causal terms, a particular type of learning should be easier during a certain period than either earlier or later varies from case to case, an issue that need not concern us here (see Bateson & Hinde, in press). Sensitive periods are not a unitary phenomenon, but a convenient label for phenomena that may have diverse causal bases.

Three examples of ways in which the existence of sensitive periods could be of interest to the social scientist may be mentioned.

The first is that the various processes of socialization and acculturation can proceed only when the organism is ready for them. For example, the child cannot learn about religion until he or she has learned to speak, and once having learned about one religion, cannot easily be converted to another. Conformity to social norms through a sense of duty, rather than to avoid punishment, requires a considerable degree of psychological development (Kohlberg, 1969).

The second concerns their possible role in the choice of marriage partners. Westermarck (1891) suggested that adequate sexual relationships are seldom formed between individuals who have grown up together. There is some evidence for this view (e.g. Shepher, 1971). If substantiated, this implies an early sensitive period for the acquisition of a standard against which subsequent sexual partners are compared. (The parallel with the mechanisms for preventing inbreeding in birds, mentioned above, will be apparent. How far such a propensity provides a basis for incest taboos is a controversial matter, to be discussed later (pp. 158–60).)

A third issue concerns the role of extrinsic factors in enhancing susceptibility for learning outside periods in which it would otherwise occur or after a comparable type of experience has already had its effect. Changes in the social situations in which an individual finds himself demand cognitive reorientation. Often this can be accomplished gradually, but sometimes, for social or other reasons, a rapid transition is required. These are often marked by *rites de passage*, many of which (e.g. initiation rituals) are frequently of a stressful nature for those involved. It may be relevant here that a common element in various military, political, religious and therapeutic attempts to change the ways humans think and behave is a combination of stress and suggestion (e.g. Sargant, 1957). There are some indications of physiological factors related to this generality. High levels of stress are associated with rapid synthesis and turnover of noradrenalin (Ursin, Baade & Levine, 1978), and noradrenalin is implicated as an important factor in brain plasticity (Pettigrew, 1982; Horn, 1985).

CONSTRAINTS ON AND PREDISPOSITIONS IN DEVELOPMENT

Of all the possible ethological contributions to the social sciences, perhaps the most important is the insistence that the development of the individual is channelled but not predetermined. It is necessary to reject on the one hand genetic determinism, and on the other the *tabula rasa* view that human behaviour is infinitely malleable, as espoused by some psychologists (e.g. Watson, 1916) and social scientists (e.g. Berger & Luckmann, 1966). Instead, we must come to terms with an important aspect of the relation between genetic constitution and experience, namely the existence of predispositions in what an individual responds to and in what he or she learns, and constraints upon what he or she can learn that are not merely limitations of capacity. These constraints and predispositions may arise from the very nature of our bodies, from the properties of our sensory/perceptual apparatus, from the motor patterns at our disposal, or from properties of the nervous system which become apparent in specific learning situations (Seligman & Hager, 1972; Hinde & Stevenson-Hinde, 1973).

Consider first how the structure of an individual's body may influence the course of its behavioural development. An obvious case arises with food selection in fishes, which grow continuously. The size and nature of food objects taken change during development. Whilst this could be due to the gradual maturation of responsiveness to successively larger prey organisms, it is more probably an effect of changing reward/cost ratios, the size of prey that gives optimal food reward for the energy expended in taking it increasing with the size of the fish. For example, a perch of 4 inches needs the equivalent 37,500 *Cyclops* (a small crustacean) per day, or about one every 2 seconds. This might just be possible, but an 8 inch perch would need 600,000 Cyclops a day, which is unlikely to be possible. Instead it takes about 4 small fish (Allen, 1935; Hinde, 1959).

A similar principle applies to some interspecies differences. The several species of finch living in any one area tend to have beaks of different sizes, and to eat seeds of sizes such that they can de-husk them efficiently with beaks of the size they possess. Thus goldfinches, with small pointed beaks, tend to select small seeds such as those of thistles, but hawfinches which have heavy beaks take cherry stones, which goldfinches would never be able to open. The bases of seed selectivity lie at least partly in experience: young birds are more catholic in their tastes than adults, and gradually come to select preferentially those seeds that they can open most efficiently, kernel weight per time spent opening the seed being an important issue. Thus the basis of the predisposition to learn to select particular types of seeds lies at least partially in the size and structure of the beak (Kear, 1962).

In the same way, it must be argued, aspects of our behaviour probably depend upon the degree of fit between our physical bodies and the aspects of the environment with which they come into contact. Whilst we can properly say that our teeth are adapted for an omnivorous diet, it is also the case that we select the foods we do in part because we can deal with them with the masticatory tools at our disposal. Temperature preferences are conditioned in part by the body's response to temperature changes, preferred work schedules by the body's responses to stresses on its circadian rhythms. (Here of course it must be remembered that the cause–effect relations are not one way: an individual's behaviour is affected by his/her nervous, endocrine, etc., systems, but the functioning of those systems is affected reciprocally by the behaviour and experience of the individual. The dialectics in Fig. 1 extend to infra-individual levels.)

Again, the nature of our sensory/perceptual apparatus ensures that we are responsive to some changes in the physical environment and not others. Unlike some animals, for instance, we do not respond (overtly) to electromagnetic fields or to light beyond the limits of our visible spectrum. Within the range of stimuli to which we are potentially responsive, some stimulus arrays are more conspicuous than others: for instance circular forms are more conspicuous than irregular ones, and the occurrence of categorical perception appears to be universal and founded in infant capacities for the discrimination of colours (von Wattenwyl & Zollinger, 1979; Bornstein, Kessen & Weiskopf, 1976), and of speech sounds (Eimas, Siqueland, Jusczyk & Vigarito, 1971; Marler, 1979; Liberman, 1979). Of particular interest is the finding that monkeys have cortical cells that respond preferentially to faces, and to some faces more than to others (Rolls, 1987). Such perceptual dispositions are clearly going to influence what we learn.

On the motor side, the patterns of walking, running and so on are similar (though not necessarily identical) in all cultures. So are sucking, chewing and the Moro, grasping, orientation and many other reflexes. Even the development of hand skills is affected by physical growth processes (neurological and mechanical), the establishment of sensory-motor relations, the assembly of basic sub-routines of skilled movements, and the learning of transformation rules whereby these sub-routines are governed and mobilized (Connolly, 1973). And as we have seen, certain expressive movements, such as smiling, laughing and crying, also have marked similarities in form in all cultures. Such patterns, once acquired (and however acquired) must influence the subsequent course of development.

Again, at the motivational level, we all seek for food and learn to repeat responses that bring us food. We withdraw from painful stimuli, and learn to avoid situations that bring us pain. More specifically, we learn responses that lead to the ingestion of sugar and avoid those that lead us to ingest formic acid: this is in harmony with the properties of our digestive system, but anteaters are constituted differently (Barash, 1977). We interact with those around us in ways that establish and constitute relationships that are in general conducive to our survival and reproduction. We seek social approval. And, at the cognitive level, we all attempt to make sense of the world, to construct our own reality (Piaget, 1929). Indeed young organisms behave as though they were equipped with rules to acquire knowledge: 'If it is new, investigate its properties' ; 'Class together things seen at the same time' (Bateson & Chantrey, 1972); 'Watch what Mum does, and imitate her' (e.g. Bandura, 1977; see also Gewirtz, 1969). All such characteristics will channel the learning that occurs, and thus the course of development.

In some cases the constraints and predispositions may be much more specific than those mentioned so far. A classic animal case is the song of the chaffinch (*Fringilla coelebs*). This bird normally has a repertoire of several songs of the same general type: each song lasts about 2.5 seconds and consists of two or three phrases and a terminal flourish. The songs develop in early spring from a rambling sub-song which has no definite duration, a wide range of notes, and no terminal flourish.

Chaffinches hand-reared from a few days of age develop only a very simple type of song, with a definite duration but only one phrase and no terminal flourish. This indicates that learning from other individuals normally plays some part in song development. Birds brought up in groups, still in auditory isolation from normal chaffinch songs, produce songs more elaborate that those of individually isolated birds, but conforming to a group pattern that differs between groups and from the normal song.

If chaffinches are reared in isolation from a few months of age, after they have heard chaffinch songs, they produce in adulthood songs that are more or less normal. This indicates that some learning of the normal pattern occurs during the early months of life, before the birds themselves start to sing. This is confirmed by the fact that birds individually isolated from independence at a few weeks of age and exposed to chaffinch song from a tape recorder during the winter subsequently produce near-normal song. Other evidence indicates that further learning occurs later.

However chaffinches will not learn any song that they hear. They will not learn representations of chaffinch song in which the notes have a pure tonal quality, or songs of (most) other species. The evidence indicates that they will learn only songs with a note quality like that of chaffinch song. Furthermore, once they have developed a repertoire of a few songs, they cannot learn fresh variants (Thorpe, 1961).

When chaffinches are exposed to song early in life, before they themselves start to sing, they learn what to sing but not how to sing it. A reasonable suggestion is that they acquire a template, or elaborate a pre-formed template, and then, during the period of transition from subsong to full song, adjust their motor output to conform to the template previously acquired (Marler, 1984). Two predictions from this hypothesis have been confirmed. First, chaffinches will learn to sit on one perch rather than another if doing so permits them to hear chaffinch song, indicating that hearing song acts as a reinforcer (Stevenson-Hinde, 1972). Second, chaffinches, deafened after exposure to full song but before song development, never produce the normal song: deafening after song development does not affect its pattern (Nottebohm & Nottebohm, 1971). However the precise mechanism is far from clear, especially since the rather amorphous sub-song produced by many species before they come into full song may contain elements of alien songs which have evidently been learned but are dropped when full song develops (Marler, *pers. comm.*).

In other species of bird, song development depends on previous exposure to the species-characteristic song, but the nature of the constraints differ. Whilst chaffinches are apparently predisposed to learn songs with notes having a characteristic structure, in other species young birds are predisposed to imitate the song of the male who rears them (Baptista & Petrinovich, 1984). But the important issue is that each species, though having to learn the species-characteristic song, is predisposed to learn that rather than others.

Another important example of a predisposition to learn concerns the association between the taste of a food and subsequent ill-effects of its ingestion. Garcia and his associates showed that rats could learn to avoid poisoned food, even though the ill-effects could not have been felt for sometime after they had eaten the food (Revusky & Garcia, 1970). It has since been shown that rats learn to associate the *taste* of a food (e.g. saccharin) with subsequent ill-effects very much more readily than other stimuli present at the time it was eaten. However, it has also been shown that rats will learn to take avoiding action on hearing a buzzer that predicts a mild electric shock more readily than they will if the shock is predicted by the taste of saccharin (Domjan & Wilson, 1972). This difference cannot be explained by a difference in the salience of the two stimuli, since the taste is more effective in one context and the sound in another. A more likely alternative is that the 'relevance' of the stimulus is the crucial issue

(Stevenson-Hinde, 1973; Shettleworth, 1973). Whilst experimental psychologists have shown that diverse examples of associative learning can be explained in terms of a general learning mechanism designed to detect causal relationships (e.g. Mackintosh, 1983; Dickinson, 1980; Logue, 1979), there is as yet no evidence as to how rats could learn that tastes are relevant to illness or sounds to electric shocks (see also Delprato, 1980).

In subsequent chapters such characteristics of structure, sensory-perceptual functioning, responsiveness to stimuli, motor patterns, motivational and cognitive processes and constraints on learning will be referred to collectively as 'propensities'. Although heterogeneous and although some (e.g. motor patterns) are directly observable and others (e.g. the propensity to seek for social approval) are inferred, they are grouped together because they share two properties important in later chapters. First, they are reasonably (though not completely) consistent across individuals (and thus have ontogenetic stability in the sense described on p. 55). This implies neither a total absence of individual variation nor genetic determinism: each has a developmental history that may depend in part on properties of the social or physical environment. Second, they all place constraints on the course of individual development, predisposing individuals to develop in some ways rather than others. Although the propensities themselves are present in all individuals, the behaviour through which they find expression, and the behaviour and psychological characteristics whose development they facilitate, may vary with circumstances and between individuals.

Because such propensities are present in all (or virtually all) individuals, and because most social scientists are interested in differences between individuals, groups or societies, social scientists may feel that such propensities are of little relevance to their problems. Yet they provide part of the input into the dialectics between the successive levels of social complexity (Fig. 1): such propensities are part of 'human nature'. Even some quite specific predispositions are present in our own species, though more difficult to demonstrate with hard data. For instance the fear of snakes is extremely widespread, but at the same time variable between individuals (Hebb, 1949; Marks, 1969). There are difficulties with the view that fear of snakes is entirely dependent on learning, and also with the view that learning has no role (e.g. Delprato, 1980), and it is at least a reasonable supposition that humans are strongly predisposed to acquire a fear of snakes, though not all individuals do so. Children brought up in an institution, who have never seen a snake, show little fear if they first encounter one at ages one and a half or two and a half years, but avoid a snake crawling on the ground from about 3 years of age (Prechtl, 1950). That such behaviour would have been adaptive in our environment of evolutionary adaptedness seems highly likely. However individuals vary greatly in the extent to which they fear snakes and much evidence (Delprato, l.c.) indicates that experiential factors, including especially witnessing adults displaying fear of a snake, are undoubtedly also important. Indeed it will be argued later (p. 141) that discussion of human fear of snakes is scarcely profitable unless it is placed against the socio-cultural background of beliefs about snakes. Many other 'irrational' fears also involve objects or situations which could have posed a threat to our ancestors – fear of strangers, the dark, being alone, falling, and so on – would have made very good sense for infants who were carried by their mothers and for whom maternal proximity was essential for protection and nurturance (Bowlby, 1969). Interestingly, comparable fears of the real dangers of the modern world, such as cars and guns, occur much more rarely. This strongly suggests that our propensities to learn have been guided by natural selection.

A comparable phenomenon has been studied in some detail in vervet monkeys. This species responds differentially and appropriately to three types of predators – birds of prey, snakes, and mammalian predators. The appropriate responses can be elicited not only by the predators themselves, but also by alarm calls from adults. Young monkeys initially have a rather generalised responsiveness – for instance they may give the response appropriate to a winged predator to a falling leaf. However they play close attention to the responses of adults, and especially to those of their mother, and this probably plays an important part in increasing the specificity of their responsiveness (Seyfarth & Cheney 1986). In such cases the behavioural predisposition seems to depend or involve both an initial predisposition to respond to objects of the same general class and to tune such responsiveness through experience.

Thus, aspects of the nature of our sensory, perceptual and motor abilities, of the structure of our bodies, of the motivational bases of our behaviour, of our cognitive predispositions and of more specific mechanisms within our brains predispose behavioural development to go in some directions rather than others, and more specifically predispose individuals to learn some things rather than others. But we are dealing only with predispositions, and the actual course of development is determined by many other factors including, of course social influences.

The nature of these social influences is itself influenced (though not determined) by, for instance, the dispositions of human adults to teach and of humans to learn from other humans. Of course young of other species also learn from adults, but in no other species is there teaching comparable with that found in our own. Anecdotal and circumstantial evidence strongly suggest that such teaching and early learning is more effective when it takes place in the context of close relationships (e.g. Tizard 1985). For all social vertebrates development involves integration into a social group: in man we can describe it as involving learning to depart from an egocentric point of view to an ethnocentric conception of reality. What is of special importance in the present context is that, in all interactions with adults whether or not they involve teaching, human children are dealing with adults who are themselves acculturated and thus behave in culture-specific ways, using culture-specific artefacts, modes of communication and symbolic mediators that are more or less characteristic of the group in which they live. Thus human development, socialization and acculturation proceed hand in hand.

The basic propensities, the constraints on and predispositions for learning, must have been influenced by natural selection: their consequences on behaviour are therefore likely to be usually adaptive, but we shall see later that, primarily because of the complexities of socialization and acculturation, they are not inevitably so.

SUMMARY

This chapter reviews some general principles of development of relevance to the social scientist. The old nature–nurture issue is reviewed briefly: dichotomies of behaviour are misleading, but dichotomies of sources of influence on the development of behaviour may be useful in leading to attempts to specify the sources of differences more precisely. The complexity of organism–environment interactions during development is stressed, and the way in which the individual's sensitivity to experience changes through development discussed. The final section concerns limitations on what an individual can learn that are not limitations of capacity: constraints on what can be learned, and predispositions to learn some things rather than others, are inherent in our nature and may play an important role in the dialectics between successive levels of social complexity. Of special importance in the present context are predispositions to teach and to learn, especially within the context of close relationships: in humans development, socialization and acculturation proceed together.

5

Development – the individual and relationships

THE SOCIAL ENVIRONMENT

In our society, most young children grow up in a nuclear family, interacting daily with one or two parents, with siblings, and from time to time with relatives and friends. In due course, through schools and peer groups, the range and variety of their interactants increase. In other societies the details differ (e.g. Whiting & Whiting, 1975), but the general pattern of a network of relationships expanding from one or more with blood relatives (including nearly always the mother) and other kin is ubiquitous. Indeed something similar occurs in many non-human primates, and was almost certainly present in, to use Bowlby's (1969) term, our 'environment of evolutionary adaptedness' (Mellen, 1981).

This network of interpersonal relationships, of which the growing child forms part, constitutes a crucially important part of his or her environment. In studying psychological development, including the processes of socialization and acculturation (or enculturation), it is therefore essential to remember that the child is a social being, formed by and forming part of a network of relationships that are crucial to its integrity and individuality (e.g. Bronfenbrenner, 1979; Clarke-Stewart, 1978). Until recently, for instance, cognitive development was seen as involving the individual organism actively developing his or her potentialities, assimilating and accommodating to experience. On a Piagetian (1929) view, equilibration processes in the individual are the primary source of development. The social environment has a largely permissive role: provided the child can explore the environment autonomously, discovering its properties by acting upon it, development will proceed in such a way that the child acquires all the basic cognitive structures. Relationships play a role, but cultural differences are largely irrelevant in the early stages.

Many developmental psychologists now see this view as underemphasizing the crucial importance of the social environment. From birth, the child's physical and cognitive development depends to a very large extent on interactions with others. Early interactions with the mother are not functionless games, but play a vital role in the child's emotional and cognitive development (e.g. Stern, 1985; Bryant, 1985). Cognitive, emotional and social factors are interwoven in complex ways in development (e.g. Radke-Yarrow & Sherman, 1985).

Turning specifically to cognitive issues, discovery is to a large extent socially mediated: through interactions with others the child learns to act on objects and to regulate interpersonal behaviour. Mainly through interiorizing what he has learned in regulating interpersonal behaviour does he come to regulate his own behaviour, and to act and think autonomously. Thus Vygotsky (1934) notes how the infant's vain attempt to reach an object elicits a reaction not from the object but from another person. If this happens a number of times, the child comes to use such movements as an indicative act aimed at someone else. They become means for initiating social interactions. Subsequently, through interactions with others the child accquires language which can then serve as a tool in mediating not only interpersonal but also personal behaviour (see also p. 74). On this view, then, pan-cultural behavioural propensities are due in part to the availability of basically similar social environments in early development. At the same time, cultural differences in personality are due in part to cultural differences in child-rearing practices, childhood relationships and the environment of development (e.g. Whiting & Whiting, 1975).

It is crucial to bear in mind that the interchange between infant and environment is an active one. Others impose themselves to a greater or lesser extent on the child, but the child also actively selects from the social experiences made available to it. As development proceeds, social circumstances are perceived along dimensions that are cognitively structured and will be perceived differently by different individuals: the individual acquires and develops socially constructed ways of behaving, of conceptualizing and interpreting the world. According to the nature of his social exposure, the child may classify his experiences in diverse ways, allocate meanings differentially, and weave together meanings in culturally specific, and beyond that in idiosyncratic, ways (e.g. Perret-Clermont, 1985).

For these reasons, we must come to terms with the relations between the child's inherent propensities and the diverse natures of the social experiences to which he or she is exposed if we are going to understand the processes of development, socialization and acculturation.

A non-human example

The developing child's social environment does not consist merely of a number of isolated individuals, but of individuals who also interact with each other in systems of increasing complexity. The relatively simpler situation in a particular species of group-living monkey can be used to exemplify the issues involved.

Young rhesus monkeys are held by their mothers virtually continuously for a few weeks, and then leave her for progressively longer periods of time. Mothers vary in their permissiveness, and this is likely to affect their infant's development. In addition the mothers at first determine which other individuals the infants will interact with – for instance the infants first encounter the adult females with whom their mothers habitually sit, and play with the offspring of these 'friends' (who are mostly close kin) of their mothers. Over time, the nature of the infant's associations changes. Those with closely related individuals become strong relationships, whilst other individuals remain as 'acquaintances' (Berman, 1982 a & b).

This is a general picture. However, we have already seen (Fig. 2) that the structure of the troop is complex, and the more precise nature of the infant's environment depends on the social position of the infant's mother in the troop – for instance whether she is a member of a small or a large matriline, with relatively few or many close relatives able to intervene on her behalf; whether the mother is dominant or subordinate in the troop, more or less able to defend the infant's interests in encounters with others; and whether the infant has few or many siblings to interact and play with when young and to dominate or be dominated by later (Hooley & Simpson, 1983).

And beyond that, demographic factors may affect the infant's social environment. Berman (in press) has data indicating that as a troop grows, the infants come into contact with more other individuals but a smaller proportion of them are close kin. The proximity of relative strangers causes mothers to become more restrictive, and the infant's social network comes again to be more focussed on close kin. This in turn may affect the lines along which group fission occurs. There are thus changes of a number of types that could affect the infant's social development (Fig. 10).

All this represents only a brief summary of an 'outsider's' view of the variability in the social environment of young monkeys. We can be confident that it would be perceived as even more diverse if we could see 'with monkey's eyes'. The social environment of the human child is at least as complex.

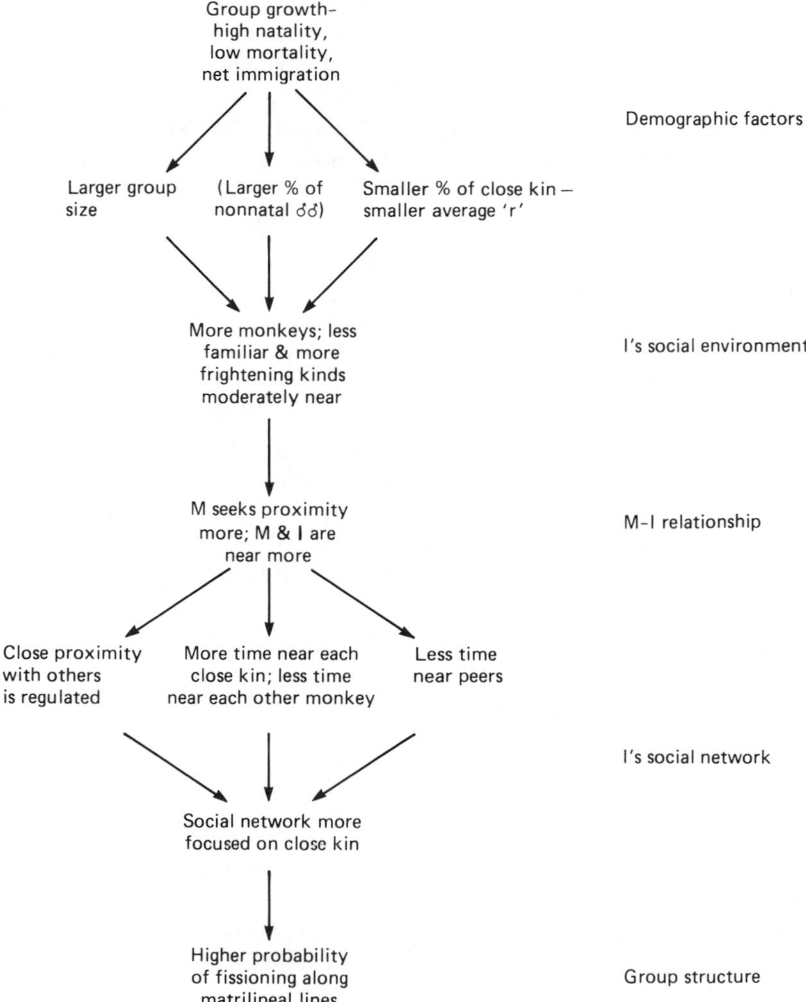

Fig. 10 Postulated relations between demograpic factors and inter-individual relations in a group of rhesus macaques (From C. Berman, in press).

THE DIFFERENTIAL CONTRIBUTION OF DIFFERENT RELATIONSHIPS

The emergence of the self as a subject, agent and reflective individual, and the emergence of the self as an object, defining itself in categories appropriate with respect to the external world, depend on interactions with other individuals (Mead, 1934; Sullivan, 1953; Harter, 1983). Given that children grow up in a complex and changing social environment, we may ask whether some relationships are more important than others in influencing socio-emotional and cognitive development. Opinions have differed on this issue. Some, and especially those with a psychoanalytic orientation, regard the mother–child relationship as the prime determinant of all future relationships (e.g. Bowlby, 1969). ('Mother' here is to be interpreted as the figure who performs the primary care-giving role.) This is in harmony with the finding that children reared in institutions with multiple care-givers may subsequently show some impairment in their ability to cope with social situations and to form social relationships. Furthermore psychological development depends in part on the imitation of competent models and on the internalization of skills first actualized in interaction with more competent individuals. As we have seen, Vygotsky (1934) argues that much of the child's early learning takes place in interaction with others. It is within the relationships he or she has established that the child relates acts to outcomes, signs with actions, and acquires language as a major mediating tool in regulating behaviour. Adults provide a very special type of learning environment for the child by presenting material within its 'zone of proximal development' – that is, within limits set by the stage that the child has already reached: the child can enter into an action or discourse suggested by an adult only if it is not too different from what it can already cope with.

However the parent–child relationship is inevitably complementary. Adults teach, provide rules, restrain, encourage and give to the world the order that children seek. Children conform, more or less, but the radically different perspectives, interests and goals of parent and child limit the real understanding that can be gained from the interaction by the child. By contrast, in interacting with peers, mutual understanding can be reached and the child can compare self with other comparable individuals (eg. Sullivan, 1953; Youniss, 1980). In addition, cognitive development is often facilitated by differences from other comparable individuals in opinion or approach to problems (Doise, Mugny & Perret-Clermont, 1974; Perret-Clermont & Brossard, 1985).

There are thus reasons for thinking that relationships with adults and relationships with peers usually play important but different roles in emotional and cognitive development. To discuss which is the more important would be a vacuous enterprise, especially as relationships within a family or group affect each other, so that parent–child, child–sibling and child–peer relationships may be interdependent to extents which vary with age (e.g. Minuchin, S., 1974; Minuchin, P., 1985). Of course, at least in most Western societies, the parent–child relationship comes first, and thus plays a role in influencing what the child can get out of subsequent relationships with peers (Hinde and Tamplin, 1983).

ASPECTS OF COGNITIVE DEVELOPMENT

The influence of social relationships on performance in tests of cognitive capacity was referred to in Chapter 2, and the importance of social interactions in cognitive development has already been mentioned briefly in this chapter. Here we may emphasize a few additional matters bearing on the importance of social relationships.

The first concerns the basic question of the nature of cognitive development. Carey (1986) has convincingly argued that many aspects of cognitive development do not depend simply on the maturation of new abilities: for instance much of the apparent increase in memory span with age disappears if nonsense syllables are used in testing, implying that the increase depends on the meaningfulness of the digits or letters used to the subject. Nor can improvements be ascribed simply to knowledge acquisition. Rather an important role is played by restructuring of the already acquired knowledge. To take a somewhat trivial example, many four year olds class plants with rocks as 'non-moving', but most ten year olds class them with animals as 'living'. It must be presumed that such changes occur in part as a consequence of discourse with others, especially adults in the early years and peers later, and are culture-specific.

The second issue concerns the importance of differences of opinion between peers. This is best illustrated by a particular example. Children were first tested on their ability for the conservation of liquids (e.g. assessing when two differently shaped containers contain the same amount of liquid). Some performed poorly on this task. A week later, each of these non-conserving children interacted with another child (of the same or a more advanced cognitive level) on a similar task until both agreed that they had the same quantity to drink. Then, after a further week, the children were re-tested on the conservation of liquids and other related tasks. Children showed more progress in ability to cope with comparable tasks in subsequent tests when they had had this opportunity to interact with a peer than did control children. It was not necessary for the partner to be more able or to give more correct answers: the important issue was the confrontation. But it was necessary that this confrontation should concern the cognitive task, and not other issues (e.g. unfairness, jealousy or blame for incompetence). Furthermore progress occurred only if the subject had reached a sufficient cognitive level (cf zone of proximal development, see p. 74): if he or she had not, the socio-cognitive conflict involved in the confrontation did not affect cognitive development. The progress might be generalized to other conservation tasks (matter, length, etc.). (Doise & Mugny, 1981; Doise, 1985; Perret-Clermont & Brossard, 1985.)

Another issue concerns the manner in which social relationships may actually enter in to cognitive operations concerned with the material world. If two flexible bracelets are laid out on a table partially curled up, some young children are unable to specify which is the longer. Yet such children can often assign correctly the larger of the two to the arm of the experimenter and the smaller to their own, whilst failing to assign them correctly to two cylinders of differing size. Furthermore, after succeeding with the human subjects they are likely to be able to generalize their ability to new problems. Again, as noted above, young children often evaluate the amount of liquid in differently shaped glasses in terms of the level it reaches, without taking into account the width of the glasses. If children are told they each merit an equal reward and are asked to share liquid equally between two differently shaped glasses, they are more likely to make cognitive progress (in terms of their ability to perform correctly on subsequent related tasks) than if the two partners' equal merits had not been stressed. The notion of 'social marking' used to explain such data postulates correspondences betwen social relations influencing the interactions of individuals in a given situation and cognitive relations between the properties of things in the material world (e.g. Doise, 1985).

Finally, the social context may influence cognitive processes. Thus while acting as street vendors, children and adolescents in Recife, Brazil, solve a large number of mathematical problems without recourse to pencil and paper. Carraher, Carraher & Schliemann (1985) tape-recorded the responses of subjects to such problems posed in the market place, and then interviewed them about the methods they had used. They were also given formal tests of comparable problems. Many children capable of solving a computational problem in the natural setting failed when it was disembedded from its context. This seemed to be primarily due to the use of different computational strategies. Thus the nature of cognitive processes directed towards solving a particular problem is affected by the social situation.

In general, then, these diverse studies illustrate that quite basic aspects of cognitive development and performance are influenced by the social situation. It hardly needs to be added that more complex properties of the child's conceptual world, how he/she perceives and classifies his experience, are crucially influenced by social factors (see Chapter 8).

ALTERNATIVE STRATEGIES

Given the diversity of micro-social situations into which many young animals and virtually all young children are born, it is not surprising to find that the course of development may vary in accordance with the prevailing conditions, and that in the majority of cases the course taken is one suited to those conditions. The migratory locust is an extreme example – the hoppers develop into an off-white, yellow, brown or black (according to the background) sedentary form or a black and orange migratory one, depending on the density of other individuals around them. Although no such dramatic difference in morphological characteristics is involved, the complexity and diversity of a young primate's social environment (see above) result in considerable differences in their social behaviour.

Consider the relationships between adult male monkeys. The adult males in a troop can usually be arranged in an approximately linear hierarchy such that A bosses B, B bosses C, and so on. Being at the top of the hierarchy carries a number of advantages in terms of access to mates, food and so on, so that animals strive to be top. But an animal which finds itself low in the hierarchy does not strive continually to defeat those above it. Rather it finds alternative means to satisfy its needs – stealth, subtlety, even deception. Thus we must describe the animal's behaviour in terms of a series of alternative strategies – 'Be boss if you can, but if you can't resign yourself and find other routes to your goals.' Of course, the use of the term strategy here carries no necessary implication of conscious planning. The goals, the range of possible means for achieving them, and the flexibility to adopt one or another, are characteristic of the species: the particular courses adopted differ between individuals, and in the same individual at different times, according to circumstances and the nature of the individual in question.

Similar issues arise with maternal styles. Altmann (1980), studying baboons in Africa, divided the mothers into those who were 'restrictive' with their infants and those who were 'laissez-faire'. In the necessarily somewhat small sample of baboons that she studied, the offspring of restrictive mothers were more likely to survive to maturity. Altmann suggests that this was because, in the early months, such infants were less exposed to kidnapping, predation, and so on. However she also stresses that other factors must be taken into consideration. With 'restrictive' mothering infant independence is achieved more slowly, so that a laissez-faire style could lead to infants better able to survive if orphaned. The balance between factors producing infant mortality and those producing maternal mortality may vary with circumstances, so that the relative effectiveness of restrictive vs laissez-faire styles may vary. For instance, mothers might be expected to become more laissez-faire as they get older, because their infants are more likely to be orphaned. Again, if the offspring of high-ranking mothers are less exposed to social dangers than those of low-ranking ones, the balance of advantages for them may swing towards a laissez-faire style. On this view there would be no best mothering style, and natural selection would act to favour individuals who showed a mothering style appropriate to the situation in which they found themselves.

That the concept of alternative strategies is applicable to human behaviour hardly needs emphasizing, but one case from the child development field is of special interest. In the Ainsworth Strange Situation procedure for assessing parent-infant 'attachment' (Ainsworth *et al.*, 1978) infants are separated from the accompanying parent for about three minutes (see p. 28). On reunion, most infants go straight to the parent and make physical contact with him or her before continuing to play with the toys provided. However, some infants actively avoid and ignore the parent even when he/she seeks their attention, and focus on toys and the inanimate environment instead. In view of the importance of the parent–child relationship to the infant such behaviour seems maladaptive. However it has been found that the mothers of such children often have an apparent aversion to physical contact with their child and are restricted in emotional expression (Main and Stadtman, 1981). In addition, the child's avoidance is often associated with traces of maternal 'anger' (George and Main, 1979). Main and Weston (1982) have suggested that avoidance is a strategy that permits the offspring of such mothers to maintain organization, control, and flexibility in behaviour. If the infant were to attempt to cling to the somewhat rejecting mother, distress and behavioural disorganization would be likely. The child thus employs alternative strategies according to the nature of the mother.

In the case of the subordinate monkey, and perhaps in that of restrictive mothering, we could regard the behaviour as a temporary adjustment to current circumstances. However there is evidence that behaviour in the strange situation has long term correlates (Bretherton, 1985). We must expect the dispositions an individual develops to cope with particular situations to become independent from the context in which they were first developed, and to be used in others (see pp. 2, 107–8). Human faculties for using symbolic mediators enormously increase the possible complexity here, for the behaviour displayed depends also on how the individual interprets the situation.

Cases such as these emphasize that variations in behaviour within a culture are not necessarily to be regarded as mere aberrations. Nor are they necessarily to be seen as due either simply to the particular experiences of the individuals concerned nor as based in genetic differences from others. Rather we may seek to interpret them, or many of them, as rooted in basic propensities that are realized in behaviour in diverse ways through dialectical relations between the individual and the particular social and cultural situation within which he/she is living.

CONTINUITIES AND DISCONTINUITIES

The view of development presented so far involves a continuing interaction between the individual and his/her environment from conception to death such that each shapes the other. Put in that way, the course of development seems like a continuum, with each experience affecting the individual to a greater or lesser extent and thus having potential repercussions throughout life. However, as we have already seen (p. 54), we must expect some childhood characteristics to be temporary devices suited to the current stage, to be subsequently demolished in the progression towards adulthood. And indeed there sometimes seem to be marked discontinuities in development. An obvious biological case is metamorphosis: the changes from caterpillar to pupa and from pupa to butterfly involve dramatic changes in structure and behaviour. In mammals the change from feeding by sucking to eating solid food may involve a switch to a quite different control mechanism (Hall & Williams, 1983).

In such cases, it might appear that experiences before the given change would have no long term significance: once pupated, the pupa seems to 'start again' and the tissues apparently reorganize to generate a butterfly. Less dramatic changes have been postulated in human development. For instance the scores of attentiveness, vocalization and smiling in two-month-old infants fail to predict their relative scores on the same measures at four months (Kagan, 1978), and a number of temporally concordant changes (increased attentiveness, inhibition, object permanence, distress in response to strangers and to separation) have been taken as evidence for a discontinuity in development towards the end of the first year (Kagan, 1980).

That the rate of development (however measured) is not constant, and that some characteristics change much more rapidly during certain periods (e.g. puberty) than others, is not to be denied. But great care is necessary before marked discontinuities in development are postulated. There are a number of reasons for believing that consistent causal chains persist through the individual's life, although they may not be immediately apparent and although they involve changes in behaviour *appearing* to imply discontinuity.

In the first place, the effects of experience may persist through marked structural change. It has been shown, for instance, that the food plant selected for egg-laying by certain moths may be affected by their experiences as a caterpillar (Thorpe & Jones, 1937), and the effects of training larval amphibians can be detected in adulthood (Herschkowitz & Samuel, 1973).

Second, the evidence for discontinuities is often misleading. The issues involved need not be discussed here (see Bateson, 1976; Hinde & Bateson, 1984), and two examples will suffice. A discontinuity is often postulated on the grounds that the rank order of individuals on a particular characteristic changes dramatically from one time to another. However it could be that one or other set of measurements was made in a period of rapid change which individuals pass through at different rates, the original order being restored thereafter. Or it could be that in one or other period the characteristic in question was at a floor or ceiling level (e.g. all individuals were able to read perfectly), so that rank order correlations lost their meaning (Bateson, 1978).

Third, a number of cases of consistencies in psychological characteristics over a wide age span have in fact been reported. For example, 53 women were assessed at 30 and again at 70 years of age. All 5 of the cognitive variables used, and 10 of the 16 personality variables, showed significant stability over this age span (Mussen, Eichorn, Honzik, Bieber & Meredith, 1980). As another example, Thomas & Chess (1982) found significant correlations between a measure of temperament along a 'difficult' to 'easy' scale at 3–5 years and a comparable measure at 18–22 years. And Richman, Stevenson & Graham (1982) found that 62% of children assessed as having problems at 3 years of age showed deviant behaviour when assessed at 8 years, as compared with only 22% of the control population. Another source of evidence lies in the persistence of the effects of a particular type of experience: for instance, children with reduced opportunities for forming close relationships over the first 2 or 3 years of life appear to have reduced abilities to form close relationships in later life, and to be under-discriminating in their displays of friendliness (e.g. Wolkind, 1974).

In such cases the possibility arises that the continuities or sequelae are due to persisting environmental influences, and in particular a persisting climate of relationships. For instance the experience of parental loss may be associated with inadequate parental care (Brown *et al.*, 1986) or institutional upbringing (Quinton & Rutter, 1986). This appears not to be the case for the effects of institutional upbringing on the subsequent ability to form close relationships, but in some other cases the presence of consistent experiential factors appears to be crucial. For instance programmes of intervention in the preschool years were earlier thought to lead to some immediate I.Q. gains but to no substantial long-term consequences. Recently, however, it has become apparent that there are longer-term sequelae involving some increases in academic achievement and a reduction in the proportion of children requiring special educational treatment (e.g. Clarke-Stewart & Fein, 1983; Lazar & Darlington, 1985).

However the evidence suggests that such effects depend on a variety of social factors including continued parental support for education, positive personality characteristics and supportive teachers. The long-term effects are thus not direct, but stem from a sequence of effects involving relationships in both home and school (Rutter, in press).

Fourth, just as consistencies may depend on the presence of persisting experiential factors, so may apparent discontinuities in the behaviour of an individual be due to changes in his or her environment and especially to changes in important relationships. In the case of dramatic discontinuities, this is often obvious enough: every school teacher knows that the appearance of problems in school may reflect trouble at home. Perhaps of more general importance, many parents adjust their parental behaviour to the requirements of their children more easily at one stage than at another. Thus Dunn, Plomin & Nettles (in press) found that parents behave with considerable consistency to successive children of the same age, but parental behaviour often changes dramatically as children grow up (Clarke-Stewart & Hevey, 1981). This raises the possibility that apparent discontinuities are related to changes in the quality of important relationships in the children's lives.

Finally, and most importantly, the multiple interacting factors that influence the individual in development may make it exceedingly difficult to identify readily the long-term effects of experience on development. As discussed earlier for consistencies across situations at the same time, continuities over time may be revealed in ways other than by comparing similar patterns of behaviour over time. What we must search for has been termed by Sroufe (1979) 'coherence across transformations' (see also Hinde & Bateson, 1984) or causal connections between experiences at one age and subsequent psychological or behavioural outcomes. At one level, this involves recognizing that the same behavioural propensity may be revealed in different ways at different ages and/or in different situations. At another, it means that we must come to terms with the ways in which one type of experience or relationship may affect behaviour of a different sort in a different context and/or at a different stage in the life history. Sroufe's work on the precursors of seductive behaviour in mothers exemplifies this (see pp. 47–8). As another example, in a study of the effects of institutional rearing Rutter, Quinton & Liddle (1983) found that the strongest effect on the women's parental styles was provided by the characteristics of the women's spouses. This, however, could be seen as an indirect effect of the institutional rearing: over half of the institution-reared women married men with psychosocial problems, as compared with 13% in the general population comparison group. Thus the childhood experiences influenced the choice of spouse, and the spouse affected the quality of parenting. And a difficult childhood can enhance the risk of psychosocial difficulties in adulthood even though none are apparent at the time (Quinton & Rutter, 1986).

Thus, because every behavioural act depends upon numerous capacities and propensities and upon aspects of the current environmental context including especially the social situation, the effects of a given experience on behaviour in either the short-term or the long-term are not always easily predictable. This is not an attempt to seek refuge from the task of understanding behavioural development in an appeal to complexity. Continuities are sometimes obvious, but their apparent absence is not in itself a reason for abandoning the search for causal sequences underlying the changes that occur. Just because the behaviour shown in every interaction depends on both participants, and because every individual changes in development, experience with individual A at time 1 can hardly be expected to produce a tendency to behave with individual B at time 2 in exactly the same way as would have been the case at time 1. Although reorganizations of psychological structures may occur, underlying coherence is often there to be found.

SUMMARY

Children grow up in a social environment, and their development is crucially affected by their relationships with others. Relationships with adults and peers not only affect each other, but may be of different significance for the child. Individuals use and develop alternative strategies in order to satisfy their needs: strategies acquired by the individual because of the current social situation at one stage may affect his/her characteristics and his behaviour in other situations at a later point in time. Although development often appears to involve discontinuities, psychological continuities are often there to be found.

6

Universal individual characteristics

WHAT QUESTIONS CAN BE ASKED?

We have seen that the analysis of behavioural development involves first the study of differences in order to implicate genetic or environmental factors in their genesis, and then study of the mechanisms of action of the factors so isolated. In one important way such an approach is inadequate for the social scientist. Although one of his major goals is indeed to seek understanding of the bases of differences in behaviour between individuals, groups or cultures, he must also understand what is common to them (Lumsden & Wilson, 1981). Explanations are needed not only for the forms that incest taboos take in different societies, but also for the fact that incest taboos, of one sort or another, are virtually ubiquitous. The anthropologist must seek to explain differences between the structures of different societies, but he must also explain why all societies are structured, and why the structures are always in some sense hierarchical. To understand human diversity, it is necessary to know something of the clay from which it is formed. To focus *exclusively* on differences, as advocated by some anthropologists (e.g. Harris, 1979) is to build a castle upon sand: at least the analysis of differences must go hand in hand with a search for common properties that will aid comprehension of the differences.

In fact the search for human universals has had a long and not always respectable history (Count, 1973). Bastian's (1881) 'psychic unity of mankind' was used as a *deus ex machina* to account for supposedly independent inventions. Some attempts to describe human universals have been based on theories of the human mind (e.g. psychoanalytic) of doubtful value in this context, and used concepts (e.g. adolescent conflict, Oedipus complex) that turned out to have more cultural specificity than was anticipated (Bourguignon, 1973). Geertz (1970) has argued that a search for Man (*sic*) '"behind," "under" or "beyond" his customs, is inevitably fruitless, because man does not exist without some form of culture. But if, instead, one looks for Man 'in' culture, 'one is in some danger of losing sight of him altogether. Either he dissolves, without residue, into time and place, a child and perfect captive of his age, or he becomes a conscripted soldier in a vast Tolstoian army, engulfed in one or other of the terrible historical determinisms . . .' Instead, Geertz recommends a focus on diversity. However in the following chapters I shall argue that these problems can be at least partially resolved by giving due attention to the level of social complexity at which human universals are being sought. So-called 'universals' at the level of sociocultural structure involve different issues from the universals that can be found at the level of individual behaviour. Because of the mutual influences within and between each level of social complexity, the socio-cultural universals are related, but related only indirectly, to the psychological characteristics of individuals.

In so far as a behavioural character is found in all individuals, the method of differences (see pp. 56–7) fails. Both genetic influences (heritability) and environmental influences on its variance will be zero, and we can make no statements about their relative importance. In special cases cross-species comparisons or pathological cases can help, but in general all that can be said is that the genetic constitution of all individuals is such that the character in question appears under the whole range of environments experienced by individuals of the species. Changes in either the genetic constitution or the environment of development could in theory affect the character, (though it is possible and perhaps likely that an effective change in one or both of these might breach the viable limits for development of any sort). We have referred to such characters as (developmentally) stable (p. 55).

In point of fact, of course, no character is absolutely constant across individuals: there is always some degree of variation in its several features. Where such variations are correlated with environmental or cultural differences, the character may be stable within the range of environments provided by each environment or culture, but not across them. The question of whether the cultural or individual variation is due to experiential differences or to genetic differences between individuals is still open, though in principle resolvable with data from (e.g.) twin or adoption studies.

For example, twin studies provide evidence that differences in perception of the Mueller-Lyer and other primary illusions amongst subjects from Western cultures have a partially genetic basis (Scarr & Kidd, 1983). There are also differences between cultures, which are held to be experientially determined (e.g. Rivers, 1901; Segall, Campbell & Herskovitz, 1966): however the latter interpretation is unproven (compare p. 57).

In so far as a given characteristic is universal, not only can we make no statements about the genetic or environmental contributions to its development, but there are also difficulties about functional questions. As discussed in Chapter 1, functional questions, like developmental ones, usually concern differences and so are strictly speaking inapplicable to universal characters. However in a loose sense we can ask 'What is this behaviour good for?' or 'What immediate consequences of this behaviour are likely to enhance the individual's survival or (inclusive, see p. 101) reproductive success?'. In some cases, where current beneficial consequences are not apparent, we may ask instead 'What *was* this behaviour good for?' As we have seen, the 'argument from design' involves two types of assumption – namely assumptions about the nature of an 'environment of evolutionary adaptedness' which differed in some respects from that in which we live now, and assumptions about the temporal stability of the character in question. Thus we must bear constantly in mind the limitations of the clues available to us. However the nature of the universal characteristics of our species that influence the development and nature of our social behaviour is an issue of considerable importance for all the social sciences, and we must not lightly discard such evidence as we have.

Furthermore, in so far as even a 'universal' shows some variation in some of its aspects, we can investigate functionally relevant sequelae of the variants. With behavioural characteristics this often runs into another difficulty – abnormalities or variants tend to involve a number of different aspects of behaviour. However, as we shall see, in some cases we can examine how far the variations in the strength of a given propensity (or in the way in which it is expressed) are correlated with variation in reproductive success.

In fact questions about function, coupled with an appreciation for the dialectics between successive levels of social complexity (Fig. 1), can give us some insights. In this and later chapters we shall consider some aspects of human behaviour of increasing complexity – focussing in this chapter on behavioural and psychological characteristics of individuals, and in subsequent ones on inter-individual relationships and aspects of sociocultural structures. The aim is not to present a comprehensive review, but to use particular cases to assess the limits of a functional approach in illuminating the nature of the characteristics concerned. To summarize the conclusions, we shall see that it can be valuable for some aspects of individual behaviour and for some relationships, even though they are subject to influences from the sociocultural structure, but that at the sociocultural level a functional approach is much less useful.

The discussion of this issue was really started in Chapter 4, where we were concerned with aspects of our make-up that affect what we learn. The emphasis there was on universal human psychological characteristics or propensities (see pp. 63–9), so perhaps it is as well to reiterate that every characteristic is subject to individual variation, and that much of that variation is to be understood in terms of differences in experience – differences that may be culture specific. This applies even to relatively elementary psychological processes. For instance, as we have seen, through language, cultural factors may influence perception: the colour terms available in the subject's language affect performance on tests of colour perception (Rivers, 1901). This, however, does not affect the argument: the variants influence the course of learning, as discussed in Chapter 4, and feed into the dialectics between levels of social complexity, as discussed in the succeeding chapters.

In this chapter we take up two aspects of the behaviour of individual humans, the first to show how changes in a particular artefact can reasonably (though certainly without proof) be ascribed to a universal behavioural propensity, and the second illustrating how cultural influences may be closely interwoven with pan-cultural propensities. In both cases argument from design, supported in the second case by comparative data, suggests (but, it must be repeated, does not prove) that the basic propensities were once of functional significance. Then we shall turn to the perhaps more interesting question of whether individual differences in the extent to which universal propensities are displayed can be interpreted in terms of reproductive function.

PREFERENTIAL RESPONSIVENESS AND ARTEFACTS

There is abundant evidence from non-human species for preferential responsiveness to certain stimulus configurations that is independent of previous experience of those stimuli: for example, a territory-holding male stickleback will court a very crude fish model that has a swollen belly, and attack one that has a red belly and is held vertically,[1] and a chaffinch which has never seen an owl will 'mob' a crude wooden model with conspicuous eyes just as it would mob a real owl.

There is some evidence that humans have elements of a similar selective responsiveness. The case of responsiveness to snakes was discussed in Chapter 4. As another example, there is evidence that we have a tendency to respond parentally to certain characteristics of babies. In most non-

[1] Recent work indicates that these responses are not quite so consistent as earlier ethological reports indicated, and that 'anxiety' and a variety of consequences of experience affect responsiveness to the stimuli. However the basic principle remains valid (Rowland & Sevenster, 1985; Baerends, 1985).

human primates (and indeed other species) young individuals have special characteristics of shape and/or colour that elicit parental behaviour from adults. Lorenz (1950) noted that many Disney cartoon animals have features that appear to be caricatures of baby characteristics – for instance, high bulging foreheads, small noses and large cheeks. A number of experimental studies were in harmony with his view that humans (at least those of Western cultures) respond preferentially to such features (Gardner & Wallach, 1965; Sternglanz, Gray & Murakami, 1977; Fullard & Reiling, 1976). Responsiveness to them appears to increase in girls around puberty and in boys a year or two later. Although it is certain that experience plays a role, the tendency to develop responsiveness to such configurations seems to be widespread and perhaps ubiquitous.

More recently further evidence that other cartoon characters owe their appearance to such propensities has come to light. Thus Mickey Mouse, at first a slightly evil mischievous individual, later acquired a more beneficent disposition. Concurrently, his nose became shorter and his forehead larger (Gould, 1980). Similar changes have occurred in the faces of teddy bears. The early ones, manufactured at the beginning of the century and associated with a story about Theodore Roosevelt on a bear hunt, were modelled on a real bear with a long snout sometimes encased in a leather muzzle. Over the years their snout has become relatively shorter and their foreheads relatively larger (Fig. 11). The change is presumably due to a process comparable with selection, those types more successful in leaving the shop shelves being more numerous there in the next year. Thus the supposition is that those types that were more successful were those that were better at eliciting parental responses in those that bought them, specific responsiveness to infant characteristics having been selected for in our environment of evolutionary adaptedness (and perhaps still being selected for) because it enhances the chances of infant survival (Hinde & Barden, 1985). There is, of course, no implication that such a basic human propensity is the only issue involved in such cases. The attractiveness of Micky Mouse or Teddy Bears depends also on fashions and social pressures of various kinds. But it seems reasonable to propose that the effectiveness of at least some of those forces arises in part from the fact that they capitalize on basic propensities.

PAN-CULTURAL AND CULTURAL INFLUENCES ON NON-VERBAL COMMUNICATION

That the signals used in human non-verbal communication have an important function in facilitating interactions and relationships between individuals cannot reasonably be doubted. They cover a spectrum from

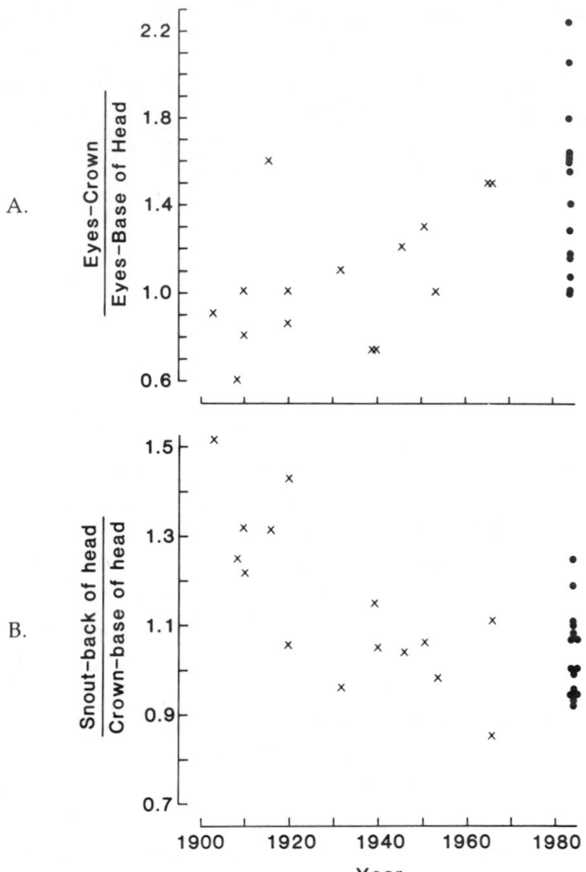

Fig. 11 Changes with time in (A) ratio of the vertical distance from eyes to crown to that from eyes to base of head and (B) ratio of distance between tip of snout and back of head to distance between top of head and its base. Crosses indicate specimens from a Museum collection of teddy bears, dots those from a shop in Cambridge in 1984.

those that are pan-cultural to those that are individually idiosyncratic. Whilst there is strong evidence that some of them have a long evolutionary history, many exemplify the action of cultural factors on a basically stable pattern. We may consider a few examples in some detail.

We have already seen that certain human expressive movements, such as smiling and crying, appear even in deaf and blind-born human infants, so that cultural influences are unlikely to play an important part in the development of their characteristic form. At the same time the situations that evoke such expressive movements, and the significance attached to

Fig. 12a Bared-teeth display or fear grin of rhesus macaque. (Drawing by Priscilla Barrett).

Fig. 12b Relaxed open-mouth display in crab-eating monkey. (Drawing by Priscilla Barrett from van Hooff, 1972).

them, differ widely between cultures and between individuals within a culture. Comparative evidence throws further light on the matter (van Hooff, 1972).

Amongst the non-human homologues of smiling and laughing are the 'fear grin' or 'bared-teeth display' (Fig. 12a) and the 'play face' or 'relaxed open-mouth display' (Fig. 12b). The former is accompanied by loud vocalizations including squeals and screams, and accompanies a tendency to flee. For instance it is often seen in cornered animals. It occurs in a wide range of mammals. It has been suggested that it evolved from elements evoked by strong aversive stimulation of the face, or as a secondary consequence of vocalizations (Andrew, 1963), or from movements of defensive aggression (van Hooff, 1972).

In higher primates the bared-teeth display occurs primarily when the animal has a thwarted tendency to flee, and is thus submissive or on the defensive, but it is also seen where other strong tendencies are thwarted, and the animal is frustrated. And in some primates the silent bared-teeth display, though normally a submissive gesture, is sometimes given by a dominant animal to a subordinate: it then appears to have a reassuring function. In yet other genera it is associated with 'lip-smacking' in contexts which suggest that it is being used as an expression of friendliness. There are thus grounds for believing that, in the course of primate evolutionary history, the silent bared-teeth display, originally having a defensive or protective pattern, came also to signify submission, non-hostility, and finally friendliness.

The relaxed open-mouth display found in many monkeys and apes resembles an expression given in aggressive contexts, but differs in that the mouth corners are not pulled forward and eye and body movements are lacking in tension. It typically accompanies boisterous mock-fighting and chasing, and it is often accompanied by an 'ohh-ahh' vocalization.

Van Hooff (1972), making a special study of chimpanzee expressive movements, used a form of factor analysis to show that the occurrence of the fifty-three most frequent behavioural elements appeared to be explicable in terms of five main causal categories which he designated 'affinitive', 'play', 'aggressive', 'submissive', and 'excitement' systems. The silent bared-teeth display was closely related to the affinitive category, the relaxed open-mouth display to the play category. Furthermore, three types of silent bared-teeth display could be distinguished – horizontal, vertical, and open-mouth: various lines of evidence indicated the former to be primarily submissive, the other two primarily affinitive.

He thus suggested that the chimpanzee silent bared-teeth display encompasses not only the phylogenetically old appeasing type, but also the more recently evolved 'friendly' types. He further suggested that the silent bared-teeth display is phylogenetically related to our smiling, and the relaxed open-mouth display to our laughing. In humans, however, as in a few non-human primates such as *Mandrillus*, the two displays have become closely related and often merge. On this view, human laughter is regarded as most closely related to the relaxed open-mouth display though somewhat akin to the open-mouth form of the silent bared-teeth face, with the smile as a less intense form of the latter, the two originally independent phylogenetic sources having merged. The human 'fear grin' remains as a fairly distinct entity.

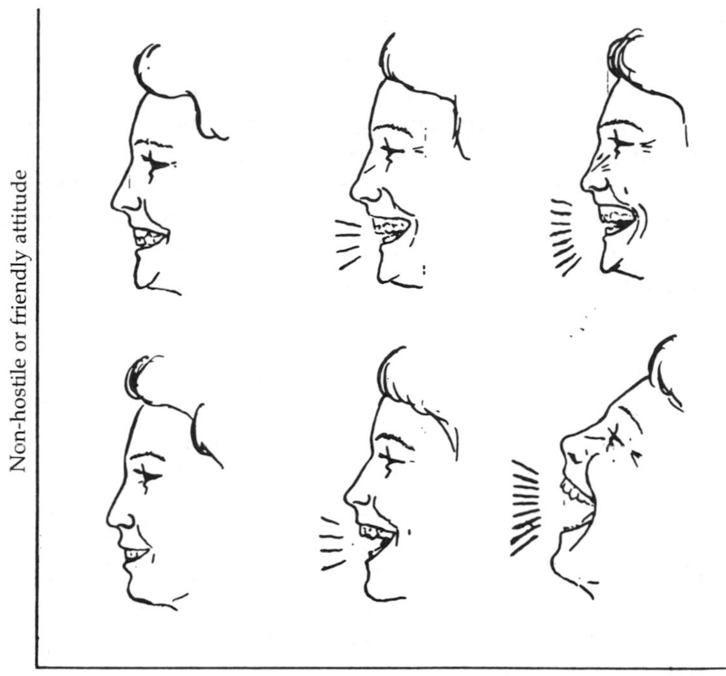

Fig. 13 Two dimensions of variation of the smile-laughter continuum. From bottom to top there is increased baring of the teeth. From left to right there is increased mouth opening and vocalization. (From van Hooff, 1972).

That this is not the whole story, however, is indicated by the fact that there are situations in which only smiling is appropriate (expressions of sympathy, appeasement) and laughter would be definitely out-of-place and even offensive, while in other situations laughter is more appropriate. Furthermore, a number of investigators have emphasized not only that there are differences in form between smiling and laughter, but also that each may vary in form in ways which are interpreted differently by an observer (Grant, 1969; Blurton-Jones, 1972; Brannigan & Humphries, 1972).

Van Hooff points out that this variation cannot be described along a single continuum, but demands at least two dimensions. One leads in its most intense form to the 'cheese' smile, used in greeting and associated with the manifestation of a non-hostile or friendly attitude. The other dimension leads to the wide-mouth laugh accompanied by 'ha-ha' vocalizations, which is especially characteristic of children's play. Fig. 13 shows how many of the variants in the smile–laugh continuum can be conceptualised in terms of two dimensions, one of 'friendliness', involving, among other things, baring of the teeth; and the other of 'playfulness', involving increased mouth opening and vocalization: whether other dimensions are also necessary to account for the whole range of variation is an open issue.

Van Hooff found this interpretation also to be consistent with studies in which human subjects were asked to place a list of adjectives and participles (e.g. jovial, roguish, meek, affable) into various 'motivational' categories (aggressive, submissive or fearful, affinitive, and playful), while other subjects were asked whether the words indicate an attitude that is accompanied by smiling or laughing. Those words that were assessed as describing affinitive moods were the ones describing a state most likely to be accompanied by a smile, while those assessed as describing a playful mood were assessed as most likely to be accompanied by a laugh.

Thus van Hooff believes that laughter and smiling involve a continuum of intergrading signals whose variation can be described in at least two dimensions. The extreme forms, the broad 'cheese' smile and the wide-mouth laugh, show formal and functional relationships to the silent bared-teeth display and the relaxed open-mouth display of lower forms. The forms of smiling and laughing most used in social interaction can be regarded as intermediates. Figure 14 represents the sort of way in which evolution could have occurred, though of course it is not to be interpreted too literally: there is, for instance, no suggestion that man has evolved from chimpanzees – only that in terms of this character man's ancestors passed through a stage not too different from that seen in modern chimpanzees.

Some evidence of other sorts supports this scheme. For instance, Krebs (cited in Blurton Jones, 1972) found that children low in dominance status at a nursery school smiled more when initiating an interaction with high-ranking children than did high-rankers when initiating interactions with low: this suggests that perhaps the use of the human smile in appeasing situations is still not so very far from that of the non-human primate's fear grin. However, van Hooff's scheme certainly does not account for all variations in smiling or laughing, as more detailed studies in which finer categories of the expressions were distinguished indicate (e.g. Grant, 1969; Brannigan & Humphries, 1972; see discussion in Hinde, 1972, p. 238–41). Furthermore van Hooff's scheme is primarily concerned with the movement patterns of smiling and laughter, and not with the contexts in which they are used. For instance, that laughter is normal behaviour at funerals in some cultures (La Barre, 1947) is open to a number of interpretations, one being that aspects other than the movement pattern itself are subject to marked cultural influences.

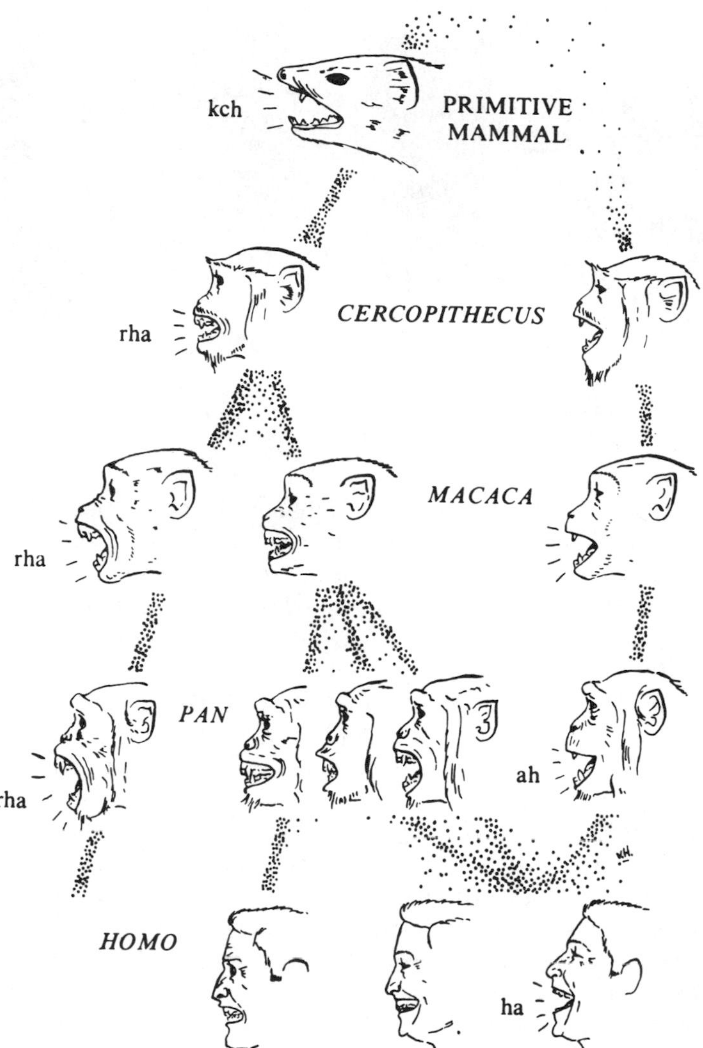

Fig. 14 The phylogenetic development of laughter and smiling as suggested by homologues in existing members of the phyletic scale leading to *Homo*. On the left is the speciation of the silent bared-teeth display and the bared-teeth scream display. The sbt-display, initially a submissive, later also a friendly response, seems to converge with the relaxed open-mouth display (on the right) a signal of play. (From van Hooff, 1972).

Fig. 15 The eyebrow flash. (Drawing by Priscilla Barrett from a photograph in Eibl-Eibesfeldt, 1972).

Another case is the eyebrow flash (Eibl-Eibesfeldt, 1972). When greeting, people of many cultures smile, nod, and raise their eyebrows with a rapid movement, keeping the eyebrows raised for about one-sixth of a second (Fig. 15). Eibl-Eibesfeldt has filmed this eyebrow flash in greeting in Europeans, Balinese, Papuans, South American Indians, and Bushmen, and has seen it in other cultures.

There is, however, some considerable variation: in central Europe reserved individuals do not use it, and in Japan it is considered indecent and suppressed. In some cultures it is used also in other contexts – for instance, we often use it as a general sign of approval or agreement, when seeking confirmation, when beginning a statement in dialogue, when flirting, strongly approving, thanking, and calling for attention during discussions. Eibl-Eibesfeldt suggests that the common denominator in these situations is a 'yes' to social contact, the eyebrow flash being used either for requesting or for approving a request for contact. It is in fact used for a factual 'yes' in Polynesia.

By looking at other contexts in which it occurs, Eibl-Eibesfeldt was able to make a suggestion as to the nature of its origin. It occurs in surprise, and in other situations associated with attention, including those involving disapproval and indignation. Eibl-Eibesfeldt suggests that the eyebrow lift of surprise was the starting point for the differentiation of several attention signals, as shown in Fig. 16. This scheme is of course purely speculative. It would be difficult to support it with comparative evidence, since among those non-human primates which move their eyebrows there is considerable variation in the manner in which they do so. Furthermore, the extent to which the changes in Eibl-Eibesfeldt's scheme are experien-

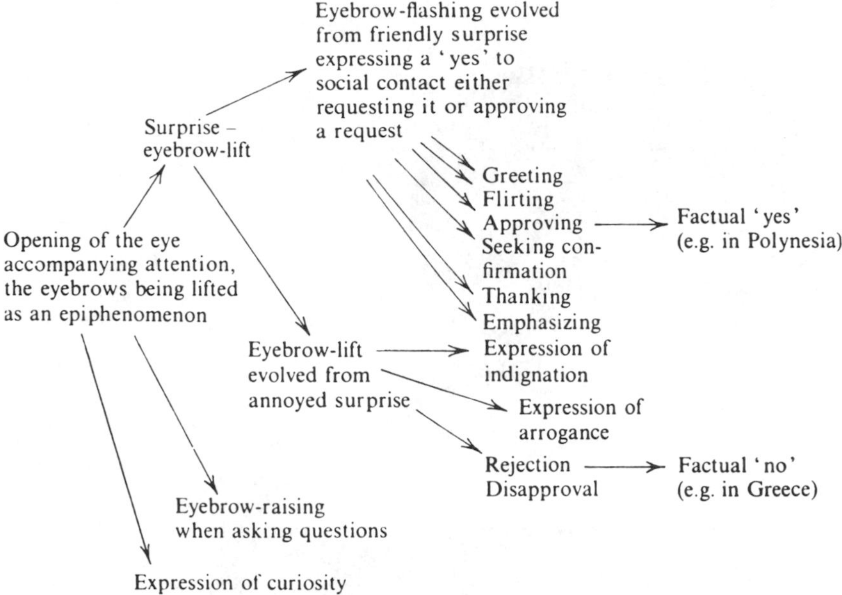

Fig. 16 Hypothesis for the evolution of eyebrow movements into signals in man. (From Eibl-Eibesfeldt, 1972).

tially induced is unknown. At most it provides a reasonable descriptive framework for displaying the relations betwen variants of the eyebrow flash, even though the precise nature of those relations is obscure (see also Eibl Eibesfeldt, 1975).

The two examples just considered concern movement patterns whose form is more or less predetermined, and each of which is related to a certain range of internal states. However, not all cross-cultural or cross-specific similarities involve the precise form of a movement pattern. Sometimes they concern general muscle tonus: a dominant rhesus monkey and one that is subordinate and dejected are readily distinguished by a naive human observer on the basis of his knowledge of comparable differences in his own species (Fig. 17 a & b). Another type of case concerns the quality of vocalizations. The shrillness of many vocalizations is related to the extent to which the lips are drawn back. Drawing back the lips is associated with fear, and shrill vocalizations tend to be associated with fear in both monkey (Andrew, 1963; Rowell, 1962) and man. In such cases the similarities between cultures or species depend not on genetically determined stability in the development of a specific movement pattern, but in the similar determination of more general aspects of behaviour (e.g. relation between muscle tonus and internal state) which lead to similarities in expressive movements.

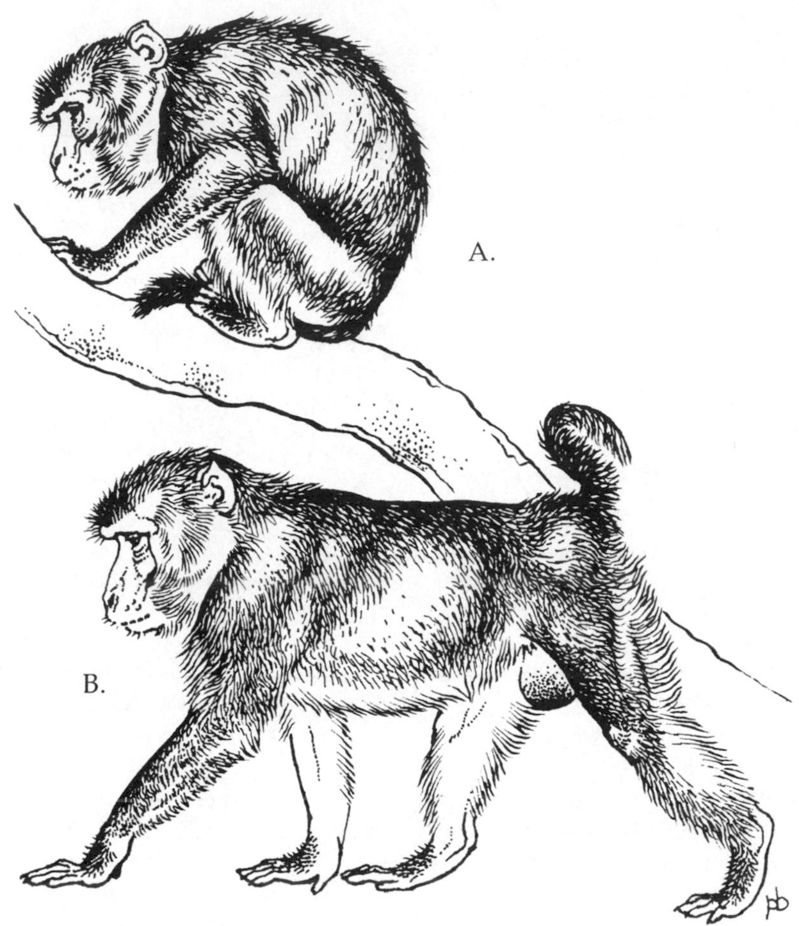

Fig. 17 Male rhesus macaques: (A) subordinate, (B) dominant. (Drawing by Priscilla Barrett).

Even where similarities do involve the form of the movement, we must remember that, as emphasized earlier, this does not imply the genetic determination of a movement pattern independently of environmental influences – the similarities may be due partly to common factors inherent in the situation predisposing individuals to develop a particular type of movement pattern. This is even more true where more complex sequences of movements are involved. The complex patterns expressing coyness, embarrassment, and flirting are a case in point. In many cultures these patterns involve bringing the hands in front of the face, mouth, or eyes. This seems to be similar to a movement seen in children wanting to hide (Eibl-Eibesfeldt, 1972) and also sometimes in chimpanzees startled by a sudden noise or movement nearby (Goodall, 1986). However, the precise way in which the hands are brought up is idiosyncratic, and the constant feature is not the movement pattern itself, but its end result. Thus the similarities are presumably a consequence of individuals learning to bring about a commonly acceptable situation, a barrier in front of the eyes, with many culture-specific influences along the way. Additional complexities may be superimposed: thus in flirting the movements are often associated with ambivalence between flight and approach, and may be accompanied by patterns inviting contact.

Many other examples could be cited. In chimpanzees, for instance, greeting by males is often preceded by some ritualized aggressive behaviour, swaggering, stamping, and so on. The actual greeting involves a variety of postures and gestures, including bobbing, bowing and crouching, touching, kissing, embracing, grooming, presenting the genital region, mounting, and occasionally hand-holding. Many of these patterns occur also in human greetings and some of them are found in many cultures. Of course, it is an open question to what extent the similarities in movement patterns involve genetically influenced stability in spite of differences in experience, or experientially determined stability in spite of genetic differences, and/or similar transferences from infantile or parental patterns, and/or similar responses to common factors in the greeting situation – for instance, differences in status leading to submissive gestures, and physical contact bringing reassurance. In any case the complexities of the greeting situation must not be forgotten. In both chimpanzee and man it not only involves minimizing the fear or expressing the pleasure that an encounter may induce, but also permits the individuals concerned to place each other in the social hierarchy. And in man greeting rituals may permit individuals to manipulate each other in a variety of ways (Goody, 1972). Such issues must be taken into account in considering their present forms (see also Kendon & Farber, 1973).

With those expressive movements whose basic form is similar across cultures, the impact of cultural influences can be seen on three other aspects. First, the nature of the eliciting factors is markedly influenced by experience: what we find amusing or sad is much influenced by the culture in which we live. Second, social experience affects the extent to which the internal state in question is expressed: for instance the degree to which anger or sexual interest is allowed to become apparent. And third, emotional states may elicit further emotional states, as when we become angered by our own fear or frightened by our own anger: these secondary emotional states may be culturally influenced and their expression superimposed to a varying degree on that of the primary one (Ekman & Friesen, 1969).

Similarities between cultures occur especially with signals that concern emotional or personal characteristics or 'affect' displays. At the other extreme, some non-verbal signals, and especially those dependent upon verbal language, are specific to particular cultures. The 'emblems' which can substitute for words, and signals that illustrate and regulate verbal interchanges, are usually culturally specific and individually learned (Ekman & Friesen, 1969; Ekman and Friesen, 1975).

We see, then, that some of the signals used in non-verbal communication are similar across cultures and even resemble movements used by our non-human relatives. The resemblances, however, concern primarily the motor pattern: other aspects of the signal differ markedly between cultures. For other signals, cross-cultural similarities can be detected only with description by consequence (see p. 12) (e.g. hiding the eyes in embarrassment), and yet others are culturally or individually idiosyncratic.

Though there are no studies that demonstrate it, it is reasonable to presume that the ability to communicate with these non-verbal signals enhances the inclusive fitness of individual non-human primates. It is also legitimate to speculate that they have, or at any rate had, a similar biological function in man. But there are no simple explanations for the nature of many of the cultural variants in terms of reproductive function. Whilst in some cases variants can be related to other aspects of the culture (for instance, not only the eyebrow flash but many expressive movements are publicly suppressed in Japan), the concept of biological function has not so far helped to explain the nature of the cultural differences – though such a possibility can not be ruled out.

VARIATIONS IN BEHAVIOUR

As discussed in Chapter 4, all individuals must be motivated by hunger; most surely have sexual inclinations; and few would get far without curiosity and a tendency to make sense of the world about them. To argue that such characteristics are ubiquitous and part of human nature, or that they are functional in the biologist's sense, would be superfluous. But what about the extent to which such propensities are manifest? Is there any evidence to suggest that the manner in which individuals vary their behaviour is adaptive? The evidence available here extends somewhat beyond the argument by design. We can ask correlational questions: do the variations in human behaviour seem to fit with predictions made on the supposition that individuals act in a way that will enhance their reproductive success (or in some cases that of their kin, see p. 101)? Although proof of adaptedness is virtually impossible to obtain, posing the question and collecting the evidence can sometimes help us to see how previously unrelated facts fit into a coherent picture, and even to interpret some apparently maladaptive aspects of human behaviour as expressions of propensities that are adaptive in other consequences.

One example is provided by Daly & Wilson's (1984) analysis of infanticide. These authors view variations in the incidence of infanticide as a manifestation of variations in a postulated parental motivation. Evolutionary theory would predict that the latter would vary in an adaptive fashion, parents devoting themselves to their offspring when such a course would enhance their inclusive fitness but husbanding their resources when it would not. An examination of the ethnographic record showed that a high proportion of the circumstances in which infanticide occurred or was permitted fell into three categories: (a) the infant was not the putative parent's own; (b) the infant's fitness potential was poor either by virtue of deformity, sickness or circumstances; or (c) the parental resources were inadequate (e.g. twins, mother unwed, economic hardship). In each of these cases, it is implied, it is adaptive for parental motivation to be low because further parental investment might not increase the parent's long-term reproductive success in proportion to its costs, and the parent might even do better to abandon this attempt, conserve resources and try again. Similar conclusions came from an examination of the infanticide statistics in Canada. For instance, the incidence decreased with the child's age, and was greater with mothers who were unmarried, or young, and in the families of step-parents. Again, in a study of 300 middle-class Los Angeles women, Essock-Vitale & McGuire (1985a & b) found that pregnancies were more likely to be terminated by voluntary abortion if the women were unmarried or uncertain of the paternity of the child.

Thus the data are in harmony with the view that infanticide is more likely to occur when the costs entailed in maternal care are high relative to the probable reproductive gains. That, of course, is very far from proving what the socio-biologist would like to prove – namely that the strength of maternal tendencies are adjusted to changing circumstances so as to enhance inclusive fitness, and that this is a consequence of natural selection (Caro & Borgerhoff Mulder, 1986). And this analysis has nothing to say about cultural variations in the acceptability of infanticide, or about the incidence of other limitations on reproduction in relation to the maintenance of socio-economic status (see pp. 166–7). Nor does it purport to say anything about the proximate factors that lead to infanticide, the incidence of which could perhaps equally well be accounted for on a frustration-induced aggression hypothesis: whilst ultimate and proximate explanations are not incompatible, such a proximate explanation in terms of behavioural tendencies adaptive in other contexts could render the socio-biological one unnecessary (see p. 49; see also Lenington, 1981, for a similar conclusion about child abuse). Nevertheless the hypothesis does co-ordinate otherwise isolated facts about infanticide into a coherent picture. Whilst not wishing to imply close similarity, this is exactly what the theory of evolution did when first propounded – it made sense of diversity. Hard proof is very much more elusive.

As another example, we may consider the question of friendly or co-operative behaviour. Is the manner in which such behaviour is shown and distributed amongst others in the individual's best interests? As a matter of fact, classical evolutionary theory, based on the view that individuals compete for resources and the fittest survive to reproduce, had difficulty in explaining why behaviour that was beneficial to others but costly to the performer (in terms of reducing his chances of surviving and reproducing) should be shown at all. Why, for instance, should an animal give an alarm call if doing so increased his own susceptibility to the predator? Such behaviour, which appears to decrease the survival chances of the actor and increase those of another individual, provides one of the central themes of sociobiology (Wilson, 1975). (Biologists like to refer to such behaviour as 'altruistic', but the term is misleading in so far as the occurrence of the behaviour can be explained in terms of long-term benefits to the individual showing it. Furthermore in everyday speech 'altruism' is defined in terms of intention, whereas the biologist implies consequence. 'Prosocial behaviour' is a more literal term, but 'altruism' has become embedded in the biological literature: see Bertram, 1982.)

Two principle hypotheses have been advanced to account for such cases. One is the principle of 'reciprocal altruism' – a good turn may be worthwhile if it is likely to be reciprocated (Trivers, 1971, 1985). For example, male baboons who do not have consorts sometimes form temporary alliances with each other. Whilst one attacks a third male who had a consort female, and thus distracts his attention, the other male mates with the female. Those males who give aid often seem to be more likely to receive aid in return (Packer, 1977). A related type of case occurs when individuals get better benefits by co-operating. It pays two pied wagtails to defend a winter feeding territory together, because each can thereby achieve a higher feeding rate (Davies & Houston, 1981).

An example where the benefits appear to be longer-term is provided by the behaviour of adolescent baboons. Young female baboons tend to direct their grooming behaviour toward the more dominant adult females in the troop, and young males to the more subordinate ones. While grooming may have some function in cleaning the fur, there is considerable evidence that it is important also in furthering interindividual relationships, analogous to the bestowal of social approval in man (Hinde & Stevenson-Hinde, 1976). The manner in which each sex distributes its grooming appears to be appropriate to its long-term needs. The young females will stay in the troop and may later profit from aid given by more dominant individuals; the young males will later leave the troop, but in the meantime can profit from practicing copulation, and are more likely to be able to mount the subordinate adult females without interference from adult males (Cheney, 1978). In a similar way much of the social life of nonhuman primates can be understood in evolutionary terms as involving individuals furthering their own interests by fostering relationships with particular others (Datta, 1983).

Other cases of prosocial behaviour can be understood in terms of 'kin selection' (Hamilton, 1964). The suggestion here is that natural selection acts or has acted to ensure that individuals not only maximize their own reproductive success, measured in terms of their descendants in subsequent generations, but also that of their relatives, who share a very high proportion of their (rare) genes, to an extent devalued according to their degree of relatedness. This is referred to as enhancing 'inclusive fitness'[2].

Selection could thus favour acts that benefit related individuals, and is more likely to do so the closer the degree of relatedness and the smaller the cost to the actor. This generalization is in fact in harmony with the data. For instance rhesus monkeys are much more likely to form coalitions with related individuals than with non-related ones (Datta, 1983). Furthermore an individual's offspring are among his or her closest kin, so acts that favour them promote the perpetuation of genes, most of which are identical with the individual's own: hence selection for parental care. But individuals are equally closely genetically related to their parents and (full) siblings, so prosocial acts directed toward them may also be in an individual's evolutionary interests. This is more the case with siblings than parents since, given two individuals equally closely related, natural selection will favour more strongly prosocial acts directed toward the one with the greater reproductive potential, and this usually means the younger. (This also implies that parents have more interest in the well-being of their young than vice-versa.) However siblings also compete with each other for parental resources, so their relationship is likely to be an ambivalent one (Hinde, 1984a).

[2] Strictly speaking, inclusive fitness includes only the offspring the animal would have had in the absence of help and hindrance from others, and only the offspring of relatives that owe their existence to the animal's help. The status of the concept, and difficulties of measuring it in practice, are discussed by Grafen (1982).

In practice, in most social species prosocial behaviour based on reciprocity and that based on kin selection are closely interwoven. Indeed, the explanations of the biologist's 'reciprocal altruism' given above are incomplete in the sense that they leave unexplained the initial spread of prosocial behaviour in a population. Except in those cases where both individuals benefit (in evolutionary terms) from the 'altruistic' act (e.g. parental care), an individual predisposed to behave co-operatively in a population of selfish individuals would be at a disadvantage, and the trait would not spread. One possible suggestion is that co-operation first became established in the population through kin selection. Selection could then favour the use of correlates of relatedness to cue co-operative behaviour. A policy of co-operating with another individual on first encounter, and subsequently behaving as the other had done (co-operatively or selfishly), would be selected for (Axelrod & Hamilton, 1981).

Now in our own species, individuals do not help all others equally, and we may ask whether the manner in which they distribute their prosocial behaviour is similar to that that would be predicted on the basis of the above two principles. *In general*, it seems to be. Individuals are more likely to help others who are likely to reciprocate than those who are not. In addition, people are more likely to help related than unrelated individuals and, amongst related individuals, are more likely to give aid the closer the genetic relationship. Furthermore, some more precise predictions about the direction of prosocial behaviour based on reciprocity or kin selection theory fit the observed facts. For instance Essock-Vitale & McGuire (1980, 1985b) found that helping amongst friends was more likely to be reciprocal than helping amongst kin; that, amongst kin, helping was an increasing function of the recipient's expected reproductive potential; and that the greater the help received, the more likely was it to come from kin. Again, competitive behaviour is much more characteristic of urban societies than of traditional rural cultures, and prosocial behaviour is more pronounced in those cultures where extended families live together and where the production system favours mutual aid (Mussen & Eisenberg-Berg, 1977; see also Hinde, 1985).

The distribution of prosocial behaviour *in general* seems to fit the predictions of evolutionary theory. Once again, proof of a direct action of natural selection is lacking: the value of the approach lies primarily in the manner in which it co-ordinates diverse facts about how and when humans help each other. However the fact that this approach is compatible with some findings about human prosocial behaviour does not mean that it explains them all. Cultural factors enter into virtually all human gift-giving – we give presents at Christmas, to particular others, and so on – and into much prosocial behaviour. Furthermore the extent and nature of the prosocial behaviour of individuals helps to establish and maintain the social structure: gifts create, maintain or affect relationships between individuals. Thus prosocial behaviour cannot be adequately understood without reference to the dialectical relations between the successive levels of social complexity. We may consider three issues arising from the application of sociobiological theories to human prosocial behaviour.

First, much human gift-giving is one-sided, one individual giving but apparently receiving relatively little in exchange, and where there is exchange, it is often insisted upon by the initial recipient. In the former respect it resembles grooming in non-human primates, where subordinate animals groom dominants more than vice versa, and it has been suggested that grooming is a means for giving and obtaining 'social approval' (Hinde & Stevenson-Hinde, 1976). Moore (1984) makes a related but somewhat different suggestion for much human gift-giving – namely that the act of begging involves also an acknowledgement of status. For example, chimpanzee males sometimes kill monkeys or other animals. After a kill, other chimpanzees cluster round the possessor of the meat and beg for pieces. Moore suggests that receiving begging is reinforcing because it is an acknowledgement of lower status by the begging individual. Meat/status exchanges could help to determine or maintain rank, and thus affect the donor's reproductive success. In humans, the gift-giver may remind the recipient of the exchange to emphasize the status difference, and the recipient may insist on reciprocation to wipe it out. Thus reciprocity could arise from basic self-interest. Selection for taking optimum advantage of reciprocal exchange could have led to the establishment of true co-operation. It remains the case that the incidence and importance of the relations between gift-giving and status, and the 'rate of exchange' between them, differ greatly between cultures: the processes involved cannot be understood independently of the socio-cultural structure. Indeed Moore's hypothesis does imply both that gift-giving affects status and thus the social structure, and that it is affected by it – and thus depends upon the dialectical relations between the levels of social complexity.

A second issue is that human groups, even in our environment of evolutionary adaptedness, probably consisted only partially of relatives. Human groups often have unilineal kinship systems, so that some close kin are not in a position to receive prosocial behaviour and some non-kin count as part of the group (Richerson & Boyd, 1978). If there is any inherent mechanism for recognizing genetic kin in humans (Rushton, Russell & Wells, 1985), it is at best weak, and the category of kin is defined primarily by culture-specific rules. It is therefore argued that many of the rules governing the distribution of prosocial behaviour must be sought along non-Darwinian lines (Cavalli-Sforza & Feldman, 1981). To counter this view, two further types of functional explanation have been advanced. First, this is just the sort of situation in which kin selection could aid the establishment, spread and maintenance of 'reciprocal altruism', especially with a propensity to 'do as you have been done by' (see above and also Morgan, 1985). The second arises from the fact that, in many societies, males primarily interact with and display prosocial behaviour towards other individuals related to them through males (e.g. brothers, paternal uncles and paternal uncle's sons): in such societies couples usually live with the husband's kin, and women are relegated to a subordinate position. In other societies the reverse applies, precedence being given to individuals related through females (siblings, maternal brothers, sister's children etc.). In the latter case the father may be relatively remote from his own offspring, the paternal role being performed by the mother's brother. This seems at first sight contrary to kin selection theory.

Alexander (1977, see also Kurland, 1979) therefore suggested, and Hartung (1985) showed, that the dispensation of prosocial behaviour to the sister's offspring occurs especially in societies in which adultery, promiscuity and divorce are common. The implication is that, in such societies, males can have relatively little confidence in their own paternity but could be confident of their relatedness to their sister's offspring, and might enhance their inclusive fitness more by directing their prosocial behaviour to them rather than to children who are supposedly their own but might in fact be unrelated. (There is of course no necessary assumption of conscious decisions here, or that paternity uncertainty is a motivating factor, but only that males are adapted to behave in a manner that furthers their inclusive fitness.)

This hypothesis fits many of the facts, but there are also problems with it. For instance, assessments of adultery and promiscuity are notoriously unreliable, and their relation to paternity uncertainty even less predictable. This makes hypothesis testing difficult. Again, in most societies showing the mother's brother's phenomenon, confidence of paternity is low, but not low enough for a man to assume that his sister's children are more closely related to him than his own putative offspring. Indeed Hartung's analysis shows that, with moderate levels of extra-marital sex, matrilineal inheritance (relative to patrilineal) is strongly advantageous to women but disadvantageous to men. This raises the questions of how matrilineal inheritance could be initiated, and how it could be enforced, if it is against the interests of the dominant controllers of wealth. One possibility is that, in former times, paternity confidence was so low that matrilineal inheritance was actually advantageous to men. Flinn (1981) has suggested a number of additional possible factors. One issue involves social pressure from uterine kin. Although a man may be more related to his own putative offspring than to his sister's children, he may tend to be more closely related to his sister's children than to his brother's if the latter's paternity is in doubt. Thus brothers may bring pressure on each other to behave prosocially to their mutual sister's children. Another factor may be frequency of divorce, making paternal prosocial behaviour not only more difficult but less certain of benefitting the putative offspring. These and other factors *could result* in a situation in which a man enhanced his inclusive fitness more by aiding his sister's children than by attempting to aid children whom he could not be certain he had fathered. However Kitcher (1985) has convincingly argued that the strategy of devoting parental care to a sister's children is open to invasion by a number of other strategies, and will not necessarily maximize the inclusive fitness of those who engage in it. He prefers an explanation in terms of proximate factors – specifically 'commonplace human desires' to help kin, displaced in situations of paternity uncertainty onto individuals with whom the man has some assurance of genetic relatedness. This leaves open the possibility that the propensity to help kin has been shaped by natural selection, but denies a role of selection in shaping the particular cultural practice observed. At the moment, the controversy rests there.

A third problem with explanations of human prosocial behaviour in terms of biological functions arises from the fact that individuals do sometimes help unrelated strangers in circumstances that could provide no chance of reciprocation. They may even sacrifice their lives. Such cases, however, do not refute the hypothesis that the *propensity* to show such behaviour is a consequence of the action of natural selection. This requires a digression.

Instances of behaviour that are maladaptive from the point of view of the individual's inclusive fitness can often be explained in terms of propensities adaptive in other contexts. We may consider two examples. An obvious one is the reed warbler that feeds a cuckoo in its nest: the response of putting food into the gape of a chick in your own nest is usually adaptive, but goes wrong when it is exploited by a cuckoo. As another example, in Britain milk is delivered in bottles that are left outside homes. Certain birds (tits, *Parus* spp) often open the bottles and drink the milk. These birds apparently peck the bottles because the bottles present certain stimuli similar to those presented by their natural food objects, and which elicit motor patterns already in their repertoire. For instance bottles with cardboard tops (now seldom used) elicited a tearing movement usually used in tearing bark off trees in searching for insect eggs. Bottles with foil tops elicit hammering comparable to that normally elicited by seeds or nuts. Milk is nutritious and bottle opening is presumably adaptive, even though blue tits have occasionally drowned in milk bottles. However tits sometimes enter houses and tear paper, books etc. In such cases they obtain no food, and are sometimes unable to find their way out again (Hinde & Fisher 1951). Apparently behavioural propensities normally adaptive for natural foods can also in changed circumstances be expressed to utilize a new food source, milk, or maladaptively, in houses. Expressions of a behavioural propensity in inappropriate circumstances are especially likely when circumstances change. However natural selection acts through the consequences of particular acts and, if inappropriate expression were markedly dysgenic, individuals who discriminated correctly between appropriate and inappropriate circumstances would presumably be selected for. Such selection for appropriate discrimination would not necessarily occur, but only if inappropriate expression brought adverse consequences.

Since this issue is of importance in later chapters, it may be generalized by caricaturing it as follows. Suppose a propensity P can be expressed in two types of behaviour. One, A, has consequences with a positive effect on inclusive fitness, and the other, B, is neutral. Natural selection could enhance A by affecting the strength of P or the connection between P and A. If a third type of behaviour C had a negative effect on inclusive fitness, the latter type of effect would be more likely. However much of the sociobiological evidence that considerations of inclusive fitness are or have been important in shaping human behaviour rests on correlations between a particular outcome and inclusive fitness. This is a proper first step, but such evidence cannot in itself show what aspect of the underlying mechanisms have been affected in enhancing the behaviour in question: indeed, most sociobiologists are not concerned with mechanism. In particular, in the above model, evidence of a correlation between the strength of A and inclusive fitness tells us nothing about whether variations in A are due to variations in an underlying propensity or to variations in the strength of the connection between the propensity and A. And if the sociobiologists' first step fails, and A is not correlated with inclusive fitness, it is a reasonable hypothesis that A is one expression of a propensity that is adaptive in other contexts.

Caro & Borgerhoff Mulder (1986) argue against the supposition that selection acts on propensities that are expressed in more than one type of behaviour on two grounds. First, since it is difficult to measure the reproductive consequences of a general propensity, it is difficult to disprove the contention that a propensity is adaptive even though some of its manifestations are not. This is correct and methodologically important but concerns a shortcoming in the evidence, not what is actually true in nature. Second, they argue that natural selection acts through particular manifestations of basic propensities: as we have just seen, this does not necessarily mean that it acts to change those particular manifestations rather than the basic propensity.

Thus, to return to the issue of the occurrence of true altruism in man, the suggestion is that it can be partially explained as the expression of normally adaptive prosocial propensities in inappropriate circumstances. This would be even more likely to occur in humans than in animals. Our cognitive and linguistic capacities not only give flexibility to our behavioural propensities, but also enable us to reify them into principles, and these principles may become incentives for action even when that action is to the detriment of the actor (Kelley, 1979). In addition, the human tendency to seek for social approval may sometimes impose heavy costs on the individual. Cultural values may demand sacrifices from individuals and individuals willingly comply. The forces that drive humans to self-sacrifice are thus not solely simple exaggerations of human propensities, nor are they necessarily mere expressions of such propensities in abnormal circumstances: rather they are in large part products of the dialectics between those propensities and the sociocultural structure. As we shall see in Chapter 8, cultural influences can magnify, distort and redirect the behavioural tendencies of individuals, even to their own disadvantage.

Thus we see that, with some exceptions, human prosocial behaviour is in general directed in ways similar to those that would be predicted from principles used to explain comparable behaviour in animals. The exceptions seem to be explicable as inappropriate expressions of propensities which are (or have been) themselves adaptive in other circumstances, or as consequences of social imperatives arising from the dialectics between successive levels of social complexity but not necessarily advantageous for the individual concerned. Such a view does not necessarily deny human ability to choose between alternative courses of action, though it does imply that the choice made does not necessarily accord with that which would be made by an omniscient observer.

We can extend this speculation to developmental issues. The extent to which it is in an individual's interests to show mostly co-operative or competitive strategies (see pp. 76–8) will depend on the social context in which he/she is living. For example, behaviour appropriate in societies organized around close kinship relationships may not be so in more complex societies where acquaintances are less likely to be related (Alexander, 1980). Consider an imaginary animal example. In a population containing few vicious fighters and plentiful resources the advantages to individuals of co-operating in group living may detract from the advantages of being an egotistical vicious fighter. In a population containing a moderate number of vicious fighters and scarce resources, it may be necessary to be a vicious fighter or succumb. But if nearly everyone is a vicious fighter it may be better to contract out and seek access to resources through stealth or deceit. This is an imaginary example, but it has a possibly important implication for studies of the development of social behaviour. We must expect the effects of a given experience not only to differ with the nature of the individual but also with the social situation in which the individual is embedded (Maynard Smith, 1979). In the longer term, which strategies are likely to be appropriate in the future will depend on the social situations likely to be encountered then. And the only data available for predicting future social situations concern current social situations. So we can legitimately ask whether the propensity to show prosocial behaviour is influenced in the expected fashion by the social situations experienced in childhood.

There is in fact some evidence that that is the case. For instance in western cultures children who have had an affectionate and/or secure relationship with one or more parents are more likely to show prosocial behaviour (e.g. Mussen & Eisenberg-Berg, 1977; Hoffman, 1983; Stevenson-Hinde, Hinde & Simpson, 1985). Deprivation of maternal care/or affection can have long-term effects in augmenting aggressiveness (Ainsworth *et al.*, 1978; Rutter, 1972; Baumrind, 1971; Martin, 1981). The suggestion is, then, that natural selection has operated to provide individuals with a tendency to show prosocial behaviour, and with mechanisms whereby the extent and direction of that behaviour is adjusted to suit both their current and their likely circumstances (see also MacDonald, 1984; Hinde, 1986). Of course, such an hypothesis is likely to be applicable only within a certain range. Whilst a range of normal childhood environments may produce appropriate adjustment to a corresponding range of adult ones, extreme childhood ones (e.g. 'over-indulgence' or extreme rejection) may not. This is yet another reason why linear relations between childhood experience and subsequent behaviour are not to be expected (cf p. 50).

Before we conclude this chapter, a caveat is in order. In this chapter, and in Chapter 4, four main points have been made. First, certain behavioural propensities (perceptual biases, responsiveness to stimulus configurations, motor patterns, constraints on learning, etc.,), though varying in strength and though their precise expression may be modifiable by experience, are virtually ubiquitous in human individuals. Whilst there may be scope for argument about particular instances, the general thesis that there are pan-cultural human characteristics, some of which differentiate us from other species, is surely undeniable. Second, it has been argued that the effects of experience on an individual depend on the nature of that individual: thus both pan-cultural and individual human characteristics may involve constraints on and predispositions concerning what is learned. This is supported by comparative evidence and, though again the details require much further research, seems in principle self evident. Third, it has been suggested that the universal propensities have been (and/or are) functional in a biological sense. Here the evidence rests almost entirely on the argument from design. In principle, the extent to which universal characteristics are functional cannot be tested (see p. 85). Nevertheless, since the question bears on the nature of human characteristics, it is not an unimportant one and the hypothesis a reasonable one. Finally, behavioural tendencies that are universally present may nevertheless vary in their strength or in the object or person to which they are expressed: we have asked whether these variations make adaptive sense. Here the argument was again primarily from design, though supported by correlational evidence, and is a purely qualitative one. Again, most variations are of the kind that would be expected if they were or are adaptive. There is no necessary implication of genetic differences between individuals in this conclusion: indeed most of the data concern variations of behaviour within individuals. But such data support the view that natural selection has favoured tendencies to acquire behaviour that is adaptive. However whilst expression of the propensities discussed (e.g. to respond to certain characteristics of babies, to smile in certain circumstances, to show prosocial behaviour more readily to kin than to non-kin, etc.) is in general adaptive, there are exceptions. These can be explained either as inappropriate expressions of behavioural tendencies that are in general adaptive, or as due to the over-riding power of aspects of the socio-cultural structure impelling individuals to behave against their own best interests. It must be acknowledged that such a conclusion is almost incontrovertible: it may still be the conclusion closest to nature.

The role of the socio-cultural context on the expression of such tendencies, and the importance of the dialectics between successive levels of social complexity, are discussed further in later chapters.

SUMMARY AND CONCLUSION

In this chapter we have examined selected categories of individual behaviour that can be regarded as part of man's nature. In so far as they are human universals, the method of differences cannot be used to assess the relative contribution of genetic and environmental factors in their development. However evidence for their developmental stability is provided by their ubiquity, and in some cases by their development in the absence of opportunities for the learning processes likely to be important in their development, and by comparisons with other primates. However we have also seen that their development may be affected, in various ways and to various degrees, by environmental and especially cultural influences.

Their ubiquity also prevents us from obtaining hard evidence about their adaptedness. But parallels between the ways in which humans vary their behaviour and the variations that would be predicted on the basis of evolutionary theory, are of considerable interest in integrating previously unrelated facts about human behaviour. Whilst the basic human propensities discussed can be seen as the product of selective forces, their expression is heavily influenced by social factors. The extent to which those social forces can themselves be seen as adaptive is discussed in later chapters.

7

Interindividual relationships

THE ADAPTIVE COMPLEX

In the last chapter some selected examples of individual psychological characteristics relevant to interpersonal relationships were discussed. We saw how experience could impose variance on a basically stable pattern, and discussed evidence compatible with the view that at least some pan-cultural individual propensities are or have been biologically functional. We also saw how some variations in behaviour fitted a selectionist model. The evidence on the latter point was correlational, but in some cases compelling, though propensities that are in general adaptive can be expressed inappropriately, or their expression can be distorted by social forces.

In this chapter we move up the levels of social complexity to consider some examples of inter-individual relationships. We shall suggest that some of their characteristics lie in the natures of the participating individuals, and are in harmony with the view that they depend on behavioural propensities that are or have been subject to natural selection. The argument rests on the biological principle that the characters (anatomical, physiological and behavioural) of every species form a co-adapted complex such that evolutionary change in one character may have ramifying effects through the whole. Thus not only do birds have wings, but most of them have neural and other physiological adaptations for flying, as well as a life-style in which flight is advantageous.

To give a more specific example, whereas most gulls nest on flat marshy or grassy areas, one species, the kittiwake, nests on cliff ledges. This presumably helps to protect the adults and chicks from predation. The kittiwake's behaviour also differs from that of other gulls in a number of ways, many of which can be regarded as evolutionary consequences of cliff-nesting. For instance the nest is much more elaborate than those of ground-nesting gulls, and the young do not run away when attacked.

These and many other characteristics in which kittiwakes differ from other gulls form a co-adapted complex related to cliff-nesting (Cullen, 1957). We shall now ask whether a similar principle applies to two sorts of human relationship.

PARENT–CHILD RELATIONSHIPS

The human mother–child relationship varies to a considerable extent between cultures and between individuals within cultures: for instance the continuous close contact between mother and baby found in many non-Western cultures indicates a mother–baby relationship very different from that found in some Western families. Nevertheless there are some universal or near-universal features, and we can ask how far aspects of maternal behaviour, of infant behaviour, and of the mother–child relationship found in the majority of cultures make sense as a co-adapted complex. We can also ask whether variants in the mother–child relationship correlate with the circumstances of one or both partners in a manner that appears to be adaptive.

We may start with some issues in which much current Western practice seems to be (or to have been until recently) aberrant – to the detriment of Western babies. Whilst fathers (but rarely other relatives) have only recently been admitted to delivery wards in the West, Kennell & Klaus (Kennell, 1986) found that a woman, usually well known to the mother, was present in 127 out of 128 societies in an ethnographic sample. In an experimental study in Guatamala, the present of a sympathetic woman providing support during labour was associated with fewer perinatal complications, a lower use of medication, shorter labour, fewer caesarian sections, and fewer infants admitted to intensive care.

Again, in only 20% of the 89 societies for which data were available did the mother deliver when on her back, side or hands and knees. In the majority she was sitting, standing, squatting, kneeling or leaning back with support. There is in fact evidence that the area of the pelvic outlet can increase by 28% during delivery on moving from the supine or back to the squatting and/or sitting position, and that the use of that position results in a reduction in the period of active labour by more than one quarter (Kennell, op. cit.)

Another example concerns the rhythm of nursing. The frequency with which mammals suckle their young varies greatly: in some species the young spend the greater part of the day attached to the nipple, while in others they are suckled once a day, or less (Table 7.1). Comparative study shows that suckling frequency is inversely related to the protein content of the milk. Human milk has a relatively low protein content, suggesting that

Table 7.1 *Properties of maternal milk in relation to suckling frequency in a range of mammalian species*

Species	Concentration	Suckling interval (approx.)
Tree shrew	Very high	48 hours
Rabbits	High	24 hours
Ungulates (cached young)	High moderate	4 hours
Ungulates (following young)	Moderate	2–3 hours
Apes	Low	1 hour
Man	Low	?

neonates should be fed more frequently than the four-hourly feeds common in many hospitals. In addition, mammalian babies that are suckled infrequently suck faster and for a shorter period than those that are suckled frequently: human babies suck very slowly (Blurton Jones, 1972). Thus by comparing man with a range of other species we get a new perspective on the appropriateness of schedule feeding: the demand feeding practiced in most non-Western cultures seems more compatible with the nature of the milk and with babies' behaviour. This view is confirmed by a comparison of breast and bottle-fed babies: bottle milk tends to be more concentrated than breast milk, and bottle-fed babies demand food less often (Bernal, 1972).

Newborn primates are relatively helpless, but their mothers must move about in search of food. Unlike some ungulates, most carry their babies with them. This is still the usual practice in many non-Western societies, and was probably the case also with early man. Such a view would be compatible with the evidence for frequent suckling cited above. Furthermore, while some mammalian mothers with relatively helpless young cache them in a nest or hiding place for long periods, this is unlikely to have been the case in early hominids: infants of caching species usually do not urinate or defecate unless stimulated by the mother, and this is not the case with human babies. In addition, the poor thermoregulatory ability of human infants is more compatible with their being carried than with their either being cached or following their mothers (Blurton Jones, 1972).

There is indeed evidence that, after birth, babies have a higher partial pressure of oxygen in their blood if in a vertical or semi-vertical position (as they are when carried by their mothers) than when lying on their backs (Kennell, 1986). Furthermore it has been suggested, on the basis of a considerable mass of evidence, that tactile, thermal and chemical stimuli from the mother contribute to the infant's breathing rhythms, and that their absence, when babies sleep away from their parents, contribute to the incidence of the sudden death syndrome (cot death) (McKenna, in press).

The continuing presence of the Moro reflex (Prechtl and Beintema, 1964) and the vestigial grasping reflex of human infants indicate that they originally held on to their mothers like other primates. With reduction of maternal body hair this must have become difficult, and carrying must have posed problems to the mother, the more so as, by analogy with modern hunter-gatherers, she was probably responsible for most of the food-gathering (Blurton Jones and Sibley, 1978).

Let us return for a moment to one of the questions posed at the start of this section – whether variants in the mother-child relationship make adaptive sense. It seems that in the three cases just discussed – certain obstetrical practices, nursing rhythms, and the extent of mother-infant proximity – the variants usual in Western cultures are not in line with the biological requirements of mother and infant. Social imperatives appear to have overridden the patterns more usual in other societies, apparently to the immediate detriment of mother and infant. Whether or not those social imperatives themselves have a biological basis – whether for instance the costs to the infant consequent upon less frequent nursing and reduced mother-infant proximity are countered by gains (in a biological or solely in a social sense) is an open issue. And of course the other side of the coin is that in the majority of societies the practices are indeed (more) in accord with the biological needs of mother and baby.

Returning to the issue of the co-adapted complex, dilute milk, frequent nursing and maternal carrying of the baby would be associated with more or less constant maternal availability – though there is no implication as to which was primary. Maternal availability would be associated also with maternal protection and with infant dependence on that protection. As we have seen (p. 68), the so-called 'irrational fears of childhood' would have made good sense in our 'environment of evolutionary adaptedness', where dangers from predators, from infanticidal fellow-members of the species (Hrdy, 1977), and from just getting lost were constantly present. Application of demographic techniques to admittedly small samples of skeletal remains suggests that mortality before the age of fourteen was probably over 50% (Acsádi and Nemeskéri, 1970). For an infant attached to its mobile mother, falling, darkness, and solitude signify real dangers and contact comfort is properly reassuring.

Nurturance and protection are but two of the resources a primate infant needs from the mother: she also cleans, guides, and so on. Natural selection ensures that each female directs her maternal care primarily to her own infant (or to those of her close relatives, see p. 101). It would not be in a female's biological interests to devote her primary care to another's offspring: on the contrary, another infant may be a potential competitor to her own, so that a mother would be better not to aid, and even to harm, unrelated infants. (Of course, given a propensity to behave maternally, a woman may show maternal care to children not her own, especially if she does not have one herself. Doing so may not only be satisfying, but bring long-term social or even reproductive benefits. The issue here concerns the effect on a female's inclusive fitness of devoting her primary care to the infant of an unrelated female in preference to her own.) Two things follow. First, it is in an infant's interests to avoid unfamiliar individuals: fear of strangers would be conducive to survival. Fear of strangers is in fact found in a wide range of species (Freedman, 1961), and it is probably no coincidence that in our own it appears about the same time as the capacity for independent locomotion.

Second, if strangers (including strange mothers) may be hostile, it will be in the infant's interests to seek nurturance and succour primarily from its own mother: the formation of a close mother–infant relationship is thus in the evolutionary interests of both. This explains much behaviour that might seem to contribute little to the long-term well-being of either. The smile and the games that mother and infant play (for example, Stern, 1977) cement and deepen the relationship between them. The smile is elicited preferentially by stimuli with the configuration of the human face (Ahrens, 1954): an interest in such a configuration is present from birth (Jirari, cited in Freedman, 1974) and may depend on special perceptual mechanisms (cf. p. 86 and Rolls, 1987). Many mothers say that they feel their babies become 'real persons' when they start to smile. The games show considerable cultural diversity, but the propensity to play such games is certainly pan-cultural.

Aspects of mother–child interaction that were presumably originally important in other ways have also come to have a function in strengthening their relationship. For instance, when confronted by a strange object, a child may first look at its mother, and only play with it if the mother signals her assent. This 'social referencing' (Emde, 1984) also strikes a chord in the mother, and enhances the relationship between them.

Other aspects of the mother–child relationship can be understood on the basis of kin selection. We have already seen (p. 101) that this predicts that parents will be more likely to sacrifice their resources for their children than vice versa. It also predicts that weaning conflict is almost inevitable, since it will be in the mother's interests to conserve her resources for the sake of future offspring whilst it is in the current infant's interest to exploit the mother (Trivers, 1974).

This case merits further consideration, because it illustrates a general principle. Consider first the general case of a mammalian mother with a single infant. Evolutionary theory makes certain predictions. It is in the interests of both parent and infant to promote the bond between them. However the positions of parent and infant are not precisely similar. Natural selection promotes parental care because the offspring carries the parent's genes, and gene survival requires the offspring's well-being. However at the same time the parent expends resources in caring for the infant, and this may reduce its chances of rearing further young. The relative importance of these two issues changes with time. When the infant is small, parental care is essential for its survival. As it grows, it demands more milk, and (except in the case of a last child) thus the cost of parental care to the parent (measured in terms of the parent's inclusive fitness) increases. At the same time parental care is likely to become less essential to the offspring. Thus the benefits of a given parental act to the infant (measured in terms of the infant's inclusive fitness) decreases when the costs to the parent are rising. In due course the costs to the mother (in terms of her long-term inclusive fitness) exceed the benefits to her in terms of the effects of her care on the current infant. Yet the infant will continue to benefit from parental care in its own right, and the cost to the mother (in terms of her ability to rear further offspring) will affect the infant's fitness less than the mother's. Whilst there are assumptions in this argument, it seems that, at a certain point, natural selection will favour the mother's withdrawing maternal care and the infant's continuing to demand it. Weaning conflict is thus firmly based in the processes of evolution (Trivers, op. cit.).

By the same token, mothers will be more prepared to expend resources on a lastborn, as there are then no future offspring to cater for. The crucial issue is that natural selection is acting not (or not only) to promote harmonious relationships between the individuals, but the interests (in terms of inclusive fitness) of each. This may lead to either co-operation or conflict, or to a mixture of the two.

Data on the mother–infant relationship in a wide range of non-human species support this view. The rate at which an infant monkey becomes independent of its mother might seem to be determined by the infant's increasing physical capacities and exploratory tendencies, but this is a misleading impression. As an infant rhesus gets older, it spends more and more time off its mother. If this were due solely to a change in the infant, we should expect the frequency with which the mother rejects the infant's attempts to gain contact to decrease. In fact the rejections increase so the opposite must be the case – the increase in the time the infant spends off the mother is controlled more immediately by changes in the mother than by changes in the infant (see pp. 50–3). This of course does not imply that the infant could not achieve independence on its own: infants reared on inanimate mother surrogates do in fact leave them more and more as they grow older. However independence is achieved more slowly than by mother-reared infants, presumably because they are never rejected (Hansen, 1966). Nor does it imply that the changes in the mother arise endogenously: they may be initiated by the infant's increasing demand for milk or its more vigorous locomotor play. However, these in turn depend on maternal care, which in turn depends on signals from the infant, and so on. Development depends on a complex interaction between parent and offspring, and the present issue is only that changes in the time the infant spends off the mother are immediately controlled primarily by changes in the mother. In practice the extent of the conflict, and the age of infant at which it becomes crucial, will vary with circumstances: one case, involving alternative strategies of restrictive and *laissez-faire* mothering in baboons, was discussed on pp. 77–8.

The question arises, can similar principles be applied to our own species? In Western societies, at least, mothers may be less interested in maximizing the number of children they could have than in the potential well-being, quality of life and status of those they do have (see pp. 106–7). However weaning conflict is common, at least in Western societies, and many human mothers do push the baby on from breast to solid food, from crib to bed, or from home to school faster than the child, if allowed to make decisions itself, would proceed. Such evidence must be treated with caution, especially since some Western child-rearing practices seem not to harmonize with the biological desiderata (see above). And in some African societies children are fed virtually as long as they wish, a postpartum sex taboo reducing the liklihood of competition from a younger sibling. The further question thus arises, are any of the cultural variations in weaning practices such as to maximize lifetime reproductive success, the relative advantages of having few well-nurtured children or many less well-cared-for ones varying with circumstances? We shall postpone this issue until Chapter 9, where a case that has been studied in some detail is discussed.

An emphasis on the biological advantages to the mother in promoting the offspring's independence, and on the role of the mother in bringing it about, is not incompatible with the emphasis placed on sensitive mothering by many writers (e.g. Ainsworth *et al.*, 1978), for that implies both responding appropriately to the infant's signals, especially when the infant is distressed, and not interfering when the infant is otherwise engaged. But it does imply that infants are unlikely to be adapted to mothers who are infinitely compliant. If it is in the biological interests of the mother to reject the infant before it is in the interests of the infant to be independent, it is likely that infants are adapted to cope with mothers who wean them before they would otherwise prefer to be weaned, and to emerge from the relationship as individuals able to cope with the social environment into which they have been born. Similar considerations may well apply to our own species, or at least to Western societies, for with sensitive mothering, weaning can be achieved with minimal conflict. Furthermore older children whose parents have used a degree of measured control seem better adjusted than children of permissive ones (Baumrind, 1971).

This brings us to the question of individual differences. Many developmental psychologists (e.g. Bowlby, 1969; Ainsworth *et al.*, 1978) have implied that mothers who behaved in an ideally sensitive way would raise an ideally well-adjusted infant. We have seen that the evolutionary viewpoint of Trivers and the data on weaning in monkeys complicate the issue by indicating that the partner in the mother–infant (or for that matter any other) relationship is unlikely to be ideal because he or she is likely to have not only different social interests, but also partially incompatible reproductive ones. Now we reach a third stage in the argument – partners are likely to depart from the ideal (if it makes sense to talk in such terms) in varying ways. Are these individual differences to be seen as mere noise in the system that come to the psychiatrist's notice when they pass acceptable limits? Or is there more to it than that? Even if they are in part the products of chance events, perhaps the effects of those events are not chance, but are guided by the forces of selection?

We saw earlier (pp. 77–8) that different styles of mothering by baboon mothers might be adaptive in different social circumstances. We also saw that a comparable type of argument could be applied to the behavioural styles of human infants with their mothers: the behaviour of infants whose proximity-seeking is mixed with some avoidance of the mother could be understood as enabling them to maintain contact with mothers who do not encourage physical contact and are restricted in emotional expression, whilst avoiding the distress and behavioural disorganization that would follow outright rejection.

Cases such as these show that a functional approach can help to make sense of variations in relationships, for at least some variants may result from the pursuit of strategies adaptive in the prevailing context. They also underline the danger in idealizing particular behavioural styles or particular types of relationship. Of course such an argument must not be taken too far: it does not imply that all aberrations are 'normal' or desirable. Furthermore any suggestions that the avoidant baby of a rejecting mother is behaving adaptively in a biological sense involves dilution of the meaning of the term 'adaptive': it is a long haul from showing an effect on the maintenance of behavioural organization in the baby to demonstrating the enhancement of its inclusive fitness. All that is being claimed is that the behaviour of an avoidant baby seems to make sense when seen as permitting the maintenance of a mother–child relationship in spite of certain maternal characteristics – a relationship important for the infant's long-term well-being.

In summary, in the preceding paragraphs we have seen how a number of diverse but rather widespread characteristics of maternal behaviour, infant behaviour, and the mother–child relationship are related to each other and would have been adaptive in our environment of evolutionary adaptedness. We have also seen that some cultural variants appear not to be in the reproductive interests of the individuals concerned – but that is an issue to which we shall return later.

MALE–FEMALE RELATIONSHIPS

An another example, we may consider the differences between the behaviour of men and women in close personal relationships. These show even greater cultural diversity, but again there are consistent trends.

In Western societies, 'Traditional sex roles prescribe that men and woman play different roles in sexual interactions. Men are expected to initiate sex, while women are expected to set limits on the couple's intimacy . . . For young men, seeing "how far you can get" often serves to affirm masculinity, to acknowledge the woman's sexual attractiveness, and to test her virtue . . . Woman's role as a limit-setter is consistent with her presumed lesser interest in sex and her greater stake in preserving a good reputation and avoiding pregnancy' (Peplau *et al.*, 1977). This statement by social psychologists poses a host of questions. Why should seduction be seen as affirming the masculinity of a seducer and not the feminity of a seductress? Why should women be presumed to have lesser interest in sex or a greater stake in preserving a reputation for sexual restraint than men? Sex-role stereotypes (see pp. 52–3) provide a basis for many sex differences in behaviour, but they in turn demand explanation.

We have already referred to prenatal, hormonal and experiental developmental causes for sex differences in behaviour (pp. 58–9) between men and women. Here we ask whether differences in sex roles reflect differences in propensities whose direction would have been adaptive in our environment of evolutionary adaptedness. The genesis of the sex role stereotypes will be discussed in Chapter 8.

The argument is that, because of their physiological differences (see below), the requirements of male and female mammals for successful reproduction are not the same. We may therefore expect natural selection in our environment of evolutionary adaptedness to have provided males and females with behavioural propensities that differed between the sexes. These differences are unlikely to have been simple, and would have involved alternative 'strategies' (see pp. 77–8) for use in different circumstances. Functional consideration of sex differences in strategies requires some knowledge about human social and sexual arrangements in our environment of evolutionary adaptedness. Here we have no hard data, but the general principle of the co-adapted complex (pp. 111–2), coupled with comparative evidence, provides some clues (Alexander, 1980; Hinde, 1984).

Comparative study of monkeys and the great apes shows that their sexual anatomy and physiology is related to the social and sexual behaviour they display. We can be sure that the same was true for the human species in its environment of evolutionary adaptedness. Thus extrapolation of the relations between anatomy, physiology and behaviour from the great apes to the known sexual anatomy and physiology of men and women permits hypotheses about early human sociosexual behaviour.

Consider first the relations between sex differences in body size, intra-sex competition, and polygyny or polyandry. If some individual males are able to fertilize several females and adult sex ratios approximate 1:1 (Fisher, 1958; Hamilton, 1967), other males may fertilize none. Thus in a polygynous species, the variance in reproductive success will be greater amongst males than amongst females. If this variation arises from differences in competitive abilities in acquiring mates, there is likely to be stronger selection for attributes leading to success in competition, such as body size in the competing sex (Trivers, 1972). In accordance with this expectation, in several groups of mammals, including the primates (Alexander, 1977; Clutton-Brock, *et al.*, 1977), there is a correlation between sex differences in body size and polygyny. (Certain apparent exceptions involve species that move around in a three-dimensional environment where locomotor ability is more important than size in fighting – e.g. the polygynous Weddell's seal, where males are smaller than females.) Assuming that similar principles applied to our own species in its environment of evolutionary adaptedness, the human sex difference in size suggests that our ancestors practised a mild degree of (simultaneous or successive) polygyny. In addition the greater muscle/body weight ratio and the greater average aggressiveness of males are compatible with the view that males competed for females (Alexander & Noonan, 1979).

Now there are some differences of opinion about the precise functional argument here. Clutton-Brock (1983) has suggested that the association between polygyny and dimorphism arises because the effects of body size on reproductive success of males and females are similar in monogamous species but not in polygynous ones. The size differentials may arise through selection favouring smaller body size in females through an association with early breeding (Willner & Martin, 1985). But in any case, the occurrence of an association between sexual dimorphism in body size and polygyny is clear, and the human sex difference in size suggests that our ancestors tended to be mildly polygynous. Whilst human familial arrangements are undoubtedly characterized by a high degree of flexibility, at the present time over 80% of human cultures are polygynous or condone polygyny (though in many of these the proportion of polygynous marriages is actually small), around 15% are monogamous, and very few are polyandrous (Ford and Beach, 1951; Murdock, 1967). The incidence of monogamy depends at least in some cases on ecological factors requiring two parents for child-rearing. Although, over the world as a whole (and including polygynous societies), most individuals live monogamously, it can reasonably be argued that this involves the suppression of polygynous tendencies (Shepher & Reisman, 1985).

It is as well to stress the nature of the evidence here. There is no proof that early humans were polygynous. All we can say is that, given the concept of a co-adapted complex, the view that our species was polygynous integrates a number of known facts about sex differences in body size, development, and behaviour (see also Alexander, 1980).

This does not mean that females did not compete. Amongst hon-human primates competition between females is ubiquitous (Hrdy, 1981) and competition may affect breeding success (Dunbar and Sharman, 1983). In human societies females compete with each other and also compete with males for power – in some societies successfully, at least in certain contexts (e.g. Sanday, 1981). Furthermore it must be emphasized that, whilst the biological argument is in harmony with greater physical strength in males, it says nothing about intelligence or other attributes. Even in male-dominated human societies, women may not readily accept subordinate status, and strive to achieve autonomy (Schlegel, 1972). It must not be forgotten that the arguments used here about sex differences apply to our (postulated, though with some evidence) environment of evolutionary adaptedness, not to all possible environments. They are also *generalizations* about sex differences: we must assume that, as today, there was extensive overlap in many characteristics between the sexes and that individuals used diverse alternative strategies to achieve their goals.

The available evidence indicates that early man lived in small groups, and analogy with modern hunter-gatherers suggests that there was a marked division of labour, with men co-operating to prey on large animals and women bonded to particular males and collecting plant foods

(Mellen, 1981). A special issue here is parental care. We take it for granted that mothers are more prone to give parental care than fathers, but it is at least conceivable that the reverse could happen – for instance in mammals, where the female has suffered the debilitating effects of pregnancy, the male might well be in a better condition to look after the young. However there are functional reasons why this should not be so. First, a female mammal can be sure that a given offspring is her own, whereas a male could have been cuckolded so that, from the point of view of biological function, paternal care would be wasted. Second, because of internal fertilization, mammalian females are forced to invest more in each offspring than do males, and the infant's early survival depends on maternal care. If an infant did not thrive, a female would have to invest more to bring a second infant to the same stage than would a male (Dawkins & Carlisle, 1976). For both these reasons, neglect of parental care imposes greater costs (in terms of reproductive success) on females than on males (Trivers, 1972; Maynard Smith, 1977).

The difference in parental involvement between the sexes is associated with differences in their reproductive strategies. Since in mammals the infant's survival depends on extended maternal care, the rate at which females can reproduce is limited by the time they need for gestation and to rear the young. By contrast, in so far as males are freed from parental duties by the females' commitment to the offspring (see above), their reproductive success is determined largely by how many females they can fertilize. We shall return to this issue shortly.

Considering another aspect of the co-adapted complex, secondary sexual organs are related to species differences in copulation patterns and socio-sexual arrangements (Fig. 18; Short, 1979). For example the chimpanzee female often mates with several males in succession and the males have exceptionally large testes and accessory glands: it has been reasonably suggested that these evolved because sperm competition occurs inside the female, so that a male who produces many sperm has an advantage. By contrast the male gorilla, who usually has exclusive access to a number of females, has relatively small testes. The relative size of the human testes is little larger than that of the gorilla's, suggesting that males had more or less exclusive access to one or more females. In other respects the human sexual apparatus, including the relatively enormous penis and sexually attractive breasts together with continuous female acceptance of the male, are all in harmony with the view that sex was important in the maintenance of male-female relationships (Short, 1979). That is not to say that this is the whole answer: some species with minimal pair-bonds nevertheless show complex sexual foreplay, and some monogamous species copulate seldom (Kleiman, 1977; Hrdy, 1981). And other

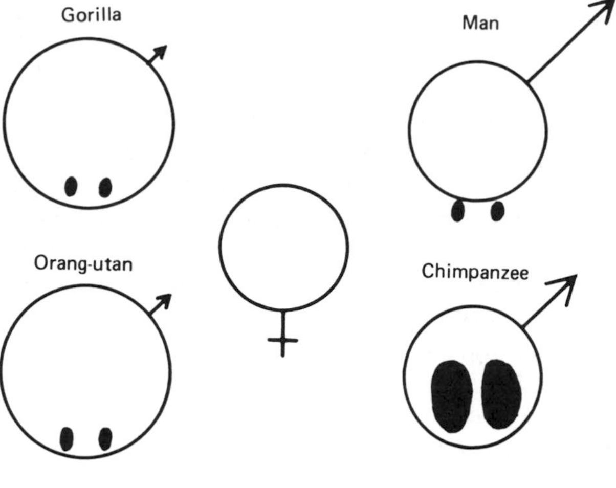

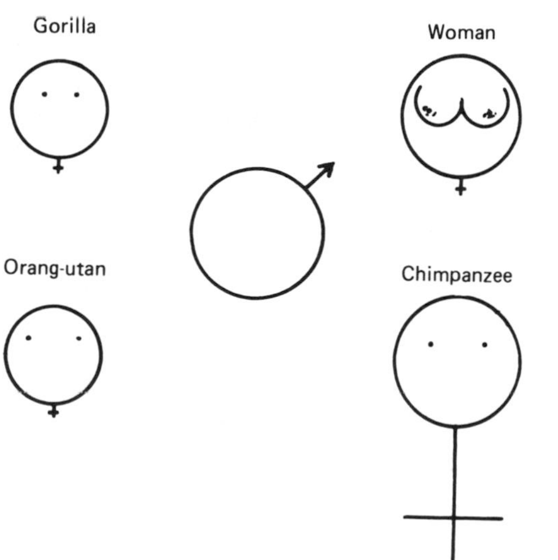

Fig. 18 The male as seen by the female, and the female as seen by the male, in man and the great apes (Short, 1979)

explanations have been advanced – some have emphasized the role of penile displays in agonistic encounters (Eibl Eibesfeldt, 1975) and others the possible significance of breast size as an indicator of nutritional state (Cant, 1981; see also Caro, 1987). But the view that human sexual behaviour is important in the maintenance of male-female relationships seems to integrate more facts than any competing hypothesis. Consider for example an interesting detailed point. If ejaculation occurs more frequently than once every 2–3 days, the semen volume and sperm density of the ejaculate decline; it has thus been suggested that we are physiologically ill-adapted to high copulation frequencies. However, since the ability to copulate does not suffer a similar decline, the data are compatible with the view that copulation has a relationship-maintaining function in addition to fertilization.

It is usually suggested that enduring male–female relationships were important because successful rearing of the offspring demanded two parents, protection and co-operation by the male being important for infant survival. Again, this may not be the whole answer. An additional suggestion is that the crucial factor in strengthening the pair bond has been not sex itself, but the concealment of ovulation. In the absence of external changes in the genitalia or marked changes in female receptivity, the male could not have told when to mate in order to ensure conception and could not have deserted the female for fear of being cuckolded (Alexander & Noonan, 1979). This could explain a male's interest in forming at least a consort relationship with a female – though maintenance of the bond once the female ceased to be receptive would have been in his interests only to the extent that his presence aided infant survival.

Now the adaptive significance that sexual assertiveness would have had for males is immediately apparent: any copulatory contact may have led to one or more descendants. This must have been much less true for females. However it has been suggested that there may have been other benefits in sexual assertiveness for females. First, in some species of non-human primates, a male taking over a group of females may kill the infants who were fathered by his predecessor: this causes the female to become receptive again more quickly, so that the new male can father his own offspring. Hrdy (1981) suggests that if males are uncertain as to whether a given offspring is their own, they will be less likely to harm it than if they were certain it was not. Thus in a multi-male society it might have paid a female to mate promiscuously throughout the cycle, so that no male could be certain who had fathered her offspring. Second, if a continued male presence was necessary for rearing the offspring, it might have paid a female to maintain a bond with one male, but to keep other males uncertain as to the paternity of her child. She might thereby have been in a better position to acquire a new male if she lost her own. Third, female sexual assertiveness might also have enabled a female to be fertilized by a male more desirable (i.e. carrying better genes) than the one with which she was bonded. Fourth, continuous sexual availability might have rendered a female more successful in obtaining resources (e.g. meat) from males, as may be the case now in chimpanzees (Teleki, 1973).

However we must also consider the costs incurred in mating. For both males and females mating must have involved some expenditure of time and energy, and entailed exposure to conflict with competing individuals, and perhaps also increased exposure to predators. For males it may also have involved expenditure of gametes which are not in infinite supply (Dewsbury, 1982). In addition, if paternal care aided infant survival any male–female bond which had been formed might have been affected by philandering. Here the situation was probably not reciprocal. Philandering by the male could have augmented his reproductive success and, if its effects on the paternal care he provided were negligible, it would not have detracted from that of his mate. It therefore would not have provided a biological reason for the female to desert, although it might conceivably have provided an opportunity for another male to take her. By contrast, philandering by the female, if known to the male, would have caused the male to fear he had been cuckolded. Without confidence in his paternity, continued paternal investment would have been unprofitable for him, and he might well have done better to transfer his allegiance elsewhere. If male assistance were necessary for infant survival, maintenance of the bond would have been more important to the female than to the male because, as we have seen, she would have had to invest more to bring another infant (or litter) to the same stage. Unless the female could call on other sources of support (another male, female kin), the bond would be likely to be more important to the female than to the male. Thus the costs to females of philandering would be greater than the costs to males.

Thus males stood to gain more from philandering than did females. Philandering may have brought greater costs to females because it could lead to a withdrawal of male support and a consequent reduction in the chances of survival of the infant. We have seen that this would matter more to the female than to the male. This background leads us to expect not only that males and females would have differed in their attitudes towards and behaviour in close relationships, but also that several partially contradictory strands might have been interwoven in each case. Mate choice may involve first a decision as to mating strategy, and then within the strategy chosen a series of tactical choices amongst potential individuals (Wittenberger, 1983), in each case the balance depending on environmental constraints (e.g. Dunbar, 1983). On the basis of these arguments the following ultimate considerations might affect the attitudes of male primates to females under circumstances in which paternal care aids offspring survival: (i) Sexual attraction to females whose characteristics, transmitted to their offspring, would increase the reproductive success of the latter. (ii) Sexual attraction to females seen as receptive, on the basis that they are impregnatable. (iii) Aversion to investing in relationships with females seen as sexually promiscuous, on the basis that any investment in their offspring might be rendered biologically valueless by their infidelity. (iv) Rather a propensity to form relationships with females seen as receptive yet potentially faithful on the basis that males mating with such females and investing resources in rearing their offspring are unlikely to be cuckolded. (v) Attraction to females whose characteristics indicate that they would rear the male's offspring successfully.

In the females' attitude to males we would expect to find: (i) Sexual attraction to males whose characteristics, transmitted to their offspring, would increase the reproductive success of the latter. These characteristics are not necessarily the same as those affecting males' attraction to females on this basis. (ii) If paternal care is necessary, a propensity to bond with males whose characteristics would make them good protectors and/or providers. (iii) A propensity to attempt to convince any male with whom they have a bond and who provides for them that he is the father of any offspring that they bear. (iv) Possibly, sexual receptivity to other males sufficient to convince them that they might be the father of the current offspring. If known, however, sexual jealousy of the bonded male might undermine (ii).

Predictions for the two sexes, based on considerations of the effects of behaviour on inclusive fitness, thus differ crucially in that males are predicted to tend to mate with more females than the one(s) in whose offspring they invest paternal care, whereas females should be more discriminating in choosing a mate and show a stronger correlation between mating preference and bonding preference.

We may now consider in more detail the nature of the observed differences between men and women in close relationships. For ease of presentation, these will be compared directly with those that would be expected, from the evolutionary argument, to have been present in early humans. Of course behaviour in close relationships differs between cultures, but it seems legitimate to start by asking how far sex differences in the societies about which we know perhaps most – those of Western Europe and the USA – can be understood in terms of propensities of the types described above. The emphasis is on the *direction* of the observed sex differences, and not on their magnitude: we shall argue later (Chapter 8) that the sex role stereotypes that so strongly influence the behaviour of men and women exaggerate any differences that might otherwise be present. And none of the differences discussed are absolute: in every case there is extensive overlap between the sexes,and the differences lie only in central tendencies.

The same-sex friendships of girls are more focussed on the dyad than those of boys: boys show a propensity to form group bonds, whilst girls are more likely to form close relationships (Hartup, 1983). Girls are more likely to distinguish between regular friendships and best friendships, the former being based on shared activities and the latter on prosocial attributes. This does not mean that men never form close friendships with other individuals, but a number of investigators have found that male and female friendships differ in quality, male friendships focussing on shared experience and activities perhaps related to a potential for co-operation, whilst female friendships emphasize intimacy and mutual emotional support (e.g. Cozby, 1973; Weiss & Lowenthal, 1975).

Turning to heterosexual relationships, a number of studies demonstrate that initial attraction is based largely on physical characteristics related to health or sexual potential, and that these are more important to males than to females (Murstein, 1979; Berscheid & Walster, 1978). (In many other species, attraction based on physical characteristics is probably more important to females than to males: perhaps in humans male physical characteristics are less closely linked to the ultimate criteria behind female choice). After the initial attraction courtship involves more or less extended negotiation about the nature and durability of the developing relationship (e.g. Duck & Miell, 1983). Whilst these are usually regarded as successive stages by social psychologists, they can also be seen as involving decisions about the adoption of alternative mating tactics by males and females.

In the pair formation stage considerable evidence indicates that women place more importance than men on choosing a dependable mate. In a study of computer dating, Touhey (1972) found that men were attracted to women who shared their sexual attitudes, women to men who shared their religious beliefs (see also Coombs & Kenkel, 1966). Rubin *et al.* (1981) found that men were more likely to endorse romantic ideas about marriage, whereas women tended to be more pragmatic, often rating economic security as highly as passion. (In another sense women are probably more romantic than men, as witnessed by the richness of romantic fiction for women: this however is related to fantasies concerning relationships, and parallels the much greater male readership of pornographic literature). In a study of sex differences in attitudes towards love, Hendrick *et al.* (1984) found that females tended to be more 'storgic' (i.e. seeing love as friendship) and pragmatic than males, whereas males tended to be more erotic and 'ludic' (i.e. instrumental, seeing love as a game). These authors see a greater female tendency to agree that it is alright to keep one's lover slightly uncertain as an exception to the tendency for females to be less ludic in their attitudes, but this could surely be seen as female strategy for cementing a bond, perhaps capitalizing on male fear of being cuckolded (cf Hrdy, cited above). (On the other hand, in dating relationships women are more likely to report emotional symptoms of being in love (Dion & Dion, 1975): it is not clear whether this is due to actual sex differences in the experience of love, or in willingness to talk about it to research workers.)

Both traditionally and in practice women prefer to marry men who are taller, whom they believe to be more intelligent, older than themselves, and successful, whereas men prefer women who are younger, attractive and likely to be good mothers and home makers (refs. in Deaux, 1976; Peplau & Gordon, 1983; Buss, 1986). This could be causally related to a marriage system in which male–male competition limits bonding to males who have achieved success by specified criteria, but it is also in harmony with the view held by some that older males acquire resources and wisdom and are better protectors than younger ones, and with the fact that younger women have a greater reproductive potential than older. A survey by Murstein (1979) again reveals differences in each sex's criteria for the other. In choosing a partner females were more concerned with the nature of the interpersonal relationships. Males, however, were concerned both with the traditional submissive role of the spouse and with her 'passion potential'.

Turning to differences in attitudes to copulation, we have seen that, in spite of modern trends towards more permissive and egalitarian attitudes, males still tend to be the ones who encourage and females the ones who limit sexual intimacy (Peplau *et al.*, 1977). A propensity to sexual intercourse even in the absence of an interpersonal relationship is much more conspicuous in males than it is in females. Male heterosexual prostitution is rare and, at least in the past, males have been found to be much more likely to be aroused by nude members of the opposite sex (Steele & Walker, 1974). Studies of attitudes towards sex are again in keeping with this general picture. Hendrick *et al.* (1984, 1985) found significant sex differences on 73 of the 102 items on their questionnaire on sexual attitudes. Males were markedly more permissive (e.g. accepting casual intercourse, approving of intercourse without commitment), and endorsed instrumentality (e.g. focussing on one's own pleasure) more than females. Females were more responsible (e.g. items concerned with communication, birth control) and tended to endorse sexual communion (e.g. the special nature of making love) as an approach to sexuality.

Again Carns (1973) found that college women were significantly more likely than college men to encounter disapproval if they revealed loss of their virginity; and that women encountered more positive reactions when the first coitus was in a loving relationship, rather than casually. Such findings are not surprising. What is interesting, however, was the finding that men received more approval when the first coitus was with a casual pick-up or prostitute than when with a loved partner. Yet such an attitude could be construed as compatible with the view that monogamously committed men were not necessarily the most biologically successful.

Thus we see that the observed social attitudes and behaviour are in line with the presumed biological desiderata of early human history – namely that it is in the male's interests to fertilize as many females as possible, and to play only a limited role in child care, whereas female reproductive success depends on the adequacy and competence of a male protector. And in so far as he takes that role, the male must be sure he is not being cuckolded. On this model, female sexual assertiveness is suppressed because the disadvantages of enhancing fears of being cuckolded in a mate or a potential mate outweigh other advantages such as raising the possibility of paternity with other men. Especially to be easy-to-get for a particular man but hard-to-get for all other men is preferred to a uniformly hard-to-get or easy-to-get woman (Walster *et al.*, 1973).

The double standard of morality has long been characteristic of Western (and many other) societies (e.g. Kinsey *et al.*, 1948, 1953; Dickemann, 1981). Although its inequity has been recognized for at least hundreds of years (Ariosto, 1521/1983), it remains a powerful force. As we have seen, it is surely related to the fact that a woman always knows that the baby inside her is her own, but a male can be cuckolded. Thus males must ensure the fidelity of their mates but, provided the bond is maintained (and risks of infection can be disregarded (Heiman, 1980)), females can permit their males some sexual licence (Barash, 1977).

The theme of bond dependence is relevant also to the issue of power strategies in close relationships. In non-egalitarian marriages in our society it is more often the man than the woman who is dominant; and female-dominated and egalitarian marriages tend to be less happy than male dominant ones (e.g. Centers *et al.*, 1971): whilst this is in keeping with the generally greater aggressiveness and assertiveness of males, it is of course susceptible also to other explanations. Compatible with the view that the bond is more important to women is the finding that women are more likely to attempt to deal with a problem arising in marriage, men to run away from it (Kelley *et al.*, 1978). An explanation not incompatible with the biological view lies in the power structure of the relationship: if men have greater power, they may gain nothing from discussing problems with a partner, but women may use confrontation as the only way to protect or enhance their position.

Many of the characteristics of the conversations of heterosexual couples can be ascribed to male assertiveness. Men do more interrupting and claim more personal space (e.g. Henly, 1977). Women are more supportive of male speakers than vice versa, asking more questions and showing more skill in indicating interest and attention (Fishman, 1978). Although men initiate more touching, women are more skilled at encoding and decoding non-verbal messages than males (Noller, 1980). Such differences are compatible with the requirements of a social situation in which males competed for females, whilst females bonded with particular males.

The question next arises, how far these gender differences in behaviour in interpersonal relationships rest on sex differences in behavioural propensities. This is a controversial area. Adkins (180, p. 390) writes 'Few unequivocal sex differences have been demonstrated (Maccoby & Jacklin, 1974): even these have been questioned on scientific grounds; and some that were demonstrated in previous decades have turned out to be greatly reduced or absent in more recent studies, due to social changes.' Nevertheless the comparative and endocrinological evidence cited in Chapter 4 cannot be dismissed: some differences are to be expected. And whilst statistical differences between the sexes in attitudes and behaviour are much affected by the task or situation chosen for the assessment, and account for only a small proportion of the variance, they are more marked in social than in asocial situations (Deaux, 1984). There is substantial evidence from a number of societies that boys tend to be more aggressive, more active and more impulsive than girls, but less susceptible to anxiety. In Western societies, females, though not less persistent or motivated in achievement-relevant situations, have less confidence in their own abilities (Block, 1983; Deaux, 1984). The achievement needs of females are more likely to conflict with their affiliative needs than are those of males, to the detriment of the former (Hoffman, 1972), and their success is more dependent on adult approval. Males are less susceptible to 'learned helplessness' (for reviews, see Maccoby & Jacklin, 1974; Block, 1983).

Sex differences in the situations that provoke anxiety may also fit into this picture. Magnusson & Oläh (1981) asked a large sample of Hungarian adolescents what situations made them anxious and why each situation was considered threatening. Although the authors emphasize the preliminary nature and possible cultural specificity of their findings, the data show that the boys were concerned about dangers to or consequent upon male assertiveness and the girls with dangers to relationships.

Finally, some issues not so obviously in harmony with the general picture must be mentioned. There is some evidence that men may suffer more severe consequences if a dating relationship terminates (Rubin *et al.*, 1981) or a marriage ends in divorce (Bloom *et al.*, 1979). The effects of who caused the break-up, and whether or not there were children, need to be studied. In addition, studies of dating couples or married partners over the last few years have revealed some sex differences which do not fit the theme of difference in basic propensities being discussed here. For instance, in college couples Peplau (1976) found females to be slightly more feminist than their partners; and Cochran & Peplau (1981 unpub. cited in Peplau & Gordon 1983, unpub.) that women emphasized independence and equality more than men. Whilst there is of course danger in this line of argument, it seems reasonable to regard these as current reactions against the more ubiquitous traditional picture, and as illustrating the complexity of the basic propensities, rather than as evidence against their existence. In any case, although they may represent a change in the sort of relationships women want, they may still reveal the importance for women of finding relationships which are right for them: it has been suggested (though without evidence) that one reason women may play a liberated role is in order to gain the respect of the kind of man who does not want a dependent submissive wife (Borgerhoff Mulder, *pers. comm.*).

Thus it seems that there are many similarities between the behaviour of men and women in close personal relationships as observed in Western society, and those that the evolutionary argument would predict our ancestors to have shown. These parallels are at least of intrinsic interest, in that they provide a way of synthesizing diverse facts about interpersonal relationships within a relatively simple framework. This synthesizing power of the parallels discussed is entirely independent of views about the means whereby the sex differences develop in individuals, and could be irrelevant to issues of inclusive fitness in man and women in present circumstances.

Should we attribute any further significance to these parallels? A number of issues must be considered.

First, the slipperiness of this sort of functional argument must not be forgotten. To cite one issue not mentioned above, female orgasm has been regarded by some as a uniquely human characteristic, and by others as not uncommon in mammals. Some have considered its occurrence to require explanation, some its non-occurrence. And some have regarded it as non-adaptive, others as functional in bond-maintenance and others as functional in promoting mating with multiple partners (Symons, 1979). Whilst the particular model of male-female relationships discussed here seems to fit the facts, it may well not be the only possible one.

Second, the parallels drawn depend to some extent on selecting facts that fit. This must be acknowledged, but it is surprising how many facts do fit, and the question is perhaps whether there is a better integrative model (see below). Furthermore the functional arguments used here are concerned first with explaining *generalities*, however interesting the exceptions may be.

Third, most human marriages are arranged, and do not occur between freely choosing partners. This, however, does not necessarily invalidate the argument. Evolutionary theory would predict that the criteria whereby potential mates are evaluated by those who arrange the marriage are likely to be closely related to those the individuals themselves would use if given a free choice. For instance parents may select husbands for their daughters who will be good providers, as well as good allies for themselves. Of course other criteria may operate, for instance where the groom's wealth goes to the bride's parents or vice versa, and generational conflicts of interest are widespread. But even if marriage is a primarily political or child-raising institution, based on co-operation between the spouses (or their kin) rather than on sex, fidelity is still a crucial issue, and sex may still be important in smoothing and cementing a relationship which has at first little of the emotional content expected in Western marriages.

Fourth, so far the data have been drawn primarily from Europe and the USA. Cultural variation in the nature of close relationships is in fact enormous, and is indeed to be expected on the current model, which is not one of biological determinism (e.g. Mead, 1950). A functional approach would indeed predict that patterns of sex-specific socialization would vary with the mating system, relative access of the two sexes to necessary resources, and so on, and thus with more general ecological and other factors (see Strathern, 1976; Sanday, 1981; Deaux, 1985; and below).

We must remember here the great gap between what people do or feel and what they say about what they do or feel. Whilst people in modern Western societies may say they support a single standard of sexual permissiveness, a double standard may continue to predominate behaviourally (Ferrell, *et al.*, 1977; Peplau *et al.*, 1977). In certain Papua New Guinea groups women, confined (by men) to special quarters because they are supposedly unclean whilst menstruating, may yet report that they are unable to persuade men to stay away (Gillison, 1980). Thus in assessing generality we must consider carefully the relative merits of data about what people do, what convention decrees that they should do, and what sources reveal that they would like to do.

Table 7.2 *Number of countries in which the aspect in question was associated more with men than with women. Based on data in Williams & Best (1982) From Hinde, R. A. (1984b)*

	No. of Countries (N = 25)	Definition (where not self-explanatory)
Affective meanings		
Favourability	12	Positive evaluation
Activity	25	
Strength	25	
Ego state		
Critical parent	23	Criticises, controls or reflects society's rules
Nurturing parent	1	Nurtures, promotes growth
Adult	25	Engages in realistic problems solving
Free child	11	Self-indulgent, spontaneous
Adapted child	0	Conforms and compromises
Psychological needs		
Dominance	25	Seeks or sustains leadership
Aggression	25	
Achievement	25	
Autonomy	25	
Exhibition	25	
Endurance	18	Persisting in tasks undertaken
Change	14	Seeking novelty
Intraception	7	Attempting to understand own behaviour or that of others
Affiliation	4	Seeking and sustaining numerous personal friendships
Order	14	Emphasizing neatness, order, etc.
Heterosexuality	5	Need to seek company of and derive emotional satisfaction from interaction with opposite sexed peers
Nurturance	0	
Succourance	0	
Deference	0	
Abasement	0	

In fact there is considerable evidence that sex differences in attitudes and behaviour within personal relationships have considerable cross-cultural generality. In the first place, cross-cultural studies reveal a surprising degree of uniformity in perceived sex differences in behavioural propensities. Williams & Best (1982) asked respondents in 25 countries from scattered parts of the world to state whether each of the 300 adjectives in a list (Gough & Heilbrun, 1965) was more frequently associated with men or women in their culture. Six items were male-associated in all countries – adventurous, dominant, forceful, independent, masculine and strong, with aggressive, autocratic, daring, enterprising, robust and stern being male-associated in all but one. Sentimental, submissive and superstitious were female-associated in all countries, with affectionate, dreamy, feminine and sensitive being female-associated in all but one.

Using the items which at least 67 per cent of respondents in the country concerned specified as characterizing males or females to represent the respective stereotypes, certain further analyses were carried out. The items were scaled for affective meanings, on the extent to which they described 5 ego states, and on the extent to which they indicated a particular need in the individual concerned (see Table 7.2). The extent to which the male and female stereotypes were associated with each of the three affective meanings, ego states and needs could thus be assessed.

Some of the data are summarized in Table 7.2. In that table, 25 means that the aspect in question was associated more with men than with women in all the countries concerned, 0 more with women than men. It will be apparent that a high proportion were uniformly or near-uniformly regarded either as masculine or as feminine characteristics. While the authors discussed various limitations in their study – for instance an over-representation of English speaking countries, and an under-representation of Eastern European and Middle Eastern countries – their data indicate surprising pan-cultural agreement. It will also be apparent that the perceived sex differences are in the same directions as those derived from functional principles (see also Segall, 1979).

Turning to aspect of relationships and socialization practices, many societies place importance on the bride's virginity but not on the groom's lack of sexual experience (e.g. Gluckman, 1950; Dickemann, 1981), and many more societies forbid adultery by wives than proscribe it in husbands (Schlegel, 1972). Male sexual jealousy of other males is widespread and strongly institutionalized in many societies: females may feel sexual jealousy (Fortes, 1949), but institutionalization of female jealousy is much rarer. Amongst the Gonja, jealousy of one co-wife for another is aroused most vehemently by the husband's attentions to the latter's child (E. Goody, 1973 and *pers. comm.*). Even in societies in which the activities of children are otherwise undifferentiated by gender, boys are given more encouragment to be aggressive and assertive (e.g. Whiting & Whiting, 1975; Goodale, 1980). Of course exceptions can be found – though one suspects fewer exceptions in what people actually do than in what they say that they do. And some of these may have a functional explanation: thus it may be to a man's advantage to claim paternity of all his wife's children, whether or not he fathered them, because they may provide labour which will contribute to the rearing of his own offspring or be exchangeable for wives and thus augment overall reproductive success (E. Goody, *pers. comm.*).

We must also ask whether the parallels between predictions of the biological model and the observed male–female differences can all be accounted for in terms of male power? Is the double standard of morality merely imposed by males because of their greater strength? It is clearly possible to relate many sex differences in behaviour to the power difference between men and woman. For instance Safilios-Rothschild (1977), discussing the consequences of social inequalities and the cultural assumptions of male superiority, has argued that women's inability to have independent access to social standing and resources leads to their developing sexual strategies that will maximize their bargaining power. One such involves a kind of sexual repression which makes sexuality a scarce resource whose value is thereby artificially increased. Several points must be made here. First, the biological argument involves sex differences in strength and fighting ability, but not necessarily in power: although male dominance is usual in human societies, it is not ubiquitous (Sanday, 1981). Second, the biological model regards the strength difference as one aspect of an adaptive complex, related to differences in reproductive strategies, rather than necessarily primary. How many of the other sex differences discussed in this chapter are to be understood solely as its ontogenetic consequences is an open issue. In any case, full understanding of power differences between men and women in any particular society requires consideration not only of sex differences in strength, but also in the control of resources, and an understanding of the relations between reproduction and production. Third, the present discussion in no way minimizes the important of social inequalities, but raises the question of their bases: understanding of these is surely necessary if they are to be removed. Cultural forces affect the nature of individuals, but the reverse is also true, and that is the dialectic with which we must come to terms – a task made the more difficult by the impact of ecological factors on its outcome (see Chapters 8 and 9). Finally, an explanation based on strength differences alone seems to account not so neatly for all the facts. For instance, it could hardly account for the differences in young children's friendships, however subtle the parental influences. The view that women express their sexuality in order to enhance its value and use it to gain status seems to demand some imbalance in sexuality in the first instance – in its nature if not in its quantity. The somewhat different view that males suppress female sexuality neglects many of the complexities: functional considerations suggests that males would not support conventions that deprived them or their relatives of sexual partners, though they might try to persuade others to adopt conventions that deprived other males. An institutionalized or inherent propensity to fear of cuckoldry provides a more economical explanation. The relative importance of the bond to females fits at least as readily into a model based on differential parental investment as into one based on power alone.

Some would prefer to regard seeking after wives and the begetting and bearing of children as routes to power or a source of labour rather than to reproductive success. But such explanations are not incompatible, for we must ask why men should seek for power. The biological model predicts male–male competition with power as a proximate goal and reproductive success as an ultimate one.

Two conclusions can be drawn. First, at least in a qualitative way, a functional approach can help to integrate a wide range of facts about male/female differences in close personal relationships that have considerable cross-cultural generality. Diverse characteristics of the behaviour of men and of women, and of male–female relationships, can be seen as inter-related and forming part of a complex that was probably adaptive earlier in human history (though is not necessarily so today). Second, in view of the evidence discussed in Chapter 4, it is not unreasonable to suppose that those differences depend partly on sex differences in behavioural propensities that are or have been adaptive. However this is not the same as saying that the differences observed are a necessary consequence, or solely a consequence, of those propensities: they vary between cultures and their development depends also on the sociocultural structure. This is discussed further in the next chapter.

SUMMARY AND CONCLUSION

In this chapter we have considered two categories of human relationships which have some characteristics that, though not ubiquitous, are present in at least the majority of human cultures – the mother–child relationship and male–female relationships. We have seen that the natures of these characteristics correspond qualitatively to those that would be predicted if individuals behaved in ways that would maximise their inclusive fitness. This of course does not prove that they have been shaped by natural selection, but it is in harmony with the view that they depend in part on basic human propensities with considerable stability and having functional importance. As we saw in the last chapter, such propensities are subject to environmental and cultural influences, and the features of relationships discussed are to be regarded only as central tendencies around which those cultural influences produce variation. And of course there is no implication that properties of relationships likely to have been appropriate for one or other party in our environment of evolutionary adaptedness are still appropriate today.

It remains to emphasize two points. First, that the argument is basically still merely an argument from design, with all its shortcomings (see pp. 17–18) – though the fact that in each case the many different properties of the relationship and of the propensities of the participants fit together adds considerably to its strength. However the argument from design applies to specified environments: it implies neither that behaviour appropriate in some circumstances is necessarily appropriate in others, nor that the course of development in one set of environments will also occur in others.

Second, nothing that has been said should be taken to imply that the nature of relationships between the sexes are driven by biological imperatives. We have already seen that social stereotypes are of overriding importance, but the possibility arises that those social stereotypes are caricatures of biological propensities. We shall discuss this in the next chapter.

Finally it must be emphasized that even the biological argument emphasizes the importance of flexibility and relative utility of alternative strategies in the light of environmental circumstances. No amount of evidence for a potential for polygyny and/or promiscuity should affect our judgement as to whether monogamous relationships can provide the best arrangement for our society – either for the rearing of children or for providing a context within which man and woman, with their similar and their divergent interests, can each reach the highest degree of self-realization. If we find evidence for sex differences in propensities to respond to socialization, we must use it to select socialization practices that will help us achieve our aims. Knowledge of our nature must be used to aid us to achieve rather than to set our goals.

8

The dialectics with higher levels

HUMAN UNIVERSALS AND VARIANTS

At the level of dyadic relationships we can find basic similarities but also many differences between societies. When we move to the levels of social structure and sociocultural structure, the emphasis must be even more on differences. However, whilst most anthropologists have been primarily interested in the differences between human cultures there have been some who attempted to list their universal features. Murdock (1967) for instance included such items as cooking, cosmology, dancing, joking, language, mourning and the propitiation of supernatural beings as universal traits of human societies. Unlike some of the individual characteristics discussed in Chapter 6, these are aspects of behaviour that cannot be identified by their form, and for which physical description (see p. 12) would be inappropriate. Not only the form that they take but also the factors that initiate them and virtually all their other characteristics may differ markedly between societies. Most of them depend, directly or indirectly, on language. In fact these so-called universals are not items or aspects of behaviour identical in different cultures but categories of items with certain characteristics in common. No so-called 'cultural universal' is actually to be found in any particular culture, only examples of the class.

Now in so far as there are categories of practices usefully described as cultural universals, they are the products of societies and they depend upon social experience. We cannot be at all sure that a group of young humans, brought up without exposure to one or other of these practices, would display the behaviour in question in adulthood (Fox, 1980). What we can say, however, is that humans are so constituted that practices of the general type specified are virtually certain to develop in human groups or, once developed, to be maintained over the generations.

At first sight, since the anthropologists' 'universals' clearly depend heavily on social experience, it would seem that we must seek for environmental factors in their development. However we must also note that, unlike some of the individual universals mentioned, most are (probably) peculiarly human characteristics. Indeed chimpanzees brought up in human families fail, so far as we can tell, to develop any of them (e.g. Kellogg & Kellogg, 1933) – though to be fair, chimpanzees have not so far been exposed to a human family environment over generations. However it is reasonable to assume that the anthropologists' universals depend ultimately on genetic differences between man and chimpanzee.

But to say that our ability to make complex tools, to use verbal language, to mourn and to dance depend on constitutional factors in which we differ from non-human species is not to say that these are characters that, like smiling and crying, will appear under virtually any environmental conditions. The anthropologists' universals are categories of practices which show some similarities but many differences between societies, which depend on social interactions and relationships, and whose properties both depend upon, and influence, the characteristics of individuals within the society. How then can we account for their generality? Since their elaboration depends upon social interactions with others, perhaps over many generations, is it reasonable to seek for their bases in universal behavioural dispositions of individuals?

At one time this was in fact a respectable route for anthropologists to follow: Frazer (1890) sought to find motives which 'have operated widely, perhaps universally, in human society, producing in varied circumstances a variety of institutions specifically different but generally alike . . .' Frazer's 'motives' seem to be equivalent to the 'propensities' and 'predispositions' used here, though the latter terms more clearly embrace the probability that learning will proceed in one direction rather than another (see p. 67) as well as motives for action. This approach has attracted criticism in the past because of a wavering uncertainty about the level of social complexity at which it should be applied, and a neglect of the dialectics between them. However we shall accept it here, arguing that whilst so-called universals can be found at each level of social complexity, any common properties they may have at and beyond the level of interpersonal relationships depend upon basic human propensities that provide constraints and predispositions for what the individual does and learns but which, in interaction with each other and with varied environmental factors, can produce diverse structural forms. This is in harmony with the views of Geertz (1970) who, having criticized the idea of human universals, advocated a 'concern with the particular, the circumstantial, the concrete, but a concern organized and directed in terms of the sort of theoretical analyses (that he had) touched upon – analyses of physical evolution, of the functioning of the nervous system, of social organization, of psychological processes, of cultural patterning, and so on – and, most especially, in terms of the interplay amongst them'.

For example, most (perhaps all) societies are hierarchically organized, though the precise forms that the hierarchical structures take are enormously variable. The hierarchical form could be accounted for by the facts that most individuals strive to outdo their fellows in at least one sphere of life (even if that be refusing to be competitive) and at least most people seek the approval of at least some others (see p. 107). Of course, such propensities did not act alone. There must have been adjustment of group size to the carrying capacity of the environment and accompanying changes in group structure (e.g. Barth, 1950); cultural innovations and influences on the environment affecting its carrying capacity (e.g. Flannery, 1969); cultural change involving special structural groupings (Adams, 1969); and increasing technological change leading to increased population density and competition between individuals, families and communities, leading in turn to, amongst other things, central political control of temporary food surpluses (Sanders & Price, 1969) However each of these could be based upon relatively few basic propensities. Although the evolution of societies is not the theme here, it is important to recognize that a relatively few human propensities, including human capacities for linguistic and symbolic abilities, must have led, not only to the tendency towards an hierarchical form found in (probably) all societies but also, under the influence of diverse environmental and historical forces, to the multitudinous hierarchical forms that societal structures take. Individual propensities influence, but do not by themselves determine, sociocultural structure.[1]

It is unnecessary to say that adequate understanding of the interplay between behavioural propensities within individuals, the interplay

[1] Lopreato (1984) has daringly presented a list of human 'predispositions' whose interactions supposedly account for many of the common features of human cultures and their variants. Although I much admire his enterprise, his 'behavioural predispositions' appear in large part to be reifications of things that most (or many) people do, at a level of analysis that already involves considerable complexity. For instance 'the urge to victimize' is said largely to explain exploitation, differential access to educational resources within a society, privilege, unfair legal treatment of the underprivileged, slavery, sacrifice, etc., and the predisposition of 'asceticism' is held to be relevant to flagellation, masochism, prohibition laws, ritualistic chastity, and even heroism. The general argument is exemplified by this sentence: 'Ascetic acts are so widespread in time and place that we may again hypothesize that they are anchored in a biological force' (p. 211). Whilst for the sake of brevity I have myself sometimes postulated 'propensities' which are little more than reifications, in general I would suggest (a) that a much more detailed psychological analysis is necessary; (b) that most acts of the type listed above have a much more complex causation than Lopreato imples; and (c) that even apparently basic propensities may not be wholly biological. Lopreato is apparently aware of these issues but does not seem adequately to allow for them in his list. I regret this comment, because Lopreato's assault on this issue is certainly a gallant one.

between individuals, and the relations between individuals and their environment, that give rise to the enormous diversity of sociocultural structures, is at present beyond our competence. However, because some biologists would like to apply principles derived from studies of animals directly to characteristics of sociocultural structure, it is worthwhile to mention one or two issues concerning the relations between properties of individuals and properties of societies.

INDIVIDUAL PROPENSITIES AND SOCIAL STEREOTYPES

Throughout the preceding chapters the importance of the dialectical relations between successive levels of social complexity has been stressed repeatedly. Consider the case of snake phobias. We have seen that these may be based in a universal predisposition to fear snakes. We have seen also that this may be enhanced by the sight of others, perhaps particularly others on whom the individual is dependent, showing fear of snakes. But the role that snakes play in our socio-cultural structure must surely also be important. In the myth of the Garden of Eden, in the Rubens paintings of snakes gnawing the genitals of those cast down in to Hell, almost wherever one looks snakes symbolize evil. And reciprocally, it seems improbable that snakes would play this role in our mythology if the predisposition were not there in the first place, though historical factors have no doubt also played an important role. The power of snake phobias can best be understood in terms of the dialectical relations between levels of social complexity. This does not mean that all such symbols have their origins in basic human propensities of this type, but many probably do. For instance lions have a significance common to many societies which presumably arises out of common human perceptions of their qualities. All that is being suggested is that such predispositions, modified and perhaps exaggerated (see below) over time by the dialectical relations between successive levels of social complexity, have played a role in many aspects of our beliefs and values.

To consider another case, in Britain and many other countries girls tend to achieve less well at mathematics at secondary schools than boys. The difference becomes important after children are about 11 years old, and concerns especially tasks in which spatial abilities are important. As the mathematics studied becomes more difficult, the proportion of the population of girls who study mathematics decreases. The differences are especially marked at the upper levels of ability (Royal Society, 1986). The decline is usually ascribed to the force of social stereotypes specifying that girls have more difficulties with mathematics than boys. For example, Williams, Woodmansee and Williams (1977) found that the adjectives 'logical' and 'rational' were associated with men more frequently than with women in England, Eire and the U.S.A. Presumably as a consequence of such a perceived difference, parents and teachers have lower expectations for daughters than for sons; this probably contributes to girls having poorer expectations about their own performance, a difference perhaps exacerbated by the attitudes of male peers; text books show a sex bias in that problems refer more often to males than to females; girls' teachers tend to be less well qualified than those of boys; girls see it as unfeminine to succeed in mathematics; and so on. The stereotypes clearly constitute an unfair handicap for women.

Whether these sex stereotypes about differences in mathematical ability can be related to inherent sex differences has been a matter of some controversy, for sex differences in performance could result from sex differences in socialization experience. However there is considerable evidence that adolescent boys are superior to girls in spatial visualization tasks that are less likely to be influenced by socialization factors (Maccoby & Jacklin, 1974; Lambert, 1978; Harris, 1979), and this is likely to be important in mathematics. The differences have been ascribed to (a) a recessive gene on the X chromosome that increases spatial ability in half of the male and a quarter of the female population (b) a hormonal difference, and/or (c) a difference in brain lateralization (Scarr & Kidd, 1983). (Girls, by contrast, tend to have superior verbal skills.) But the differences in abilities relevant to mathematics are far too small to account for the observed differences in achievement. Indeed it is often considered impolitic to refer to them, in that to acknowledge their possible existence contributes to the reality of the stereotype. However it remains a real possibility that the stereotype is linked to very small mean differences, which are then exaggerated because it is in the interests of one or other party to do so. If the effects of the stereotype are to be countered, we must come to terms with its bases. An understanding of how the stereotype develops may help us to change it.

As another example, we may consider once again the question of sex and gender differences in interpersonal relationships. We have seen that these depend in part on pre-natal and pubertal hormonal influences and in part on social experience (pp. 58–60). We have also seen that many of the basic differences are of a type that, so far as the evidence goes, would have been adaptive in our environment of evolutionary adaptedness (p. 119–36). However the differences are differences in mean values between the sexes, and not absolute. Many women are more assertive, more aggressive, more sexually promiscuous, than many men. By contrast, the stereotypes that operate in Western societies (or did until recently) imply a much greater separation than that. Men are seen as more assertive than women even though some women are much more assertive than many men; and women are seen as less promiscuous than men though some men are much more faithful than many women. The stereotypes are grossly inaccurate when applied to individuals.

How then do the stereotypes come to distort reality? One issue involves social categorization. A common propensity in human individuals, perhaps related to language use, involves attempts to define themselves in relation to the world in which they live (Kelly, 1955). One means to that end involves social categorization: we see ourselves as members of some groups and not as members of others. Furthermore individuals tend to interpret their social environment in ways that enable them to see their own group as favourably distinctive from others. In particular, they tend to treat members of the out-group as undifferentiated items in a social category and to perceive movement from the in-group to the out-group as difficult by exaggerating the differences between them (Billig, 1976; Tajfel, 1978; Hamilton, 1981; Brewer & Kramer, 1985). Attitudes towards their own and other groups are related to their self esteem. Now in reproduction and in food acquisition, men and women have long played different parts in human society. Not surprisingly, therefore, a basic issue in an individual's social identity concerns the gender he or she perceives him or herself as having. The differences between men and women become exaggerated, attributes irrelevant to the initial distinction become assimilated to the stereotype, and people come to see men and women as opposites (Deaux, 1985). Seen from this perspective, then, gender stereotypes exaggerate minor differences by processes that are inherent to the development of the self concept. That of course does not mean that the stereotypes are unalterable, though they may be resistant to change (Williams and Giles, 1978).

Nor does that mean that that is the only mechanism at work. That outlined above is likely to operate in all cases of ingroup–outgroup differentiation. In each particular case there may be particular factors at work that exacerbate the process. For one thing, denigration of the outgroup may enhance an individual's status in the ingroup, especially, if there is conflict or competition between them (Doise, 1978). In the particular case of gender stereotypes, exaggeration may also be to the individual's advantage. If a male's assertiveness augments his value as a co-parent, we must expect males to display and indeed to exaggerate assertiveness in order to influence female choice. It may be in the interests of at least the more powerful males to bolster the importance of assertiveness as a male characteristic, in order to direct female choice towards themselves, giving them access to the female they would choose. Reciprocally, if fidelity enhances the value of a female as a co-parent, females will display characters indicative of fidelity which, by enhancing their acceptability to all males, gives them access to the male they would choose. Clearly mechanisms that would enhance pre-existing small differences can be envisaged.

Such exaggerations could clearly operate against the interests of many individuals: they result in men who are not by nature assertive being regarded as unmanly and being perhaps less likely to be successful in obtaining mates, and in assertive women being labelled as unfeminine. But the suggestion is that the stereotype results from small real differences which are exaggerated by the processes involved in the acquisition of social identity, perhaps to the advantage of most members of one or other sex, or indeed of both sexes. The precise extent of the exaggeration differs between cultures (Williams and Best, 1982).

Comparable principles can probably be applied to other stereotypes. It appears that many group and national stereotypes have some basis in reality and are based on small initial differences (Campbell, 1967; Peabody, 1985). That there may be advantages to either in-group or out-group members or both in promoting them seems possible.

The values and norms that concern interpersonal relationships within a culture are an aspect of reality in that they provide goals towards which behaviour is directed, but they also often exaggerate reality in the sense that they specify ways in which people should behave or would like to behave rather than the ways in which people actually do behave. In many cases, at least, it is relatively easy to see that it is to the advantage of at least some individuals that this should be the case. Parents want their children to behave 'better' than children usually do, rulers and ecclesiastics try to bend the behaviour of individuals in ways which they see, egotistically or altruistically (in the everyday sense), as appropriate.

Nothing that is being said here implies that all precepts, norms, values or stereotypes necessarily involve exaggeration or distortion. The point being made is that many do, that some of the mechanisms that operate are at least partially understood, and that such aspects of the sociocultural structure can affect individual behaviour and augment existing tendencies. That in turn raises further questions about the evolutionary forces that shaped the propensities that lead to, for instance, in-group/outgroup differentiation. At this point it is easy to be carried away by speculation but, in addition to the probable advantages to the individual of group loyalty, it was hinted above that such propensities may be important in the formation of the self-concept in conditions of group living.

THE SOCIOCULTURAL STRUCTURE

That brings us to the ways in which relationships are patterned in the social structure and to the symbolic structure, with its accompanying myths and legends, which are the prime concern of many anthropologists. The present approach is entirely compatible with Hugh-Jones's (1979) view that 'The anthropologist must regard the ancestral cosmos as an imaginary projection of present experience, but at the same time it is a projection which both controls present experience and forms an integral part of it' (p. 1). The myths and legends reflect, form part of and affect the complex interplay between the natures of individuals and of their relationships (themselves influenced by the sociocultural structure), the economic organization and conditions of the society in which they live, and the ecological factors that affect them.

Full understanding thus requires both a psychological analysis of the ways in which the sociocultural structure is formed by the properties of the human mind, and a sociological analysis of the ways in which individuals, internalizing the symbols of the culture, come to experience the culture as part of themselves and themselves as part of the culture (e.g. Durkheim, 1912). These are issues beyond the scope of this book, but two matters, arising in part from preceding chapters, must be emphasized. The first is that the sociocultural structure is the product of brains that were shaped by selection acting in the empirical world of actual behaviour, and as such is likely to be related (though not directly), through the successive dialectics indicated in Figure 1, to the behavioural propensities, attitudes, fears, hopes and anxieties of individuals. Thus the cultural practices, rituals and beliefs which symbolize, exacerbate and/or ease the conflicts and problems that individuals face in their lives will not be understood until the natures of those individuals are understood.

Myths represent ways of coming to terms with the cognitions and emotions experienced by individuals, with sex, with the natural environment, with death and with life itself (Barth, in press). They are, however, collective constructions, elaborated not (usually) by single minds but by intercommunicating minds, with both similar and conflicting points of view. In many societies myths and other beliefs, values and customs are the responsibility of particular categories of individuals, who can therefore shape them to manipulate the behaviour of others to their own ends or according to ways they deem appropriate. In any case, at least in non-literate societies, myths must be seen as in a continuous process of creation.

Consider once more the question of sex differences in behaviour. We have seen that there are differences in behavioural propensities between men and women, which are exaggerated in social stereotypes. We must seek understanding of how these differences affect the dialectics between interactions, relationships, social structure and institutions. Given the differences between them, we must expect men and women to have differing cognitive models of society, and it will not be surprising that myths often reflect the different strands in each sex's perception of the other. Woman may be portrayed in one context as evil, radically different from and dangerous to men (Because of their power to cuckold? Because they are alien, coming from other, often hostile, groups?), and/or as epitomizing all that is good (Nurturant for the man's child?). In the same culture there may be glaring ambiguities between ascriptions of strength and weakness to women (Strathern, 1972). Similarly men may be portrayed as inconstant and promiscuous self-seekers, or as knights errant, the maiden's protector (see Ariosto, 1521/1983, for examples of all of these). We must expect the particular socialization practices, values and myths prevalent in each society to interact with each other and with environmental factors. For instance, Williams & Best (1982), in a study of sex stereotypes, found that the prominence of the Virgin Mary and of female saints in the Catholic religion was associated in Catholic countries with a female stereotype which was more favourable and less weak than that in Protestant countries. Similarly the importance of female figures in Hindu religion and their absence from Muslim religion was associated with a more favourable female stereotype in India than in Pakistan. (Indians in South Africa, however, were aberrant.) Sanday (1981) has documented similar principles over a much wider range of societies.

Furthermore cultural differences may be related to environmental factors, operating through the behaviour of individuals on the nature of interactions, relationships and sociocultural structure (see Sanday, 1981). For example, the nineteenth-century American West demanded assertive males, and an ideology grew up which fostered the notion of women as civilizing agents, who subdued the rowdy anti-social males (Rogers, 1978). Similarly in many present-day peasant societies ideologies of masculine virility are matched by high values of modesty, chastity and passivity in women (Harris, 1980).

Perhaps it is appropriate to emphasize yet again that the importance of the dialectics do not rest on an assumption of biological determinism. We must expect them to be affected by a variety of factors, such as the economic possibilities for a woman to support herself (and her children), the extent to which the residential arrangements make cuckoldry possible, the economic possibilities for polygyny and the reproductive value of offspring of different sexes. Such issues are themselves constrained by ecological factors (Borgerhoff Mulder, 1983). The dialectics will also be affected by historical factors, embodied in the norms, values and institutions of the sociocultural structure. The influences of behavioural propensities on relationships, social structure and sociocultural structure, and vice versa, remain to be unravelled whatever the sources of the behavioural propensities. However if sex differences in behavioural propensities occur, we had best know about them. Such knowledge may be an essential ingredient for understanding the most complex aspects of human societies, and could help us to construct the sort of society that we want. We must come to terms with the influence of the nature of individuals on society, as well as the influence of society on the individual. We must see this as mediated by dialectics involving successively higher order social phenomena. And we may understand these dialectics better when we see human propensities as possibly involving predispositions as well as the effects of socialization.

The second matter to be emphasized in this section involves a further warning against the presumption of direct correspondences between behavioural propensities and particular aspects of the sociocultural structure. This is not merely the fact that each myth, each legend, each practice depends on numerous behavioural propensities of many individuals and each propensity affects many aspects of the sociocultural structure. Beyond that, we must examine the extent to which the belief systems of a given culture can be considered as mutually isolated subsystems.

In more complex societies, where different aspects of the sociocultural structure are determined primarily by different groups of individuals, those aspects may be largely independent of each other. And some contradictions can be tolerated by individuals: for instance it seems that in public Trobriand islanders professed ignorance of the link between intercourse and conception, but in matters of personal relationships they behaved as though they were aware of it (Powell, cited Barnett, 1969). (A little introspection makes it painfully unnecessary to seek for further examples of contradictions that we tolerate in our belief-systems). On the other hand, dissonance (Heider, 1958; Newcomb, 1961; Kelley, 1971) within each area of life must be minimized. Furthermore there seem to be links between different cognitive domains. This is an issue that has come up several times in different forms in preceding chapters. For instance Carey's (1986) view of cognitive development implies the progressive differentiation and restructuring of cognitive domains involving new (and presumably largely culturally specific) ways of classifying concepts – with, for example, biological 'theories' differentiating from 'psychological' ones as the child grows up (p. 75). From a quite different perspective, research on social marking (p. 76) implies the application of known relations between persons to relations between objects. And we have seen how attitudes to men and women may be related to the nature of the deity accepted by the culture (p. 146).

From yet another viewpoint, some anthropologists perceive relations between the different domains of a culture. Lévi-Strauss (1955) has sought these in basic mental structures, attempting by cross-cultural comparisons to find fundamental properties of the human mind (see evaluation by Leach, 1970). Others have attempted to trace parallels between conceptual linkages in one domain with those in another: for instance Firth (1936) regarded Tikopia ideas of the soul as a re-statement of social structure at a symbolic level (see also Radcliffe-Brown, 1922; Malinowski, 1929; Tambiah, 1969). Our behaviour in any one context may be affected by principles derived from others – for instance decisions about the appropriateness of a marriage contribution may depend on kinship, prestige, economics, and so on (Keesing, 1967; 1971).

Of even greater interest are attempts to compare such parallels across societies. For instance Douglas (1966) attempted to establish parallels between cultural and personal goals, and between perceived boundaries in the environment and the perceived nature of the self. She suggested that attitudes to the body might parallel those to society, so that ritual activities and attitudes concerning boundaries and orifices of the body reflect those in the wider community. Thus an individual's attitude to a dead body may have parallels with his or her attitude to dissolution of the body politic.

Barnett (1969) followed this lead in an analysis of ethnographies of three New Guinea societies – the Trobriand islanders, the mountain Arapesh and the Manus. The Manus make clear distinctions between themselves and outsiders, between most of their village (regarded as safe), and other parts of their village together with the land outside (full of dangers). They build houses on separate atolls and visiting is not encouraged. In their attitudes to their own bodies they stress control and shame, and many aspects of their culture emphasize the differences between the sexes. They see their 'inner soul' as constantly in danger of attack from outside. In other words, boundaries are important at cultural, interpersonal and intrapersonal levels. At the other extreme, Trobrianders travel widely, regarding their journeys as reasonably safe because they are protected by beneficent supernaturals. There are flying witches, as well as hostile trading partners and adverse winds, but these are believed to be controllable by human magic. Lacking fear of bad parts in either their bodies or their minds, they are free to express themselves. They enjoy their bodily functions, decorate themselves and show considerable sexual equality. They are craftsmen, regard singing and dancing as important, and in general see both 'inside' and 'outside' as basically safe and controllable. They live in formally constructed villages which are regarded as organized wholes with mutually dependent parts, just like the human body and personality. In many respects the Arapesh are intermediate. Cultural boundaries are not emphasized and there is only a gradual differentiation between those who are 'like us' and those who are not. There are 'good' and 'bad' areas both inside and outside the village. Beliefs about bodily functions are also split: part of their sexuality and their blood is good, the other is dangerous and can lead to destruction or death. They emphasize both male–female opposition and co-operation, and have poorly constructed houses arranged in no particular order. Barnett (op. cit.) draws further parallels concerning the social structure and views about supernatural beings in these societies.

Now it is of course easy to suggest that, with the diversity of human societies and the diversity of practices within each, such parallels and contrasts are the product of selective fishing in a well-stocked sea. To that the only answer is that data from other societies pointing in the same direction are available. The point being made here is that not only the tendency to reduce dissonance within domains, but also correspondences between domains may well be important in the cognitive development of individuals. Coherence across cognitive domains presumably becomes less possible, the more complex and differentiated the society – and the resulting conflict and contradiction may exert forces that generate cultural change. But both the tendency towards coherence and structural complexity make *simple* correspondences between beliefs and institutions at the sociocultural level and the propensities of individuals even less probable. Rather the sociocultural characteristics reflect behavioural propensities in ways that combine, invert or distort them in diverse ways. They may even function in supressing them – as for example initiation rites may help to break mother–son ties in some societies (Herdt, 1981; Keesing, 1982), whilst where initiation is not closely tied to adolescence, the parent–child relationship changes more gradually (Fortes, 1949). All of which may sound like an escape through the plea that it is all very complicated, but should more properly be seen as a plea for principles, comparable to those we are beginning to have for the patterning of interactions within relationships (p. 38) that will explain how taboos and myths are related to behavioural propensities and other factors (including ecological ones) that shape and are shaped by them.

SUMMARY AND CONCLUSION

In the preceding chapters on universal human propensities and on human relationships circumstantial or indirect evidence was used to support hypotheses that, by the nature of things, cannot be proven. This chapter has been equally speculative. Yet the view that characteristics of human social structures and sociocultural structures are rooted in the behavioural propensities of individuals is reasonable, and indeed inevitable. It in no way denies the important influence of sociocultural structure on social structure, or of either on relationships or individuals or of external environmental/ecological factors on all of these. But this chapter has emphasized how small potential differences between the sexes may be magnified in social stereotypes to become part of the sociocultural structure and reflect back on the natures of individuals, and how belief systems may both reflect or distort and affect behavioural propensities. The relations between levels of social complexity are dialectical ones, with mutual influences at each level and two-way influences between levels. Simple isomorphism between features of sociocultural structure and human propensities are thus extremely improbable. Human propensities do more than set limits to the sociocultural structure, but are not themselves to be identified with particular aspects of that structure. Nevertheless the relations between the two are potentially understandable in terms of psychological mechanisms.

9

How far is the concept of adaptedness useful at the higher levels?

THE NATURE OF THE PROBLEM

Let us retrace some of the issues discussed in the last few chapters. Many aspects of selective responsiveness and many simple movement patterns are developmentally stable, and in many cases their inclusion in the repertoire of individuals must have brought,and may still bring, biological advantages. By the same token, many other human behavioural propensities – to seek food, to be assertive, to be curious, to make sense of the world, to learn from others and so on, are part of human nature, of biologically adaptive significance and likely to have been evolved under the influence of natural selection. These ubiquitous propensities and other characteristics of our species, and the inter-relations between them, guide (but do not determine) the course of learning. As a result some general properties of relationships, though influenced also by aspects of the sociocultural structure, can be related to behavioural propensities elaborated under the influence of natural selection and tend to be functional for the individual concerned. But most characteristics at the level of social structure and sociocultural structure can be seen only as very indirect consequences of a variety of individual behavioural propensities and other factors.

At this point it is important to remind ourselves that it is easy to reify the concept of culture as a system of practices and beliefs accepted by a group of individuals. This is a static conception (see pp. 4–5). Individuals are confronted by previously more or less defined practices and beliefs: acceptance of some is imposed by societal forces, but in other cases individuals have some capacity to choose from those available, and to modify or distort to varying degrees those that they assimilate. The manner in which individuals 'choose' from, assimilate and accommodate to the practices and beliefs of the society we see as the biases of the individual, and presume that in 'choosing' individuals are affected by the perceived fit between the beliefs and practices available, their own perceived needs, and the physical and social environment. However even when institutions or cultural practices are not imposed, individuals are constrained in their choices in a number of ways.

First, the dynamics of the transmission of information will depend on the extent to which it is vertical (parent to child), oblique (members of preceding generation other than parents to child) or horizontal (between members of the same generation) (Cavalli-Sforza & Feldman, 1981).

Second, whilst in simple societies individuals may be exposed to virtually all aspects of the sociocultural structure of the preceding generation, in more complex ones there may be a differential distribution of knowledge resulting from expert or privileged categories of individuals (e.g. Cavalli-Sforza & Feldman, 1981; Lumsden & Wilson, 1981; Richerson & Boyd, 1978; Boyd & Richerson, 1985).

Third, individuals have tendencies to acquire beliefs from particular others, to conform with the peer group and so on: the mode of transmission will affect the nature of cultural change.

Fourth, choice is constrained by other psychological mechanisms in individuals. For instance the desirability for compatability and coherence between the many aspects of the sociocultural structure (pp. 147–9) may affect the manner in which individuals assimilate and accommodate to societal characteristics. Each 'choice' made may constrain future freedom of choice. Thus, as discussed in the previous chapter, each aspect of the sociocultural structure is not isomorphous with a particular individual propensity but may be shaped by diverse psychological characteristics and environmental forces.

In general, dependence on cultural transmission may be in the best interests of individuals: Boyd & Richerson (1985) have shown that, given certain assumptions, individuals may do better to accept the traditions of the society than to risk the errors and incur the costs of seeking to work out new ways of behaving for themselves. This does not mean that tradition *necessarily* works to the advantage of individuals: the Yakuts, when driven back by the Mongols towards the sub-arctic regions of Siberia, persisted in their attempts to preserve a horse-oriented culture in an environment unsuited to it, until they eventually imitated the reindeer breeders around them (Godelier, 1974).

Now in theory, cultural change could be initiated in three ways. First, genetic mutations could occur in individuals, and if selectively advantageous, spread through the population. Such a process would be comparable to that which must occur in the case of sickle-cell anaemia, which is deleterious in the homozygous state but confers some immunity to malaria in individuals heterozygous for the relevant gene: in general, the incidence of the gene varies with the incidence of malaria (Livingston, 1958). There is, however, no evidence that current cultural differences depend directly on genetic differences.

Second, the physical or non-human environment could change. In the short-term, by ontogenetic processes this could produce changes in the needs and/or nature of individuals, in their relationships and, immediately or in the course of at most very few generations, in the sociocultural structure. Such processes could underlie cultural differences related to environmental ones (see pp. 160–4). In the longer term, an environmental change could involve changes in the forces of natural selection, so that over a considerable number of generations the genetic structure of the population changed. Such an effect would be comparable with that which must have been involved, for instance, in the divergence of white and pigmented human skin in adaptation to different environments. As we have seen, however, evidence for a genetic basis for cultural differences is lacking.

Third, cultural change could result from social change. This could involve conflict between social groups and/or the assimilation of one group by another. Or cultural change could arise from differences and competition between individuals within the society. It could arise from attempts to resolve the contradictions likely to be inherent in the sociocultural structure of any society. Or it could arise from innovations produced by members of the society aiming to improve their situation, or by diffusion from other societies (e.g. Cavalli-Sforza and Feldman, 1975), or simply from 'noise' in the processes of communication between individuals or between generations. However it arises, a cultural innovation may or may not be acceptable to individuals and may or may not be transmitted. In the longer term, natural selection is likely to favour mechanisms for filtering and transmitting cultural change so that *in general* those transmitted enhance the survival or inclusive fitness of individuals (Boyd & Richerson, 1985).

Wilson (1978) has suggested that changes in the sociocultural structure are subject to selection at three levels: (a) Selection according to their emotional input and acceptability under contemporary social conditions; on the present view, this might involve compatability with behavioural propensities selected on the basis of their expression in other contexts, and would also embrace the influence of historical factors on the contemporary scene (Bock, 1980); (b) Selection by the extent to which they meet the ecological demands of the environment; and then (c) Selection by the extent to which they affect gene frequencies. The extent to which the last of these is important in practice is a matter of considerable controversy. Cultural differences could be affected by the first and possibly the second, but be neutral with respect to the third. But in any case the three processes are not independent: selection by emotional input and acceptability may depend on psychological mechanisms that have themselves been geared to select cultural attributes that enhance the ability of their carrier to survive and reproduce.

In fact, suggestions that the psychological processes of individuals might mediate in genetic selection have come from a number of quarters. For instance Henry (1959), impressed by the relations between stress, psycho-somatic disorders and female reproductive dysfunction, suggested that a genetic susceptibility to such dysfunction would be passed on differentially under different conditions. Speculating on that basis, Bourguignon (1973, p. 1085) suggested that personality may 'be seen as directly related not only to the evolution and continuity of culture; it may also be seen as a mediating factor in the processes of biological evolution of a species exposed to the sociosymbolic stresses of a cultural environment'. More recently, Wilson (1975; Lumsden & Wilson, 1981) have elaborated mathematical models of the processes that might be involved in such 'gene–culture co-evolution'. Although it is clear that differences in at least some of their 'epigenetic rules' (that translate into the 'behavioural propensities' discussed here) are based in genetic differences, and although mathematical models show that genetic change could occur over a reasonable time span, their approach needs to be married to analyses of how cultural transmission actually occurs, and of how the mechanisms of cultural transmission may themselves be affected by selective forces (Boyd & Richerson, 1985).

A closely related issue concerns the extent to which the manner in which individuals select from and modify the cultural practices to which they are exposed can lead to the spread of practices that actually detract from the genetic fitness of individuals. Adapting an account of cultural transmission elaborated by Cavalli-Sforza & Feldman (1981), Boyd & Richerson (1985) have devised mathematical models which enable them to consider ways in which non-adaptive traits could spread. For instance persons of high status could display traits or propagate cultural practices that were imitated by others even though not conducive to their inclusive fitness.

Here, therefore, we shall focus on the questions of whether properties at the level of sociocultural structure can themselves be seen as biologically advantageous and, if so, whether there is any evidence that natural selection has acted through them to affect the propensities of individuals. Is it a 'good thing'' that a society should be hierarchically organised, that there should be particular clear distinctions between permissible and non-permissible practices, that food should be cooked in this way but not that, that there should be exaggerated but culture-specific ideas about the differences between men and women?

REFINING THE QUESTIONS

Before we tackle such questions it is necessary to be a bit more specific about what we mean by 'a good thing', about precisely whom we are thinking about as beneficiaries, and about the limitations of the evidence we can muster.

(i) *Propensities or behaviour?* At the risk of being repetitious, it is worth emphasizing that much of the argument in this book is based on the supposition that behavioural propensities may be expressed in situations other than those in which natural selection acts or has acted to enhance them. The paradigm is the feeding techniques of tits, evolved in coping with natural food sources, which may also be applied advantageously on milk bottles or disadvantageously in houses (see pp. 105–6). Whether natural selection would operate to eliminate disadvantageous expressions in the longer term is of course a further issue.

(ii) *Which are the relevant consequences?* Natural selection acts to enhance the inclusive fitness of individuals. Thus to a biologist, the only beneficial consequences are those that relate to reproductive success. Often reproductive success, and especially inclusive fitness over generations, is hard to measure, so that in pursuing questions of adaptedness it is necessary to be content with assessments of presumed correlates of inclusive fitness: however the measurement of inclusive fitness is the biologists' long-term aim.

Now at this point it is necessary to take a strategic decision. One could set up the hypothesis that (virtually) all aspects of the sociocultural structure of all societies will eventually be shown to favour the inclusive fitness of individuals. Such a view, which seems to be implicit in the writings of some (but not all) sociobiologists, then dictates the course of research. Evidence of advantages to inclusive fitness is advanced in the more tractable cases, and (perhaps as a first step) ingenious explanations devised in others. Since proof in this field can by the nature of things rarely be absolute, the distinction between 'evidence' and ingenious explanations is not always easy to disern (e.g. Kitcher, 1985, for a forceful critique).

The second possible strategy is to accept from the start that selection acting through the consequences of each cultural practice on inclusive fitness is not the only means whereby the relative frequencies of each cultural practice is determined. On this view the extreme position taken by some sociobiologists is at best a cry of faith: at least some cultural practices must be seen as the consequences of behavioural predispositions adaptive in other contexts but as themselves having no (or even a negative) effect on inclusive fitness. In that case, the goal must be to specify criteria for identifying to which aspects of the sociocultural structure a functional (in a biological sense) approach can profitably be applied.

To regard this as a strategic decision is perhaps to caricature the positions of some research workers, but may help to clarify the issues. The second course is the one taken here. Let us take on board from the start the possibility that behavioural propensities adaptive in another context may give rise to cultural practices that themselves have no effect on inclusive fitness. For instance imitation may enhance inclusive fitness in some contexts, but lead to the acquisition of modes of behaviour that have neutral or even deleterious consequences in others (Boyd & Richerson, 1986). Or propensities adaptive as a means to an end may become ends in themselves. Many aspects of Western culture can be interpreted in this way: for example, increasing education is associated with negative effects on fertility (see Cochrane, 1979). Or, as a more everyday issue, eating is necessary for growth and survival, but for the gourmet the means is an end. It is of course still the case that if a behavioural expression has negative consequences for inclusive fitness, either the propensity or that particular expression of it will be selected against in the longer term.

In addition we must remember that cultural change may be caused by, accompanied by and/or give rise to inequalities amongst individuals and contradictions amongst beliefs. Thus at any one time not all individuals will profit from all the socio-cultural characteristics of a society. Furthermore those characteristics are to be seen as a product of its history as well as of the natures of some of the individuals within it (Bock, 1980).

Of course there are limits. Individuals who adopt cultural practices inimical to their inclusive fitness may be less likely to pass on those practices to offspring (though of course they may be perpetuated in other ways). And societies of individuals who adopt practices such that the replacement rate becomes lower than the death rate over an extended period could not survive. But the important point is that many aspects of social structure or sociocultural structure may have effectively neutral effects on the inclusive fitness of most individuals, and negative effects on that of some. Whilst the study of adaptedness must concern itself with outcomes, natural selection operates on processes with numerous outcomes, only some of which are relevant to the course of change.

In attempting to demonstrate a role of natural selection, therefore, investigators are unlikely to be able to show that every cultural characteristic is adaptive, but at best that only some are, and that others stem from propensities of individuals adaptive in other contexts. This might seem to lighten their load, but it also raises other difficulties. How are they to know which characteristic to study? Of course they could select characteristics most likely to have consequences for inclusive fitness – marriage systems rather than mourning systems, for instance. But if not all cultural practices are adaptive, the hypothesis that cultural practices are reproductively significant is unfalsifiable, since failure to find an adaptive outcome can be explained away by saying that the practice is a by-product of a propensity giving rise to other practices that are themselves adaptive (Caro & Borgerhoff Mulder, 1987). And if there is evidence that a given characteristic enhances the fitness of individuals, how can one know that this is not due to the selection of one of the (say) one in twenty characteristics that have such an effect by chance? These are real difficulties, but they do not in principle render the enterprise hopeless. What they mean, however, is that the sociobiologist cannot *prove* his case by picking social characteristics likely to have adaptive value and showing that they do enhance inclusive fitness, though that may be one way to proceed at the moment. Ultimately he or she will require a much more detailed understanding of the dialectics between individual propensities and the higher levels of social complexity that is at present available. Only then can the relations between propensities with some (current or former) adaptive consequences and their multiple other end-results be teased apart.

(iii) *Beneficial to whom?* Taking the narrow biological view of beneficial as meaning enhancing inclusive fitness, we must ask whose inclusive fitness is referred to? Some practices could enhance the inclusive fitness of all individuals in the group. For instance war with a neighbouring group in which every warrior stood an equal chance of gaining an extra wife, or cultural conventions that mitigated against inbreeding, or increased the nutritional value of food, could have direct effects on the inclusive fitness of all individuals (Durham, 1976). Or there could be indirect effects: practices that enhanced group cohesion, that minimized intra-group tensions and contributed to harmony, could provide a background conducive to enhanced inclusive fitness for all.

In such cases the evidence for an effect on inclusive fitness, or indeed on any aspect of reproductive performance, must once more be indirect, since we can never compare two societies identical in all respects except for the practice or belief in question. At best we can establish correlations across groups in similar environments between the extent of a given practice and population increase or decrease, or use the argument from design to show that differences in the practice were appropriately related to different conditions.

But some cultural practices are likely to enhance the inclusive fitness of some individuals at the expense of others. The pursuit of any limited resource – wealth, cattle, wives, etc., – whose possession enhances reproductive success will automatically decrease that of other individuals (cf Alexander, 1981). Thus the sort of evidence we must look for here will involve comparisons between individuals within a society: for instance do those individuals who are most successful in accumulating wealth leave most offspring? And we must remember that if natural selection has operated to produce individuals who, in their own particular circumstances, support cultural practices that favour their own inclusive fitness, it may also have favoured propensities in other individuals to cheat the system to favour their own ends. Whilst some individuals may seek riches that augment their reproductive success, others may use stealth or cunning or cuckoldry to achieve the same end. Each individual must endeavour to select from alternative strategies according to his circumstances, and his success must be judged against those circumstances.

Let us consider some possible examples.

DO CULTURAL PRACTICES AUGMENT THE INCLUSIVE FITNESS OF INDIVIDUALS?

It follows, from the preceding discussion, that the answer to this question is likely to be that some do and some don't, and that proof is going to be hard to find (see e.g. Kitcher, 1985). But in some cases the evidence is of considerable interest, and we may consider some examples.

(i) *Cultural universals; the incest taboo*

One much discussed but very controversial case is that of incest taboos. Limitations on inbreeding are probably present in all human societies. Since inbreeding can reduce biological success, biologists have not been tardy in assuming that such taboos were the product of natural selection. Furthermore (see p. 60–2) it has been shown that, in some animal species, individuals are more sexually attracted to those who are a little bit different from those with whom they have grown up than they are to others who are very strange or very familiar (Bateson, 1980). This, coupled with data suggesting that humans who had been reared together were not sexually attracted to each other (Shepher, 1971; Wolf, 1966; but see Kaffman, 1977), suggested a possible mechanism. Natural selection had produced an unconscious inhibition against mating with very familiar individuals (Westermarck, 1891).

Lumsden & Wilson (1981) have used this case to illustrate the way in which genetically influenced propensities could be translated into cultural practices. Using a set of apparently reasonable assumptions (though see Kitcher, 1985), they have elaborated a model which appears to approximate closely the incidence of brother–sister incest avoidance across societies (see also van den Berghe, 1983). At this point, anthropologists may raise a variety of objections. They argue that such a biological approach says nothing about the cultural diversity of incest taboos, and that in many societies categories of persons with whom mating is forbidden overlap only very partially with those of genetic relatedness (e.g. Sahlins, 1976). Each society has its own way of classifying kin, with the nature of the categories used and the extent to which they overlap with biological relatedness differing between societies (Goody, 1973). Observation of the rules of kinship within any one society is often an essentially moral matter, and appears at first sight to be independent of economic, political or biological consequence (Fortes, 1969). If anything, in many societies property inheritance may be a more potent influence on marriage customs than incest avoidance (Goody, 1976). In Australia the kinship systems used to become increasingly complex towards the interior of the continent: it has been suggested that this was related to the greater aridity of the environment, which enforced greater mobility, greater risk of catastrophes, greater need for access to territories of neighbouring groups, and thus a more complex system for regulating social intercourse (Yengoyan, in Lee & DeVore, 1968).

Now it must be pointed out that in this instance the Lumsden & Wilson model was concerned only with brother–sister incest, and not with the range of other relatives to whom the taboo might be applied. Furthermore it was not concerned with the differences between societies in the natures of the taboos. Nevertheless the fact that the taboos are not always closely related to genetic kinship clearly poses a problem. Although it has been argued that kin selection could operate even when the degree of coincidence between the kinship classification and genetic relatedness is quite small, it seems more likely that kinship systems have multiple other consequences, unrelated to incest avoidance, whose relative importance varies with circumstances (e.g. Fox, 1980).

Alexander (1977) and Bateson (1983, 1986), however, have elaborated the view that, perhaps in a pre-linguistic era, our ancestors evolved by natural selection a preference for mating with somebody who was a little but not too different from close relatives, thereby avoiding the maladaptive costs of both inbreeding and outbreeding (Westermarck, 1891). Bateson further suggests that, independently, a tendency to conformity appeared. Those who behaved differently from the norm were discouraged. This applied particularly to people who became sexually interested in close relatives or strangers. As language evolved, prohibitions about mating were transmitted to the next generation. On this view the prohibitions on mating with close relatives, though correlated with biologically-based constraints, did not arise as a direct result of natural selection through the consequences of inbreeding.

This scenario provides a possible way of accounting not only for the cultural universality of an incest taboo, but also for cultural differences. These should be related to the categories of persons who are familiar from early life. Thus if children grow up with some types of cousins but not others, the more familiar types of cousins should be the more likely to be prohibited as sexual partners. This is true in many societies. Bateson admits, however, that other factors, such as power and property, may also influence the nature of culturally transmitted marriage rules, and this is undoubtedly the case. In many Arab societies, for instance, alliances between brothers may be associated with marriages between their children (see also above). Thus Bateson's hypothesis is an important start, but needs to be extended. Incest taboos are part of the socio-cultural structure, and may be affected by considerations of resource management and inheritance as well as serving to prevent inbreeding. On this view, then, biological considerations of inbreeding/outbreeding may contribute to, but do not determine, the occurrence of incest taboos, and cannot explain their diversity. Constraints at the individual level against mating with familiar individuals may serve to bolster a cultural inhibition, but it is the latter that is most important in affecting the behaviour of individuals, and its force and precise nature will be affected by other aspects of the sociocultural structure and the ecological situation (see also pp. 161–3). The view of incest taboos as an adaptation to prevent in-breeding is simplistic.

(ii) *Correlations across societies*

There has been a persisting group of anthropologists who have attempted to relate cultural differences to ecological factors. Although their work may have been facilitated by biological ecologists (e.g. Lack, 1954, 1966; Crook, 1964; Williams, 1966), it had much earlier roots (e.g. Radcliffe-Brown, 1922), but flowered later (e.g. Barth, 1950, 1956; Harris, 1968, 1974; Sahlins, 1964; Rappaport, 1968; Vayda, 1969).

In general, the thrust of much of this work has been towards the conclusion that societies adjust to their environments in the same sort of way as the body adjusts to temperature changes (see footnote p. 14). For example amongst animals the advantages of territorial defence depend upon the concentration and availability of resources (food, mates), so that it may or may not be worthwhile to expend energy on territorial defence in order to obtain exclusive access to the territory's resources. A similar model has been applied to several groups of North American Indians, and accounts for the observed variations in territoriality (Dyson-Hudson & Smith, 1978). The Paiute lived in an area of abundant and predictable rainfall, where wild grass seeds were reliably available: they lived in permanent villages and defended linear stretches of land along the rivers. During the winter they depended on Pinon-pine nuts, which were superabundantly available in specific locations in the nearby mountains. Territorality was there much relaxed. By contrast the Shoeshone Indians lived in short-grass prairies where food was sparse, ephemeral and unreliable. During the summer months they moved around as nomadic family groups, and did not defend any area as a stable territory. During the winter the Shoshone also depended on locally superabundant Pinon-pine nuts, and families gathered to form temporary villages in productive pine groves. Thus the degree or nature of territoriality correlated in each group and season with the demands of the environment.

In considering such data, it is of course important not to lose sight of the complexity of human territory and other forms of property. In many societies, rights of use or access differ with the level of social complexity – for instance hunting territory may be appropriated jointly but tools and weapons individually. Furthermore the manner in which resources are shared is as important as, and interwoven with, the manner in which they are owned (Godelier, 1979). Nevertheless, the study of such complexities within societies is not incompatible with the study of the nature of differences between societies, and of how those differences arose.

As another example, most human societies are polygynous, a fair proportion are monogamous, and polyandry is rare (see p. 121). Apart from the industrial societies, monogamy occurs principally in hunter–gatherer societies, and is ascribed to the presumed importance of a paternal contribution for infant survival. Polygyny occurs especially (though not exclusively) in agricultural societies, especially in those in which women play an economic role in hoe farming and where it is possible for males to accumulate wealth which the more successful ones can exchange for rights in women (van den Berghe, 1979). In advanced agricultural societies, however, other factors enter in and there is usually a trend towards monogamy (or at least to non-endowed second marriages). This is related to the practice, common as land becomes scarce, of endowing women as well as men with property. On marriage the dowry must be 'matched' with property brought by the husband. Since he must thus commit his property to obtain a wife of the right standing, a second union is unlikely unless the couple are without heirs, in which case the second woman is likely to have the status of a concubine (Goody, 1976).

But at least in less differentiated societies there is a broad relation between marriage type and the nature of the economy, and this relation is of the general type that might be expected if at least some individuals (i.e. not slaves, priests, etc.) were maximising their reproductive success within the constraints to which they were subject.

Other ecological anthropologists have tended to isolate specific aspects of the culture that are relevant to and change with environmental factors, whilst other aspects of the culture are relatively independent of them (e.g. Steward, 1968). Rappaport (1968) related cultural cycles in a particular ritual involving the killing of pigs to changes in the human and in the pig populations. Although the ritual seemed to be unrelated to ecological conditions, Rappaport argued that it played a direct role in ecological adjustment. Elsewhere (Rappaport 1971) he has suggested that ritual is a device for exchanging cultural, ecological and demographic information across the boundaries of local social groups. However, quite apart from possible shortcomings in the evidence (Kitcher, 1985), such suggestions have little bearing on process. Whilst the practices in question may have beneficial consequences, (or, perhaps more accurately, form part of a complex system that has such consequences), this is unverifiable, and there is in any case no evidence about the processes through which this situation arose. A 'fit' between societal practices and the environment does not necessarily imply selection for those particular practices, as some sociobiologists might claim, or even selection between groups. At most it implies that man's propensities are such that, within limits, sociocultural structures can accommodate to circumstances. But, within limits, that is little more than a truism. Whilst research of this type is potentially of great interest, such considerations seem always to apply.

More recently, research on the relations between ecology and sociocultural structure has focussed on the consequences for the reproductive success of individuals. One example concerns the differences in birth spacing between societies. Lee (1972) has shown that Kalahari hunter-gatherers, unlike women in many other non-Western societies, space their children widely, reproducing about once every four years. This at first sight suggests that they are not maximising their reproductive success. However the women gather a great deal of their food, and have to carry their babies with them as they do so. Lee argued that the weight the mothers have to carry increases with shorter intervals between births, the increase from giving birth every three years instead of every four being much greater than that of giving birth every four years instead of five. In addition, birth spacing is reduced if the Bushmen become settled. Thus the wide spacing of births seems to be an adaptation to the hunter-gatherer way of existence in the sparse habitat occupied.

Blurton-Jones (1986; Blurton-Jones & Sibly, 1978) has taken this argument one stage further. The need to carry two children will reduce the amount of food a mother can carry at a time when her family needs more. Yet there is a strong selective advantage in having as many children as possible, provided they can be reared successfully. It is thus necessary to ask whether the increased costs of closer birth-spacing would not be worth paying. By making certain reasonable assumptions about food-gathering strategies etc., Blurton-Jones & Sibly calculated the back-loads a mother must carry for various inter-birth intervals if her family is to be adequately nourished. The maximum safe back load corresponded with that which the bushman women do actually carry, and predicted child mortality at each inter-birth interval. The evidence is thus in harmony with the view that the inter-birth interval is set by the load-carrying capacity of the mothers, and that the observed interval of four years is in fact optimal for maternal reproductive success. This in fact is only part of a wider picture of the way in which the Bushman way of life is constrained by their need to find food near water (Lee & DeVore, 1968). However it suffers from the problem of all optimality[1] analyses – the nature of the constraints on the situation. There is considerable evidence that time is not a limiting factor for finding food in Bushman groups, and it is reasonable to ask, for instance, whether a change in the division of labour or some other aspect of the sociocultural structure, involving for instance more male participation in gathering, might not increase the inclusive fitness of both sexes.

Although cross-cultural studies have established considerable differences in other aspects of parental behaviour, their relations either to local environmental conditions or cultural requirements have been subject to little investigation. However some differences between cultures are associated with differences in physical and in personality development, some of which may be significant in this way (Mead, 1950; Ainsworth, 1967; Bourguignon, 1973; Whiting & Whiting, 1975). Relating child-rearing practices to subsequent reproductive success is likely to be a hazardous undertaking both because of the time necessary for longitudinal studies and because the style likely to be optimal for any particular environment changes with age of child.

Other examples of correlations between cultural practices and eco-

[1] In animal studies it is possible to erect a theoretical model and assess quantitatively how far the observed behaviour compares with that which would be expected, given that the animal is the sort of animal that it is and the circumstances are what they are (e.g. Maynard Smith, 1977, 1978; Krebs, 1976). The last two clauses are crucial and limit the conclusions that can be drawn from such optimality analyses. In particular, they cast doubt on the significance of optimality analyses of human behaviour of the type discussed here (see also Hinde, 1982, p. 118–20).

logical conditions could be cited. Whilst much of the earlier work was interpreted in terms of benefits to the group as a whole, many of the cultural differences can equally well be seen as enhancing the inclusive fitness of individuals. The evidence is convincing in so far as the variations in cultural practice examined *seem to fit* the apparent requirements of the environment. What is not clear is how far the argument can be taken. The diversity of cultural practices, including that amongst cultures in closely similar environments (e.g. Barth, in press), is great: each surely cannot represent an adaptive peak, immune to invasion by other practices. As we have seen, other forces – historical inertia, the need for intra-cultural coherence, and so on – must operate, and the ecological constraints can provide only a broad framework for their action. In any case, even where the correlations are in harmony with the view that inter-cultural differences have adaptive consequences for the individuals involved, they still fall far short of demonstrating an action of natural selection on those practices. The evidence is correlational and 'by design'. Furthermore, and more importantly, there is nothing to indicate whether natural selection acted to shape the initial propensities before the cultural practices arose, or acted through the consequences of those practices themselves.

To be fair, however, it must also be said that natural selection is always difficult to prove in specific instances, and its acceptance depends in large measure on the range of facts that it integrates. On that basis, the search for correlations between cultural practices and ecological conditions is certainly a worthwhile enterprise, but needs to be accompanied by an investigation of the mechanisms through which the cultural differences arise or are maintained.

(iii) *Correlations within societies: the goals of assertiveness*

We now turn to cases where the evidence for adaptedness comes from comparisons between individuals.

One category of studies concern the goals that men set themselves. A universal human (and especially male) characteristic can be described as assertiveness, though the goals that men set themselves vary widely and differ between cultures and sub-cultures. The question arises, does success in achieving these culturally-determined goals augment reproductive success?

In a classic study of the Turkmen of Persia, Irons (1979) has shown that those individuals who are most successful at accumulating wealth also tend to be those with the greatest reproductive success. In a further analysis Irons (1980) showed that the data could not be accounted for on the group selection hypothesis (pp. 15–16) that bridewealth is a conventionalized token limiting fertility as population density increases, and was compatible with the individual selection hypothesis that reproduction increases as net wealth per individual increases. Whilst such a generalization does not apply to modern Western societies (see below), a number of studies elsewhere (reviewed by Betzig, Borgerhof Mulder & Turke, in press) show correlations between status or wealth and family size to date (Yąnamamö Indians, Chagnon, 1980; Trinidadians, Flinn, 1986). In addition, controlling for age, reproductive success increases with wealth on the Melanesian atoll of Ifaluk (Turke & Betzig, 1985) and with hunting success amongst the Ache of Paraguay (Kaplan & Hill, 1985). Even more to the point, lifetime reproductive success increased with rank amongst the Portuguese élite of the fifteenth and sixteenth centuries (Boone, 1986), and with number of cows or acres of land in the Kenyan Kipsigis (Borgerhoff Mulder, 1987). In the latter study, the data indicated that the greater reproductive success of wealthy men was due to their ability to pay bridewealth and not through greater access to modern medicines. Furthermore the bridewealth paid was greater for earlier-maturing women, who in turn had higher life-time reproductive success (Borgerhoff Mulder, 1987a & b).

A number of other studies reviewed by Betzig *et al.* (op. cit.) demonstrate an association between success in male–male competition and factors likely to promote reproductive success, such as the number of wives or conjugal unions. Such studies, however, fall short of demonstrating that the connection is a causal one. Irons (1980) advances considerable evidence for a causal link from wealth to reproductive success, and for a weaker link in the reverse direction, but does not prove them. It remains alternatively or also possible that the association is due to a third factor – good entrepreneurs could also be randy, or assertiveness could operate both in the marital bed and in the market place. However, although the data are not complete (and other shortcomings are noted by Betzig *et al.*, op. cit.), they are in harmony with the basic hypothesis that 'individuals will compete for scarce resources that aid in reproductive success' (Irons, 1980, p. 438). The fact that what constitutes wealth differs between societies is consistent with the view that members of societies 'define their goals to make them correspond with those things which will increase the probability of a high inclusive fitness' in the particular context in question (Irons, 1979, p. 258). The data support the view that there has been selection for male characteristics of generalized assertiveness or acquisitiveness coupled with an ability to direct them to enhance inclusive fitness. But the goals towards which individuals direct their assertiveness or acquisitiveness are culturally determined, and depend in part upon historical and environmental factors. The processes by which cultural differences in such matters come to be established remain to be analysed. The sociobiological hypothesis has so far had little to say about the historical and environmental forces that influence cultural characteristics or about the psychological mechanisms whereby they produce their effects.

In any case the picture is not uniform. In modern Western societies, the correlation between wealth and reproductive success does not hold. Indeed, the relation between reproductive success and wealth, economic success or aptitude is an inverse one (Vining, 1986). Furthermore, it cannot reasonably by doubted that, in Western societies, individuals may invest large amounts of effort in competing for resources that do not have the effect of increasing reproductive success. Irons (1980, p. 438) has argued that the basic hypothesis that 'individuals will compete for scarce resources that aid in reproductive success' would be disproved by data showing that 'individuals invest large amounts of effort in competing for a resource which does not have this effect'. Western societies provide such data. The sociobiologist must either show that the resources competed for do in fact enhance inclusive fitness, or regard such competitiveness as the biologically neutral expression of a propensity adaptive in other circumstances.

On the latter tack, one way out lies in the supposition that individual characteristics of assertiveness/acquisitiveness (within limits) have indeed been selected for, but that in modern Western and some other societies the conditions under which they promote individual fitness no longer apply. To be specific, the welfare state rarely permits children to starve, and imposed monogamy prevents males using wealth to acquire additional mates (Dawkins, 1986). In addition the historical and environmental (including sociocultural) forces that determine goals are no longer aligned with enhancing inclusive fitness. Thus, under certain conditions, the more able individuals may be able to display behavioural propensities not linked to reproductive success in a way that was less possible earlier in human history. Barkow & Burley (1980) have made a specific suggestion in this direction. They argue that hominid intelligence allowed women to anticipate the dangers, pains and inconveniences of childbirth. However other traits, such as concealed ovulation, continuous sexual receptivity, male dominance and strong sexual desire overrode the inhibitory effects of fear of childbirth. Barkow & Burley argue that modern culture, and especially modern methods of birth control, enable women to circumvent the link between sexual desire and pregnancy, and to pursue other goals. This is an interesting but entirely speculative hypothesis, compatible with the view that goals are not necessarily set by considerations of inclusive fitness. It remains the fact that the more endowed individuals tend to reproduce less fast than their less well endowed peers. How far such a process could proceed without disruption of the culture is discussed by Vining (1986).

What constitutes wealth is specific to the culture, and wealth is often correlated with prestige, i.e. the receipt of attention with some degree of attention or approbation; it has thus also been suggested that prestige should correlate with reproductive success (cf. p. 103) (Hill, 1984). Hill found that, in societies at or above the subsistence level, prestige and reproductive success were related. However, with the accumulation of surplus wealth sources of prestige irrelevant to reproductive success appear, so that reproductive success and sociocultural success appear to become decoupled. Indeed sociocultural success may take precedence, as in rich families who limit their reproduction to keep their estates intact – though data on longer term reproductive success are mostly lacking. Hill's conclusion has been criticized by Kaplan (1985) who, taking a conventional sociobiological stance, argues that humans are designed by natural selection to evaluate information and choose options such that their behaviour does maximize inclusive fitness. He thus discounts Hill's view that individuals may seek prestige at the expense of reproductive success. However Hill (1985) replies that much human behaviour in complex societies seems to be reproductively neutral and we had better face that fact rather than 'sweep it under the biological carpet in the hope that no-one notices'. It remains the case that prestige could have been associated with reproductive success earlier in human history, but this is unprovable.

(iv) *Correlations within societies: mate choice*

Another set of issues concerns the extent to which the choice of mate affects inclusive fitness. Whilst the fidelity of their wives is of crucial importance for the inclusive fitness of men (see pp. 122–6), women are likely to choose men who are good providers. There is evidence from at least one non-Western society (Kipsigis, Borgerhoff Mulder, 1986) that this is indeed the case. In many societies, a man's qualities as a good provider affect how many wives he gets. A woman (or her parents) would then be expected to choose a husband to maximize her reproductive success by taking into account both his qualities as a provider and how many wives he had already (Orians, 1969). Consistent with this, amongst the Kenyan Kipsigis Borgerhoff Mulder (1987) found no differences in either wealth available per wife or number of children raised between monogamously and polygamously married Kipsigis women. However the generality of this finding remains to be established.

Male–male competition can result in a highly stratified society, and the advantage of a polygynous marriage may then be linked to the status of the potential husband. Given that, it would be advantageous to a female to attach herself (or, in the case of arranged marriages, for parents to attach their daughters) to an already married man only if that gave her and her offspring greater access to resources than association with an unmarried man. Thus theory would predict polygyny more in the higher strata of society than in lower ones. Throughout a considerable range of stratified societies, this seems to be the case – with a predominance of unattached males, or even polyandry, at the bottom of the social scale. In harmony with this, dowry payments are more characteristic of higher social strata, and the payment of bridewealth of the lower ones. Furthermore, it has been argued that the high status grooms would have more to lose by being cuckolded: their brides must provide not only a dowry but must have their virginity and fidelity guaranteed. In keeping with this, the claustration and defence of women has in fact been most acute in the higher levels of a number of stratified societies (Dickemann, 1981). Thus there is a parallel, but no more, between the observed distribution of marriage types across social classes and the predictions of evolutionary theory. As Kitcher (1985) has pointed out in this and other contexts, the phenomena could be accounted for in terms of proximate factors – for instance the greater ability of high status males to attract mates. The distribution of polygyny, dowries, etc., between social classes within societies could be the result of selection for propensities conducive to individual inclusive fitness before the current situation arose, and not through natural selection acting contemporaneously.

(v) *Correlations within societies: further examples*

Another frequently cited example concerns a further application (see p. 101) of kin selection theory to social structure. In a previous chapter we saw that the modern theory of natural selection predicts that individuals will attempt to ensure not only their own survival and reproduction, but also that of their close relatives. Kin selection theory is consistent with certain aspects of individual behaviour – for instance the distribution of parental care (pp. 116–17) and of prosocial behaviour (pp. 100–7). It can be applied also to certain aspects of human group structure. For instance, an analysis of an axe-fight amongst the Yąnamamö Indians of Venezuela was in harmony with the view that individuals chose to take risks to aid kin rather than non-kin, and when villages fission individuals appear to choose to remain with kin and to assert themselves in ways that are more predictable on the basis of genetic relatedness than from a knowledge of their kinship classification and kinship term usages. In addition males enter into coalitions with related males and this augments their ability to acquire multiple wives and thus enhance their reproductive success (Chagnon, 1980; Chagnon & Bugos, 1979). Whilst such data are consistent with the selectionist hypothesis, they can also be interpreted more economically in proximal terms. For example, Kitcher (1985) has shown that the axe-fight data can be accounted for in terms of ties only to *close* kin and in terms of village loyalty, with no tendency to make distinctions between more distant kin. Again, data on village fissioning in this society have been modelled by Lumsden and Wilson (1981) to substantiate their theory of gene-culture co-evolution, but Kitcher points out that their approach underestimates the importance of personal relationships and political and sexual rivalries in determining who stays and who leaves. It is of course open to the sociobiologists to reply that the concern here is with the consequences of behaviour: whatever the mechanism, kin help each other more than non-kin,and tend to stay together. The question of whether that is the consequence through which natural selection has acted, or whether it is reached as a result of propensities selected for on other consequences, remains open.

Another example concerns the economics of hunting. Classical anthropological theory has argued that hunter gatherers have limited needs and so limit what they take from available resources. Biological theory would suggest that they adjust their hunting time to optimize their inclusive fitness. Hawkes *et al.* (1985) made three predictions that would differentiate between these two views. On a limited-needs view hunters should hunt for less long on days when returns are good, and for less long when efficient technologies are available (guns or arrows), and skilled hunters should hunt for less long than unskilled ones. Optimality theory would predict the opposite. On the whole predictions of the optimal foraging model were fulfilled by data from a Paraguayan Indian group and elsewhere, but additional postulates (e.g. that men with wives incur high costs in hunting, when they cannot protect their wives) were sometimes necessary.

SUMMARY AND CONCLUSION

The studies reviewed in this chapter certainly do not do justice to the work of ecological anthropologists and sociobiologists. Nevertheless they are perhaps sufficient to indicate the sorts of evidence that are, and are likely to be, available concerning the relations between aspects of socio-cultural structure, ecological conditions and the inclusive fitness of individuals. In general, the data are in harmony with the view that cultural differences depend upon behavioural propensities which have themselves been shaped across the generations by natural selection, but whose specific expression in any one culture or any one individual depends upon the complex dialectics between successive levels of social complexity as well as upon ecological and historical factors. This would incorporate the views that individuals are endowed (through the action of natural selection) with the ability to devise alternative strategies to cope with the vicissitudes of their particular situation, but also allows for the fact that the basic propensities are sometimes expressed inappropriately. It implies that we do not have to find adaptive significance in every variant of sociocultural structure in every society.

Thus in comparisons between societies there is evidence that some (but by no means all) differences are appropriate for their different circumstances. Looking at societally held goals, for example, there is evidence that in many societies those more successful in acquiring the goals deemed appropriate in the culture in question have greater reproductive success. But there is no evidence that this was a result of natural selection acting on individuals exhibiting the cultural practices in question: it can be more economically understood as an effect of basic propensities that may have preceded the elaboration of the practices under consideration. The flexibility to adjust goals to current needs may have been acquired long before the societies under discussion came into being (cf Irons, 1979, 1980), with cultural selection determining the specific goals.

In general, the utility of the biologist's functional approach, clear with respect to individual propensities and apparent in their dyadic relationships, is attenuated when it comes to the sociocultural structure. Not surprisingly, the evidence is strongest when it concerns practices closely related to basic propensities (e.g. acquisition of wealth, p. 164–7) or to practices directly concerned with reproduction (e.g. birth spacing, p. 162–3). By contrast, evidence about the adaptedness of many other practices or beliefs, or about the adaptive significance of cultural differences in such matters, is (with a few exceptions) almost absent. And it is hardly surprising that the more complex the socio-cultural structure, the less likely are functional questions about its details to be illuminating. Indeed models of cultural evolution show that, given certain characteristics of the population, traits that are neutral or maladaptive to a degree could spread (see p. 156; Boyd & Richerson, 1985).

Where aspects of the sociocultural structure lead to behaviour that is neutral or maladaptive in terms of the inclusive fitness of individuals, some explanation is called for. Several have been considered in the preceding pages. One is that the behaviour in question is adaptive, *really*. If only we could measure inclusive fitness adequately, we should find that it was augmented by the behaviour in question. This is the goal of the extreme human sociobiologist (p. 155). A second is that the behaviour in question is due to inappropriate or excessive expression of a propensity that is ordinarily adaptive: this could for example account for gluttony (p. 156), and possibly for some cases of self-sacrifice (pp. 105–7), but leaves open the question of why the motivation of the individual should have been excessive. 'Pathology' is not in itself an adequate explanation.

A third and related explanation of behaviour that is neutral or detrimental to inclusive fitness is that it represents the expression of a propensity that was functional in our environment of evolutionary adaptedness but, because conditions have changed, is no longer so. This is probably a true explanation in many cases (e.g. the irrational fears of childhood, p. 114), and consideration of explanations along these lines can help us to integrate diverse facts about human behaviour (e.g. the characteristics of relationships, Chapter 7; the ontogeny of prosocial behaviour, pp. 107–9). However such explanations are usually only partial, and may be unprovable. They must usually be supplemented by the fourth type of explanation – namely that the behaviour in question is primarily controlled by aspects of the sociocultural structure, which is itself only distantly related to the basic propensities of individuals on which natural selection acted. Such an explanation must be invoked, for instance, in many cases of self sacrifice. This is not to abandon the Darwinian perspective, but involves accepting that (a) selection ensured that individuals were endowed with their psychological propensities and with the capacity to vary and direct them, in the main before the sociocultural structures in which they now operate came into being; and (b) that the properties of the sociocultural structure are complex, influenced by many but diverse psychological propensities of individuals, by similarities and by conflicts of interest between individuals, and by historical and ecological factors.

To adapt an analogy used by Gould & Lewontin (1979) and Bock (1980), aspects of the sociocultural structure at any one time can be likened to a Gothic cathedral. It is the product of many different skills and many different propensities. Some of its characteristics can be seen as functional – it is impressive, instils certain emotions in members of the culture, keeps out the weather, and so on. But most such functions are to be interpreted only in relation to a whole set of beliefs and other characteristics of the sociocultural structure and of the natures of individuals. Some aspects of its structure are to be interpreted as directly relevant to those functions, like the pillars, arches and fan vaulting that support the roof. Other characters, like the bosses between the spaces of the fan vaulting, are secondary, but still contribute to the overall effect. Even some differences between the cathedral and a mosque can perhaps be seen as adaptations to local conditions. But differences between Gothic cathedrals are less easily described in functional terms. They express rather the idiosyncratic propensities of the builders – and the interactions between those propensities within each individual who contributed. They express also the history of each edifice. Whilst each cathedral has a certain unity, there is also a clash of styles which reflects that history and the circumstances of its construction.

Where this analogy falls down, of course, is in the time dimension. Sociocultural structure is subject to continuous change whereas, judged by the time span of our own lives, the cathedral seems static and enduring. We must not forget that institutions, beliefs and other aspects of the sociocultural structure are dynamic processes, in continuous flux.

It is thus suggested that any attempt to apply evolutionary theory to aspects of human behaviour must come to terms with two issues. First, whilst some human behaviour is primarily influenced by basic propensities of one sort or another, virtually all is influenced by social forces, and some is primarily determined by the values and norms, or by the rights and duties attendant upon roles in institutions, of the sociocultural structure. For instance it has been suggested that snake phobias probably depend heavily on the role of snakes in mythology; that choice of mate is controlled primarily by cultural norms, rather than by inherent tendencies in individuals not to copulate with familiar individuals; that self-sacrificial patriotism stems from values imposed by society on the individual rather than being only an inappropriate expression of the behavioural propensities of individuals; that the sex stereotypes of major importance in affecting the gender-role development of individuals are exaggerations and distortions of differences between the sexes, and so on.

The second issue concerns the need to understand the genesis of the sociocultural structure in all its complexity before attempting to assess the relation between behaviour determined by that structure and inclusive fitness. The basic propensities of humans contribute to the values and norms of the society, but there is no isomorphism between them. The incest taboo is not a direct expression of the tendency not to mate with familiar individuals, but is influenced also by many other factors to do with resource management and the inheritance of property and indeed the whole structure of society. Gender stereotypes result in part from forces inherent in the formation of the self concept, and do not merely express basic differences between the sexes – though the latter play their part in the formation of the stereotypes.

As a final example, let us return to the case of modern warfare. We have seen (p. 8) that this is an institution, with prescribed roles for soldiers, politicians, munitions workers, and so on. It is the rights and duties attendant upon those roles that constitute the primary motivating forces for the individual. Elementary aggressiveness plays little part in the soldiers' actions: they are guided by obedience, duty, a propensity to co-operate, and so on. But aggressiveness does play some part in the maintenance of the institution itself: the rousing speeches of the politicians which lend force to the institution of war depend largely on their appeal to an aggressive (and/or aggressively defensive) imagery and to aggressive propensities in individuals. Attempts to apply evolutionary theory to the propensity for aggression may lead to interesting and important results; attempts to apply evolutionary theory to the institution of war, or to the roles it prescribes, are less likely to be successful. But an understanding of the part in the institution of war played by propensities to be co-operative, to show group solidarity, to sacrifice one's own interests for others, to be obedient to authority, as well as by the propensity to be aggressive, may contribute substantially to world peace.

Epilogue

My former mentor, W. H. Thorpe, used to say that at some times and in some contexts it was important to push the frontiers of ignorance back, while at other times or in other contexts it was important to synthesize knowledge already gained. This book has aimed at synthesis. The discussion has touched on ethological studies of animals, principles of biological evolution, aspects of developmental psychology, cognitive psychology and social psychology, and also on anthropology. Inevitably the treatment has been superficial in many places – the fault arises from the shortcomings of my own competence. But I hope I have contributed towards convincing (a) both biologists and social scientists that close attention to the distinctions between and dialectical relations between successive levels of social complexity are essential; (b) social scientists that the biologists have not a little to offer them; and (c) biologists that they must be armed with humility in the face of the complexity of human cognitive functioning and social systems if their contribution is to be effective.

Bibliography

Acsádi, G. & Nemeskéri, J. (1970) *History of Human Life Span and Mortality*, Akadémiai Kiadó, Budapest. (Cited Mellen, 1981).

Adams, R. M. (1969) *The Rise of Urban Society*. Chicago: Aldine.

Adkins, E. K. (1980) Genes, hormones, sex and gender. In Barlow, G. W. & Silverberg, J. (eds). *Sociobiology: Beyond Nature/Nurture*. Boulder, Colorado: Westview.

Ahrens, R. (1954) Beiträge zur Entwicklung des Physiognomie und Mimikerkennes. *Z. exp. ang. Psychol.*, **2**, 412–54, 599–633.

Ainsworth, M. D. S. (1967). *Infancy in Uganda*. Baltimore: Johns Hopkins University Press.

Ainsworth, M. D. S., Blehar, M. C., Waters, E. & Wall, S. (1978) *Patterns of Attachment*. Hillsdale, N. J.: Erlbaum.

Alexander, R. D. (1977) Natural selection and the analysis of human sociality. In C. E. Goulden (ed.) *Changing Scenes in the Natural Sciences, 1776–1976*. Philadelphia: Academy of Natural Sciences.

Alexander, R. D. (1980) *Darwinism and Human Affairs*. London: Pitman.

Alexander, R. D. (1981) Evolution, culture and human behavior: some general considerations. In R. D. Alexander & D. W. Tinkle (eds.) *Natural Selection and Social Behavior*. New York: Chiron.

Alexander, R. D. & Borgia, G. (1978) Group selection, altruisim and the levels of hierarchical organization of life. *Ann. Review of Education & Systems*, **9**, 449–74.

Alexander, R. D. & Noonan, K. M. (1979) Concealment of ovulation, parental care and human social evolution. In Chagnon, N. A. & Irons, W. (eds.) *Evolutionary Biology & Human Social Behaviour*. N. Scituate, Mass: Duxbury.

Allen, K. R. (1935) The food and migration of the perch (*Perca fluviatilis*) in Windermere. *J. anim. Ecol.*, **4**, 264–73.

Altmann, J. (1980) *Baboon mothers and infants*. Cambridge, Mass: Harvard Univ. Press.

Andrew, R. J. (1963) The origin and evolution of the calls and facial expressions of primates. *Behaviour*, **20**, 1–109.

Archer, J. & Lloyd, B. (1985) *Sex and Gender*. Cambridge: Cambridge University Press.

Ariosto, L. (1521/1983) *Orlando furioso*. Oxford: OUP.

Ashmore, R. D. & Del Boca, F. K. (1986) *Social Psychology of Female–Male relations.* New York: Acad. Press.

Axelrod, R. & Hamilton W. D. (1981) The evolution of cooperation. *Science,* **211,** 1390–6.

Baerends, G. P. (1985) Do the dummy experiments with sticklebacks support the IRM concept? *Behaviour,* **93**, 258–77.

Bandura (1977) *Social Learning Theory*. Prentice Hall: Englewood Cliffs, N. J.

Baptista, L. F. & Petrinovich, L. (1984) Social interaction, sensitive phases and the song template hypothesis in the white-crowned sparrow. *Anim. Behav.,* **32,** 172–81.

Barash, D. P. (1977) *Sociobiology & Behavior*. New York: Elsevier.

Barkow, J. H. & Burley, N. (1980) Human fertility, evolutionary biology, and the demographic transition. *Ethol. and Sociobiol.*, **1**, 163–80.

Barlow, G. W. (1962) Ethology of the Asian Teleost, (*Badis Badis*): IV. Sexual behavior. *Copeia*, **2**, 346–60.

Barnett, L. E. (1969) *Concepts of the person in some New Guinea societies*. Thesis submitted for M. Phil. University of London.

Barth, F. (1950) Ecologic adaptation and cultural change in archeology. *American Antiquity*, **15**, 338–9.

Barth, F. (1956) Ecologic relationships of ethnic groups in Swat, North Pakistan. *Amer. Anthropologist*, **58**, 1079–89.

Barth, F. (1967) On the study of social change. *Amer. Anthrop.*, **69**, 661–9.

Barth, F. (in press) *Cosmologies in the Making: a Generative Approach to Cultural Variation in India & New Guinea*. Cambridge: Cambridge Univ. Press.

Bastian, A. (1881) *Der Völkergedanke im Aufbau einer Wissenschaft von Menschen* Berlin: Ferd. Dümmlers.

Bates, J. E. (in press) Temperament in infancy. In J. D. Osofsky (ed.) *Handbook of Infant Development*. 2nd edition. New York: Wiley.

Bateson, P. P. G. (1976) Rules and reciprocity in behavioural development. In Bateson, P. P. G. & Hinde, R. A. (eds.) *Growing Points in Ethology*. Cambridge: Cambridge Univ. Press.

Bateson, P. P. G., (1978) How does behaviour develop? In Bateson P. P. G. & Klopfer P. H. (eds.) *Perspectives in Ethology*, **3**. New York: Plenum.

Bateson, P. P. G. (1979) How do sensitive periods arise and what are they for? *Animal Behaviour*, **27**, 470–86.

Bateson, P. P. G. (1980) Optimal outbreeding and the development of sexual preferences in the Japanese quail. *Zeits. f. Tierpsychol.*, **53**, 231–44.

Bateson, P. P. G. (1983) Optimal outbreeding. In Bateson, P. P. G. (ed.) *Mate Choice*. Cambridge: Cambridge Univ. Press.

Bateson, P. P. G. (1986) Sociobiology and human politics. In Rose, S. & Appignanesi, L. (eds.) *Science & Beyond*. Oxford: Blackwell.

Bateson, P. P. G. (1987) Biological approaches to the study of behavioural development. *Int. J. Behavioural Development*, **10**, 1–22.

Bateson, P. & Chantrey, D. (1972) Retardation of discrimination learning in monkeys and chicks previously exposed to both stimuli. *Nature*, **237**, 173–4.

Bateson, P. & Hinde, R. A. (in press) Developmental changes in sensitivity to experience. In Barnstein, M. H. (ed.) *Sensitive Periods in Development*. Hillsdale, N. J.: Erlbaum.

Bateson, P. P. G. & Martin, P. (in press) *The Origins of Behaviour*: Cambridge: Cambridge Univ. Press.

Baumrind, D. (1971) Current patterns of parental authority. *Devel. Psychol. Mono.* **4**, (1, Pt 2).

Belsky, J. & Isabella, R. A. (1985) Marital and parent–child relationships in family of origin and marital change following the birth of a baby: a retrospective analysis. *Child Dev.*, **56**, 342–9.

Benedict, R. (1961) *Patterns of Culture*. Boston: Houghton Mifflin.

Bem D. J. & Funder, D. C. (1978) Predicting more of the people more of the time. *Psychol Rev.*, **85**, 485–501.

Berger, P. L. & Luckman, T. (1966) *The Social Construction of Reality*. New York: Doubleday.

Berghe, P. L. van den (1979) *Human Family Systems: an Evolutionary View*. New York: Elsevier.

Berghe, P. L. van den (1983) Human inbreeding avoidance: culture in nature. *Behavioral & Brain Sciences*, **6**, 91–136.

Berman, C. M. (1982a) The ontogeny of social relationships with group companions among free-ranging infant rhesus monkeys. 1. Social networks and differentiation. *Animal Behaviour*, **30**, 149–62.

Berman, C. M. (1982b) The ontogeny of social relationships with group companions among free-ranging infant rhesus monkeys. II. Differentiation and attractiveness. *Animal Behaviour*, **30**, 163–70.

Berman, C. M. (in press) Demography and mother–infant relationships: implications for group structure. In J. E. Fa & F. H. Southwick (eds.) *The Ecology and Behaviour of Food-Enhanced Primate Groups*. New York: Alan Liss Inc.

Bernal, J. (1972) Crying during the first 10 days of life, and maternal responses. *Developmental Medicine and Child Neurology*, **14**, 362–72.

Bernstein, I. S. (1981) Dominance: the baby and the bathwater. *Behaviour & Brain Sciences*, **4**, 419–58.

Berscheid, E. & Walster, E. H. (1978) *Interpersonal Attraction*, (2nd ed.) Reading, Mass: Addison-Wesley.

Bertalanffy, L. von (1952) *Problems of Life*. London.

Bertram, B. C. R. (1982) Problems with altruism. In Kings College Sociobiology Group (eds.) *Current Problems in Sociobiology*. Cambridge: Cambridge Univ. Press.

Betzig, L. L., Borgerhoff Mulder, M. & Turke, P. M. (in press) Human reproductive behavior: introduction and a review. In *Human Reproductive Behaviour: a Darwinian Perspective*. Cambridge: Cambridge University Press.

Billig, M. (1976) Social psychology & intergroup relations. *European Monographs in Social Psychology*. London: Acad. Press.

Block, J. (1981) Some enduring and consequential structures of personality. In Robin, A., Aronoff, J., Barclay, A. M. and Zucker, R. A. (eds.). *Further Explanations in Personality*. New York: Wiley.

Block, J. H. (1983) Differential premises arising from differential socialization of the sexes: some conjectures. *Child Development*, **54**, 1335–54.

Bloom, B. L., White, S. W. & Asher, S. J. (1979) Marital disruption as a stressful life event. In G. Levinger & O. C. Mules (eds.) *Divorce and Separation*. New York: Basic Books.

Blurton-Jones, N. G. (1972) (ed.) *Ethological Studies of Child Behaviour*. Cambridge: Cambridge Univ. Press.

Blurton-Jones, N. G. (1986) Bushman birth-spacing: a test for optimal interbirth intervals. *Ethol & Sociobiol.*, **7**, 91–106.

Blurton-Jones, N. & Sibly, R. (1978) Testing adaptiveness of culturally determined behaviour. In V. Reynolds & N. Blurton-Jones (eds.) *Human Behaviour & Adaptation*. London: Taylor & Frances.

Bock, K. (1980) *Human Nature & History*. New York: Columbia University Press.

Boone, J. L. (1986) Parental investment and elite family structure in preindustrial states. *Amer Anthropologist*, **88** (in press).

Borgerhoff Mulder, M. (1983) Social organization & biology. *Man*, **18**, 786–7.

Borgerhoff Mulder, M. (1985) Polygyny threshold: a Kipsigis case study. *National Geographic Research Report*, **21**, 33–9.

Borgerhoff Mulder, M. (1987a) Kipsigis bridewealth payments. In Betzig, L. L., Borgerhoff Mulder, M. & Turke, P. W. (eds). *Human Reproductive Behavior: a Darwinian Perspective*. Cambridge: Cambridge Univ. Press.

Borgerhoff Mulder, M. (1987b) Reproductive success in three Kipsigis cohorts. In Clutton-Brock, T. H. (ed.) *Reproductive Success*. Chicago: Univ. Chicago Press.

Bornstein, M. H., Kessen, W. & Weiskopf, S. (1976) The categories of hue in infancy. *Science*, **191**, 201–2.

Bossema, I. & Burgler, R. R. (1980) Communication during monocular and binocular looking in European jays. *Behaviour*, **74**, 274–83.

Bourguignon, E. (1973) Psychological Anthropology. In Honigmann, J. J. (ed.) *Handbook of Social and Cultural Anthropology*. Chicago: Rand McNally.

Bowlby, J. (1969) *Attachment and Loss*. **1**. *Attachment*. London: Hogarth.

Boyd, R. & Richerson, P. J. (1986) *Culture and the Evolutionary Process*. Chicago: Chicago University Press. (not consulted.)

Brannigan, C. & Humphries, D. (1972) Human non-verbal behaviour. In Blurton-Jones, N. G. (ed.) *Ethological Studies of Child Behaviour*. Cambridge: Cambridge Univ. Press

Bretherton, I. (1985) Attachment theory: retrospect & prospect. In Bretherton, I. & Waters, E. (eds.) Growing points of attachment theory and research. *Monog. Soc. Res. Child Development*, **50**, 1–2.

Brewer, M. B. & Kranmer, R. M. (1985) The psychology of intergroup attitudes & behavior. *Ann. Rev. Psychol.*, **36**, 219–43.

Bronfenbrenner, U. (1979) *The Ecology of Human Development*. Cambridge, Mass: Harvard Univ. Press.

Brown, G. W., Harris, T. O. & Bifulco, A. (1986) The long-term effects of early loss of parent. In M. Rutter, C. E. Izard, & P. B. Read. (eds.) *Depression in Young People*. New York: Guildford.

Bryant, P. (1985) Parents, children & cognitive development. In Hinde, R. A.,

Perret-Clermont, A.–N. & Stevenson-Hinde, J. S. (eds.) *Social Relationships & Cognitive Development*. Oxford: Oxford Univ. Press.

Burling R. (1986) The selective advantage of complex language. *Ethology & Sociobiology*, **7**, 1–16.

Buss, D. M. (1986) Sex differences in human mate selection criteria: an evolutionary perspective. In C. Crawford, M. Smith & D. Krebs (eds.) *Sociobiology and Psychology: Issues, Ideas and Findings*. Hillsdale, N. J.: Erlbaum.

Campbell, D. T. (1967) Stereotypes and the perception of group differences. *Amer. Psychologist*, **22**, 817–29.

Cant, J. G. H. (1981) Hypothesis for the evolution of human breasts and buttocks. *Amer. Nat.* **117**, 199–204.

Carey, S. (1986) *Conceptual Change in Childhood*. Cambridge, Mass.: M.I.T. Press.

Carns, E. E. (1973) Talking about sex: notes on first coitus and the double standard. *Journal of Marriage and the Family*, **35**, 677–88.

Caro, T. M. (1985) Intersexual selection and cooption. *J. theor. Biol.*, **112**, 275–7.

Caro, T. M. (1987) Human breasts: unsupported hypotheses reviewed. *Human Evolution*, in press.

Caro, T. M. & Borgerhoff Mulder, M. (in press) The problem of adaptation in the study of human behaviour. *Ethology and Sociobiology*.

Carraher, T. N., Carraher, D. W. & Schliemann, A. D. (1985) Mathematics in the streets and in the schools. *Brit. J. Develop. Psychol.*, **3**, 21–29.

Cavalli-Sforza, L. L. & Feldman, M. W. (1981) *Cultural Transmission and Evolution*. Princeton, N. J.: Princeton Univ. Press.

Centers, R., Raven, B. H. & Rodrigues, A. (1971) Conjugal power structure: a re-examination. *American Sociology Review*, **36**, 264–78.

Chagnon, N. (1979) Mate competition, favouring close kin, and village fissioning among the Y̨anamamö Indians – In Chagnon, N. & Irons, W. (eds.) *Evolutionary Biology & Human Social Behavior*. N. Scituate, Mass: Duxbury.

Chagnon, N. (1980) Kin selection theory, kinship, marriage and fitness among the Y̨anamamö Indians. In Barlow, G. W. & Silverberg, J. (eds.) *Sociobiology: beyond nature/nurture*. Boulder: Westview Press.

Chagnon, N. & Bugos, P. E. (1979) Kin selection and conflict: an analysis of a Y̨anamamö Ax fight. In Chagnon, N. & Irons, W. (eds). *Evolutionary Biology & Human Social Behavior*. N. Scituate, Mass: Duxbury.

Chandler, M. J. (1985) Social structures & social cognition. In Hinde, R. A., Perret-Clermont, A.-N. & Stevenson Hinde, J. (eds). *Social Relationships & Cognitive Development*. Oxford: Oxford Univ. Press.

Changeux, J. P. (1983) *L'Homme Neuronal*. Paris: Fayard.

Cheney, D. (1978) Interactions of immature male and female baboons with adult females. *Anim. Behav.* **26**, 389–408.

Chisholm, J. S. (1983) *Navajo Infancy*. New York: Aldine.

Clarke-Stewart, K. A. (1978) And daddy makes three: the father's impact on mother & young child. *Child Development*, **49**, 466–78.

Clarke-Stewart, K. A. & Fein, G. G. (1983) Early childhood programs. In M. M. Haith & J. J. Campos (eds.) *Infancy and Developmental Psychobiology*. Vol. 2, P. Mussen (ed.) *Handbook of Child Psychology*. New York: Wiley.

Clarke-Stewart, K. A. & Hevey, C. (1981) Longitudinal relations in repeated observations of mother–child interaction from 1 to 2 1/2 years. *Devel. Psychology*, **17**, 127–45.

Clarke, A. M. & Clarke, A. D. B. (1976) *Early Experience*. London: Open Books.

Clutton-Brock, T. H. (1983) Selection in relation to sex. In D. S. Bendall (ed.) *Evolution from Molecules to Men*. Cambridge: Cambridge Univ. Press.

Clutton-Brock, T. H., Harvey, P. H. & Rudder, B. (1977) Sexual dimorphism, socionomic sex ratio and body weight in primates. *Nature*. **269**, 797–800.

Cochrane, S. H. (1979) *Fertility and Education: What do We Really Know*? Johns Hopkins University Press.

Collins, J., Kreitman, N., Nelson, B. & Troop, J. (1971) Neurosis and marital interaction. III Family roles and functions. *Brit J. Psychiatry*, **119**, 233–42.

Condry, J. C. & Ross, D. F. (1985) Sex and aggression: the influence of gender label on the perception of aggression in children. *Child Development*, **56**, 225–33.

Connolly, K. (1973) Factors influencing the learning of manual skills by young children. In Hinde, R. A. & Stevenson-Hinde, J. (eds.) *Constraints on learning: Limitations and Predispositions*. London: Acad. Press.

Coombs, R. H. & Kenkel, W. F. (1986) Sex differences in dating aspirations and satisfaction with computer-selected partners. *Journal of Marriage and the Family*, **28**, 62–6.

Count, E. W. (1973) *Being and Becoming Human*. New York: van Nostrand Reinhold.

Cozby, P. C. (1973) Self disclosure: a literature review. *Psychological Bulletin*, **79**, 73–91.

Crook, J. H. (1964) The evolution of social organisation and visual communication in the weaver birds (Ploceinae). *Behaviour Suppl*. No. 10, 1–178.

Cullen, E. (1957) Adaptations in the kittiwake to cliff-nesting *Ibis*, **99**, 275–302.

Daly, M. & Wilson, M. (1984) A sociobiological analysis of human infanticide. In Hausfater, G. & Hrdy, S. B. (eds). *Infanticide: comparative & evolutionary perspectives*. New York: Aldine.

Darwin, C. (1871) *The Descent of Man*. London: John Murray.

Darwin, C. (1872) *The Expression of the Emotions in Man and the Animals*. London: John Murray.

Datta, S. (1981) *Dynamics of dominance among rhesus females*. Ph.D. thesis, Cambridge University.

Datta, S. B. (1983) Relative power and the maintenance of dominance. In Hinde, R. A. (ed.) *Primate Social Relationships*. Oxford: Blackwell.

Davies, N. B. & Houston, A. I. (1981) Owners & satellites: the economics of territory defence in pied wagtails. *J. Anim. Ecol.*, **50**. 157–80.

Dawkins, R. (1976) *The Selfish Gene*. Oxford: Oxford University Press.

Dawkins, R. (1986) Wealth, polygyny, & reproductive success. *Behavioural & Brain Sciences*, **9**, 190–1.

Dawkins, R. & Carlisle, T. R. (1976) Parental investment, mate desertion and a fallacy. *Nature*, **262**, 131–3.

Deaux, K. (1976) *The Behavior of Women and Men*. Monterey, Calif.: Brooks/Cole.

Deaux, K. (1984) From individual differences to social categories. *American Psychologist*, **39**, 105–16.

Deaux, K. (1985) Sex and gender. *Ann. Rev. Psychol.*, **36**, 49–81.

Delprato, D. (1980) Hereditary determinants of fears and phobias, A critical review. *Behaviour Therapy*, **11**, 79–103.

Dewsbury, D. A. (1982) Ejaculate cost and mate choice. *Amer. Nat.*, **119**, 601–10.

de Waal, F. B. M. (1982) *Chimpanzee Politics*. New York: Harper & Row.

Dickemann, M. (1981) Paternal confidence and dowry competition: a biocultural analysis of purdah. In R. D. Alexander & D. W. Tinkle (eds.) *Natural Selection and Social Behaviour*. New York: Chiron Press.

Dickinson, A. (1980) *Contemporary Animal Learning Theory*. Cambridge: Cambridge Univ. Press.

Dion, K. K. & Dion, K. L. (1975) Self-esteem and romantic love. *Journal of Personality*, **43**, 39–57.

Dobzhansky, T., Ayala, F. J., Stebbins, G. L. & Valentine, J. W. (1977). *Evolution*. San Francisco: Freeman.

Dodge, K. A. (1980) Social cognition and children's aggressive behavior. *Child Development*, **51**, 162–72.

Doise, W. (1978) *Groups and Individuals*. Cambridge: Cambridge University Press.

Doise, W. (1985) Social regulations in cognitive development. In R. A. Hinde, A.-N. Perret-Clermont & J. Stevension-Hinde (eds.) *Social Relationships and Cognitive Development*. Oxford: Oxford University Press.

Doise, W. & Mugny, G. (1981) *Le Développement Social de l'Intelligence*. Paris: Inter Éditions.

Doise, W. & Mugny, G. (1984) *The Social Development of the Intellect*. Oxford: Pergamon.

Doise, W., Mugny, G. & Perret-Clermont, A-N. (1974) Ricerce preliminari sulla sociogenesi delle strutture cognitive. *Lavoro educativo*. Vol. 1.

Doise, W., Mugny, G. & Perret-Clermont, A–N. (1975) Social interaction and the development of cognitive operations. *European Journal of Social Psychology*, **5**, 367–83.

Domjan, M. & Wilson, N. E. (1972) Specificity of cue to consequence in aversion learning in the rat. *Psychonomic Sci.*, **26**, 143–5.

Donaldson, M. (1978) *Children's Minds*. London: Fontana.

Douglas, J. W. B. (1975) Early hospital admission and later disturbance of behaviour and learning. *Devel. Med. Child Neurol.* **17**, 456–80.

Douglas, M. (1966) *Purity and Danger*. London: Routledge & Kegan Paul.

Duck, S. & Gilmour, R. (eds.) (1981) *Personal Relationships*, 1–3. London: Acad. Press.

Duck, S. W. & Miell, D. E. (1983) Mate choice in humans as an interpersonal process. In P. Bateson (ed.) *Mate Choice*. Cambridge: Cambridge University Press.

Dunbar, R. I. M. (1983) Life history tactics and alternative strategies of reproduction. In P. Bateson (ed.) *Mate Choice*. Cambridge: Cambridge University Press.

Dunbar, R. I. M. & Sharman, M. (1983) Female competition for access to males affects birth rate in baboons. *Behav. Ecol. Sociobiol.* **13**, 157–9.

Dunn, J., Plomin, R. & Nettles, M. (in press) Consistency of mothers' behavior towards young siblings. *Developmental Psychology*.

Durham, W. H. (1976) Resource competition and human aggression: a review of primitive war. *Quart. Rev. Biol.*, **51**, 385–415.

Durham, W. H. (1978) The co-evolution of human biology & culture. In Blurton Jones, N. & Reynolds, V. (eds.) *Human Adaptation & Behaviour*. New York: Wiley.

Durkheim, E. (1897) *Suicide*. New York: Free Press.

Durkheim, E. (1912) *The Elementary Forms of the Religious Life*. New York: Free Press.

Dyson-Hudson, R. & Smith, E. A. (1978) Human territoriality: an ecological reassessment. *Amer. Anthrop.* **80**, 21–41.

Ehrman, L. & Parson, P. A. (1976) *The Genetics of Behavior*. Sunderland, Mass: Sinauer.

Eibl-Eibesfeldt, I. (1972). Similarities and differences between cultures in expressive movements. In Hinde, R. A. (ed.) *Non-verbal Communication*. Cambridge: Cambridge Univ. Press.

Eibl-Eibesfeldt, I. (1975) *Ethology*. New York: Holt, Rinehart & Winston.

Eimas, P. D., Siqueland, E. R., Jusczyk, P. & Vigorito, J. (1971) Speech perception in infants. *Science*, **171**, 303–6.

Ekman, P. & Friesen, W. V. (1969) The repertoire of non-verbal behaviour: categories, origins, usage and coding. *Semiotica*, **1**, 49–98.

Ekman, P. & Friesen, W. V. (1975) *Unmasking the Face*. Englewood Cliffs, N. J.: Prentice-Hill.

Emde, R. (1984) The affective self. In Call, J. D., Galenson, E. & Tyson, R. L. (eds.). *Frontiers of Infant Psychiatry*. New York: Basic Books.

Endler, N. S. & Magnusson, D. (1976) Toward an interactional psychology of personality. *Psychol. Bull.*, **83**, 956–97.

Engfer, A. (1986) *Stability and change in perceived characteristics of children 4 to 43 months of age*. Paper presented at the Second European Conference on Developmental Psychology, Rome, Italy, September 1986.

Engfer, A. & Schneewind, K. A. (1982) Causes and consequences of harsh parental treatment. *Child Abuse and Neglect*, **6**, 129–39.

Essock-Vitale, S. M. & McGuire, M. T. (1980) Predictions derived from the theories of kin selection and reciprocation assessed by anthropological data. *Ethology & Sociobiology*, **1**, 233–43.

Essock-Vitale, S. M. & McGuire, M. T. (1985a) Women's lives viewed from an evolutionary perspective. 1. Sexual histories, reproductive success and demographic characteristics of a random sample of American women. *Ethology and Sociobiology*, **6**, 137–54.

Essock-Vitale, S. M. & McGuire, M. T. (1985b) Women's lives viewed from an evolutionary perspective. 2. Patterns of helping. *Ethology and Sociobiology*, **6**, 155–73.

Evans-Pritchard, E. E. (1940) *The Nuer*. Oxford: Clarendon Press.

Ferrell, M. Z., Tolone, W. L. & Walsh, R. H. (1977) Maturational and societal changes in the sexual double-standard: a panel analysis (1967–71; 1970–74) *Journal of Marriage and the Family*, **39**, 255–71.

Feshbach, S. (1970) Aggression. In Mussen, P. H. (ed.) *Carmichael's Manual of Child Psychology*. Vol II. New York: Wiley.

Firth, R. (1936) *We, the Tikopia*. London: Allen & Unwin.

Fisher, R. A. (1958) *The Genetical Theory of Natural Selection*. (Originally published in 1930). New York: Dover Press.

Fishman, P. M. (1978) Interaction: the work women do. *Social Problems*, **25**, 397–406.

Flannery, K. V. (1969) The ecology of early food production in Mesopotamia. In A. P. Vayda (ed.) *Environment & Cultural Behavior*. New York: Natural History Press.

Flinn, M. (1981) Uterine vs agnate kinship variability and associated cousin marriage preferences: an evolutionary biological analysis. In R. D. Alexander & D. W. Tinkle (eds.) *Natural Selection and Social Behaviour*. New York: Chiron.

Flinn, M. V. (1986) Correlates of reproductive success in a Trinidadian village. *Human Ecology*, in press.

Ford, C. S. & Beach, F. A. (1951) *Patterns of Sexual Behavior*. New York: Harper & Row.

Fortes, M. (1969) *Kinship and Social Order*. Chicago: Aldine.

Fouts, R. S. (1975) Capacities for language in great apes. In Tuttle, R. H. (ed.) *Socioecology and Psychology of Primates*. The Hague: Mouton.

Fox, R. (1980) *The Red Lamp of Incest*. London: Hutchison.

Frazer, J. G. (1890) *The Golden Bough*. London: MacMillan.

Freedman, D. G. (1961) The infant's fear of strangers and the flight response. *J. Child Psychology & Psychiatry*, **4**, 242–8.

Freedman, D. G. (1974) *Human Infancy: an Evolutionary Perspective*. Hillsdale, N. J.: Erlbaum.

Freeman, N. H. Lloyd, S. & Sinha, C. G. (1980) Infant search tasks reveal early concepts of containment and canonical usage of objects. *Cognition*, **8**, 243–62.

Frolov, I. T. (1985) Genes or culture? A Marxist perspective on humankind. *Biology & Philosophy*, **1**, 89–107.

Fullard, W. & Reiling, A. M. (1976) An investigation of Lorenz's 'babyishness'. *Child Dev.*, **7**, 1191–3.

Gardner, B. T. & Wallach, L. (1965) Shapes of figures identified as a baby's head. *Percept. & Motor skills*, **20**, 135–42.

Gartlan, S. (1968) Structure and function in primate society. *Folia Primatologia*, **8**, 89–120.

Geertz, C. (1970) The impact of the concept of culture on the concept of man. In E. A. Hammel (ed.) *Man makes Sense*. Boston: Little, Brown.

Geertz, C. (1973) *The Interpretation of Cultures*. New York: Basic Books.

Gelles, R. J. (1973) Child abuse as psychopathology: a sociological critique and reformulation. *Amer J. Orthopsychiatry*, **43**, 611–21.

George, C. & Main, M. (1979) Social interactions of young abused children. *Child Dev.*, **50**, 306–18.

Gewirtz, J. (1969) Levels of conceptual analysis in environment – infant interaction research. *Merrill-Palmer Quarterly*, **15**, 7–47.

Gillison, G. (1980) Images of nature in Gimi thought. In C. MacCormack & M.

Strathern (eds.) *Nature, Culture and Gender*. Cambridge: Cambridge University Press.

Gluckman, M. (1950) Kinship and marriage among the Lozi of Northern Rhodesia and the Zulu of Natal. In A. R. Radcliffe-Brown & D. Ford (eds.) *African Systems of Kinship and Marriage*. London: Oxford University Press.

Godelier, M. (1974) Anthropology and biology: towards a new form of co-operation. *Int. Soc. Sci. J.* **26**, 611–35.

Godelier, M. (1979) Territory and property in primitive society. In Cranach, M. von, Foppa, K., Lepenies, W. & Ploog, D. (eds.). *Human Ethology*, Cambridge: Cambridge University Press.

Goffman, E. (1959) *The Presentation of Self in Everyday Life*. New York: Doubleday Anchor.

Goldfoot, D. A. & Wallen K. (1978) Development of gender role behaviors in heterosexual and isosexual groups of infant rhesus monkeys. In Chivers, D. J. & Herbert, J. (eds.) *Recent Advances in Primatology*, I. London: Acad. Press.

Goodale, J. C. (1980) Gender, sexuality and marriage. In C. MacCormack & M. Strathern (eds.) *Nature, Gender and Culture*. Cambridge: Cambridge University Press.

Goodall, J. (1986) *Chimpanzees of Gombe*. Cambridge, Mass: Harvard Univ. Press.

Goodenough, W. H. (1963) *Cooperation in Change*. New York: Russell Sage.

Goody, E. (1972) 'Greeting', 'begging', and the presentation of respect. In J. S. La Fontaine (ed.) *The Interpretation of Ritual*, London: Tavistock.

Goody, E. (1973) *Contexts of Kinship*. Cambridge: Cambridge University Press.

Goody, J. (1968) *Literacy in Traditional Societies*. Cambridge: Cambridge Univ. Press.

Goody, J. (1976) *Production & Reproduction*. Cambridge: Cambridge Univ. Press.

Goody, J. Introduction to Barth (in press) *Cosmologies in the Making: a Generative Approach to Cultural Variation in Inner New Guinea*. Cambridge: Cambridge University Press.

Gough, H. G. & Heilbrun, A. B. Jr. (1965) *Adjective Check List Manual*. Palo Alto, CA: Consulting Psychologists Press.

Gould, S. J. (1980) *The Panda's Thumb*. Harmondsworth, Middlesex: Penguin.

Gould, S. J. & Lewontin, R. C. (1979) The Spandrels of San Marco and the Panglossian paradigm: a critique of the adaptationist programme. *Proc. Roy. Soc. B.*, **205**, 581–98.

Goy, R. W. (1978) Development of play & mounting behaviour in female rhesus virilized prenatally. In Chivers, D. J. & Herbert, J. (eds.) *Recent Advances in Primatology*. **1**, London: Acad. Press.

Grafen, A. (1982) How not to measure inclusive fitness. *Nature*, **298**, 425–6.

Grant, E. C. (1969) Human facial expression. *Man*, 525–36.

Grossmann, K. E., Grossmann, K., Huber, F. & Wartner, U. (1981) German children's behaviour towards their mothers at 12 months and their fathers at 18 months in Ainsworth's strange situation. *Int. J. Behav. Dev*, **4**, 157–81.

Hall, W. G. & Williams, C. L. (1983) Suckling isn't feeding, or is it? A search for developmental continuities. *Adv. Study Behav.*, **13**, 219–54.

Hamilton, D. L. (ed) (1981) *Cognitive Processes in Stereotyping and Intergroup Behaviour*. Hillsdale, N. J.: Erlbaum.

Hamilton, W. D. (1964) The genetical theory of social behaviour. *J. theor. Biol.*, **7**, 1–52.

Hamilton, W. D. (1967) Extraordinary sex ratios. *Science*, **156**, 477–88.

Hansen, N. R. (1955) Causal chains. *Mind*, **64**, 289–311.

Harris, L. J. (1979) Sex differences in spatial ability. In M. Kinsbourne (ed.) *Asymmetrical Function of the Brain*. Cambridge: Cambridge Univ. Press.

Harris, M. (1968) *Cows, Pigs, Wars and Witches*. New York: Random House.

Harris, M. (1974) *Cultural Materialization: The Struggle for a Science of Culture*. New York: Random House.

Harris, O. (1980) The power of signs: gender, culture and the wild in the Bolivian Andes. In C. MacCormack & M. Strathern (eds.) *Nature, Gender and Culture*. Cambridge: Cambridge University Press.

Harter, S. (1983) Developmental perspectives on the self system. In Hetherington, M. (ed.) *Mussen Handbook of Child Psychology*, Vol. IV. New York: Wiley.

Hartung, J. (1985) Matrilineal inheritance: new theory & analysis. *Behavioral & Brain Sciences*, **8**, 661–88.

Hartup, W. W. (1983) Peer relations. In P. H. Mussen (ed.) *Handbook of Child Psychology*, Fourth Edition. Vol. IV. New York: Wiley.

Hawkes, K., O'Connell, J. F., Hill, K. & Charnov, E. L. (1985) How much is enough? Hunters and limited needs. *Ethology & Sociobiology*, **6**, 3–15.

Hebb, D. O. (1949) *The Organization of Behavior*. New York: Wiley.

Heider, F. (1958) *The Psychology of Interpersonal Relations*. New York: Wiley.

Heiman, J. R. (1980) Selecting for a sociobiological fit. Commentary on Symons in *The Behavioral and Brain Sciences*, **3**, 189–90.

Hendrick, C., Hendrick, S., Foote, F. H. & Slapion-Foote, M. J. (1984). Do men and women love differently? *J. social & personal Relationships*, **1**, 177–95.

Hendrick, S., Hendrick, C., Slapion-Foote, M. J. & Foote, F. H. (1985) Gender differences in sexual attitudes. *J. pers. soc. Psychol.*, **48**, 1630–42.

Henley, N. M. (1977) *Body Politics: power, sex and nonverbal communication*. Englewood Cliffs, N. J.: Prentice-Hall.

Henry, J. (1959) Culture, personality & evolution. *Amer. Anthropologist*, **61**, 221–6.

Herdt, G. H. (1981) *Guardians of the Flute: Idioms of Masculinity*. New York: McGraw Hill.

Herschkowitz, M. & Samuel, D. (1973) The retention of learning during metamorphosis of the crested newt (*Triturus cristatus*). *Anim. Behav.* **21**, 83–5.

Hill, J. (1978) The origin of sociocultural evolution. *Journal of Social Biological Structures*. **1**, 377–86.

Hill, J. (1984) Prestige and reproductive success in man. *Ethology and Sociobiology*, **5**, 77–95.

Hill, J. (1985) Prestige and reproductive success in man: a reply to Hillard Kaplan. *Ethology & Sociobiology*, **5**, 119–20.

Hinde, R. A. (1959) Behaviour and speciation in birds and lower vertebrates. *Biol. Rev.* **34**, 85–128.

Hinde, R. A. (1961) The establishment of parent-offspring relations in birds, with some mammalian analogies. In W. H. Thorpe & O. L. Zangwill (eds.) *Current Problems in Animal Behaviour*. Cambridge: Cambridge University Press.

Hinde, R. A. (1968) Dichotomies in the study of development. In J. M. Thoday & A. S. Parkes (eds.) *Genetic and Environmental Influences on Behavior*. Edinburgh: Oliver and Boyd.

Hinde, R. A. (1972) (ed.) *Non-verbal communication*. Cambridge: Cambridge Univ. Press.

Hinde, R. A. (1975) The concept of function. In G. P. Baerends., C. Beer & A. Manning (eds.) *Function and Evolution in Behaviour*. Oxford: Oxford University Press.

Hinde, R. A. (1976) Interactions, relationships and social structure. *Man*, **11**, 1–17.

Hinde, R. A. (1979a) *Towards Understanding Relationships*. London: Acad. Press.

Hinde, R. A. (1979b) The nature of social structure. In Hamburg, D. A. & McCown, E. R. (eds.) *The Great Apes*. Menlo Pk, Calif.: Benjaming/Cummings.

Hinde, R. A. (1982) *Ethology*. Oxford: Oxford University Press.

Hinde, R. A. (ed.) (1983) *Primate Social Relationships*. Oxford: Blackwell.

Hinde, R. A. (1984a) Biological bases of the mother–child relationship. In Call, J. D., Galenson, E., Tyson, R. L. (eds) *Frontiers of Infant Psychiatry*. New York: Basic Books.

Hinde, R. A. (1984b). Why do the sexes behave differently in close relationships. *J. social and personal Relationships*. **1**, 471–501.

Hinde, R. A. (1986) Some implications of evolutionary theory and comparative data for the study of human prosocial and aggressive behaviour. In Olweus, D., Block, J. & Radke-Yarrow, M. (eds). *Development of Antisocial & Prosocial Behavior*. Orlando: Acad. Press.

Hinde, R. A., Perret-Clermont, A–N. & Stevenson-Hinde, J. (eds) (1985) *Social Relationships & Cognitive Development*. Oxford: Oxford Univ. Press.

Hinde, R. A. & Barden, L. (1985) The evolution of the teddy bear. *Anim. Behav*. **33**, 1371–3.

Hinde, R. A. & Bateson, P. P. G. (1984) Discontinuities versus continuities in behavioural development and the neglect of process. *Int. J. Behav. Devel.*, **7**, 129–43.

Hinde, R. A. & Dennis A. (1986) Categorizing individuals: an alternative to linear analysis. *Int. J. Behav. Dev*. **9**, 105–19.

Hinde, R. A. & Fisher, J. (1951) Further observations on the opening of milk bottles by birds. *Brit. Birds*, **46**, 393–6.

Hinde, R. A. & Hermann, J. (1977) Frequencies, durations, derived measures and their correlations in studying dyadic and triadic relationships. In Schaffer, H. R. (ed.) *Studies in Mother–Infant Interaction*. London: Acad. Press.

Hinde, R. A. & McGinnis, L. (1977) Some factors influencing the effects of temporary mother–infant separation – some experiments with rhesus monkeys. *Psychological Medicine*, **7**, 197–222.

Hinde, R. A. & Stevenson-Hinde, J. S. (1973) (eds.) *Constraints on Learning: Limitations and Predispositions*. London: Acad. Press.

Hinde, R. A. & Stevenson-Hinde (1976) Towards understanding relationships: dynamic stability. In Hinde, R. A. & Bateson, P. P. G. (eds.) *Growing Points in Ethology*. Cambridge: Cambridge University Press.

Hinde, R. A. & Stevenson-Hinde, J. S. (1987) Interpersonal relationships and child development. *Develop. Review.*

Hinde, R. A. & Tamplin, A. (1983) Relations between mother–child interaction and behaviour in pre-school. *Brit. J. Develop. Psychol.*, **1**, 231–57.

Hines, M. (1982) Prenatal gonadal hormones and sex differences in human behaviour. *Psychol. Bull.*, **92**, 56–80.

Hoffman, L. W. (1972) Early childhood experiences and women's achievement motive. *Journal of Social Issues*, **28**, 129–55.

Hoffman, M. (1983) Empathy, guilt & social cognition. In Overton, W. F. (ed.) *The Relationship between Social & Cognitive Development*. Hillsdale, N. J.: Erlbaum.

Homans, G. C. (1961) *Social Behaviour: its Elementary Forms*. London: Routledge and Kegan Paul.

Hooff, J. A. R. A. M. van (1962) Facial expressions in higher primates. *Sym. Zool. Soc. Lond.*, **8**, 97–125.

Hooff, J. A. R. A. M. van (1972) A comparative approach to the phylogeny of laughter and smiling. In Hinde R. A. (ed.) *Non-verbal Communication*. Cambridge: Cambridge Univ. Press.

Hooley, J. & Simpson, M. J. A. (1983) Influence of siblings on the infant's relationship with the mother and others. In Hinde, R. A. (ed.) *Primate Social Relationships*. Oxford: Blackwell.

Horn, G. (1985) *Memory, Imprinting and the Brain*. Oxford: Oxford Univ. Press.

Hrdy, S. B. (1977) Infanticide as a primate reproductive strategy. *Am. Scient*, **65**, 40–9.

Hrdy, S. B. (1981) *The Woman that Never Evolved*. Harvard: Harvard University Press.

Hugh-Jones, C. (1979) *From the Milk River*. Cambridge: Cambridge Univ. Press.

Humphrey, N. (1976) The social function of intellect. In Bateson, P. & Hinde, R. A. (eds.) *Growing Points in Ethology*. Cambridge: Cambridge Univ. Press.

Humphrey, N. (1986) *The Inner Eye*. London: Faber & Faber.

Irons, W. (1979) Cultural and biological success. In Chagnon, N. & Irons, W. (eds.) *Evolutionary Biology and Human Social Behaviour*. N. Scituate, Mass: Duxbury.

Irons, W. (1980) Is Yomut social behaviour adaptive? In Barlow, G. W. & Silverberg, J. (eds.). *Sociobiology: beyond Nature/Nurture?* Boulder, Colorado: Westview.

Jaspers J. M. F. & Leeuw, J. A. de (1980) Genetic-environment covariation in human behaviour genetics. In Kamp, L. J. T. van der et al., (eds.) *Psychometrics for Educational Debate*. Chichester: Wiley.

Kaffman, M. (1977) Sexual standards & behavior of the kibbutz adolescent. *Amer J. Orthopsychiatry*, **47**, 207–17.

Kagan, J. (1978) Continuity & stage in human development. In Bateson, P. & Klopfer, P. (eds.) *Perspectives in Ethology*, **3**. Social behaviour. New York: Plenum.

Kagan, J. (1980). Four questions in psychological development. *Int. J. Behav. Devel.*, **3**, 231–41.

Kaplan, H. (1985) Prestige & reproductive success in men: a commentary. *Ethology and Sociobiology*, **5**, 115–18.

Kaplan, H. & Hill, K. (1985) Hunting ability and reproductive success among male Ache foragers. *Current Anthropology*, **26**, 131–3.

Kawamura, S. (1963) The process of sub-culture propagation among Japanese macaques. In Southwick, C. H. (ed.) *Primate Social Behaviour*. New York: van Norstrand.

Kear, J. (1962) Food selection in finches with special reference to interspecific differences. *Proc. zool. Soc. Lond.*, **138**, 163–204.

Keesing, R. M. (1981) *Social Anthropology: a Contemporary Perspective*. New York: Holt Rinehart & Winston.

Keesing, R. M. (1982) Introduction. In Herdt, G. A. (ed.) *Rituals of Manhood*. Berkeley: Univ. Calif. Press.

Kelley, H. H. (1971) *Attribution in Social Interaction*. Morristown, N. J.: General Learning Press.

Kelley, H. H. (1979) *Personal Relationships*. Hillsdale, N. J.: Erlbaum.

Kelley, H. H., Cunningham, J. D., Grisham, J. A., Lefebvre, L. M., Sink, C. R. & Yablon, G. (1978) Sex differences in comments made during conflict within close heterosexual pairs. *Sex Roles*, **4**, 473–91.

Kelley, H. H., Berscheid, M. E., Christensen, A., et al., (1983) *Close Relationships*. New York: Freeman.

Kellogg, W. N. & Kellogg, L. (1933) *The Ape and Child*. New York: McGraw Hill.

Kelly, G. A. (1955) *The Psychology of Personal Constructs*. Norton.

Kendon, A. & Farber, A. (1973) A description of some human greetings. In Michael, R. & Crook, J. H. (eds.) *Comparative Ecology & Behaviour in Primates*. London: Acad. Press.

Kennell, J. (1986) *John Lind Memorial Lecture*. World Congress of Infant Psychiatry, Stockholm.

Kenny, D. A. (1975) Cross-lagged panel correlation: a test for spuriousness. *Psychol. Bull.*, **82**, 887–903.

Kenrick, D. T. & Stringfield, D. O. (1980) Personality traits and the eye of the beholder. *Psychol. Rev.*, **87**, 88–104.

Kinsey, A. C., Pomeroy, W. B. & Martin, C. E. (1948) *Sexual Behavior in the Human Male*. Philadelphia: W. B. Saunders.

Kinsey, A. C., Pomeroy, W. B., Martin, C. E. & Gebhard, P. H. (1953) *Sexual Behavior in the Human Female*. Philadelphia: W. B. Saunders.

Kitcher, P. (1985) *Vaulting Ambition*. Cambridge, Mass.: M.I.T. Press.

Kleiman, D. G. (1977) Monogamy in mammals. *Quarterly Review of Biology*, **52**, 39–69.

Kohlberg, L. (1969) Stage and sequence: the cognitive developmental approach to socialization. In D. A. Joslin (ed.) *Handbook of Socialization Theory and Research*. Chicago: Rand McNally.

Krebs, J. R. (1976) Review of E. O. Wilson's *Sociobiology*. *Anim. Behav*, **24**, 709–10.

Kummer, H. (1971) *Primate Societies: Group Techniques of Ecological Adaptation*. Chicago: Aldine Atherton.

Kummer, H. (1982) Social Knowledge in free-ranging primates. In D. R. Griffin (ed.). *Animal Mind, Human Mind*. Berlin, Springer-Verlag.

Kurland, J. (1979) Paternity, mother's brother & human sociality. In Chapman, N. A. & Irons, W. (eds) *Evolutionary Biology & Human Social Behavior*. N. Scituate, Mass: Duxbury.

Lack, D. (1954) *The Natural Regulation of Animal Numbers*. Oxford: Clarendon Press.

Lack, D. (1966) *Population Studies of Birds*. Oxford: Clarendon.

Lamb, M. (1981) *The Role of the Father in Child Development*. New York: Wiley.

Lambert, H. H. (1978) Biology and equality: a perspective on sex differences. *Signs: Journal of Women in Culture and Society*, **4**, 97–117.

Lazar, I. & Darlington, R. B. (1985) Lasting effects of early education. *Monog. Soc. Child. Dev.*, **47**, Ser. No. 195.

La Barre, W. (1947) The cultural basis of emotions and gestures. *J. Personality*, **16**. 49–68.

Leach, E. (1964) Anthropological aspects of language. Animal categories & verbal abuse. In E. H. Lenneberg (ed.) *New Directions in the Study of Language*. Cambridge, Mass.: M.I.T. Press.

Leach, E. (1970) *Lévi-Strauss*. London: Fontana.

Leach, E. (1972) The influence of cultural context on non-verbal communication in man. In Hinde, R. A. (ed.). *Non-verbal Communication*. Cambridge: Cambridge University Press.

Lee, R. B. (1972) !Kung spatial organization. *Human Ecology*, **1**, 125–47.

Lee, R. B. & DeVore I. (eds) (1968) *Man the Hunter*. Chicago: Aldine.

Lehrman, D. S. (1953) A critique of Konrad Lorenz's theory of instinctive behaviour. *Quart. Rev. Biol.* **28**, 337–63.

Lehrman, D. S. (1970) Semantic and conceptual issues in the nature-nurture problem. In Aronson, L. R., Tobach, E., Lehrman, D. S. and Rosenblatt, J. S. (eds.) *Development and Evolution of Behaviour*. San Francisco: Freeman.

Lenington, S. (1981) Child abuse: the limits of sociobiology. *Ethology and Sociobiology*, **2**, 17–29.

Lévi-Strauss, C. (1955) *Tristes Topiques*, Paris: Plon.

Lewontin, R. C. (1970) The units of selection. *Anim. Rev. Ecology & Systematics*, **1**, 1–18.

Liberman, A. M. (1979) An ethological approach to language through the study of speech perception. In Cranach, M. von, Foppa, K., Pepenies, W. & Ploog, D. (eds.) *Human Ethology*. Cambridge: Cambridge Univ. Press.

Light, P. & Perret-Clermont, A–N. (1986) Social construction of logical structures and social construction of meaning. *Dossiers de Psychologie, Univ. de Neuchatel*, No. 27.

Livingstone, F. B. (1958) Anthropological implications of sickle cell gene distribution West Africa. *Amer. Anthropologist*, **60**, 533–62.

Logue, A. W. (1979) Taste aversion and the generality of the laws of learning. *Psychological Bulletin*, **86**, 276–96.

Lopreato, J. (1984) *Human Nature and Biocultural Evolution*. Boston: Allen & Unwin.

Lorenz, K. (1935) Der Kumpan in der Umwelt des Vogels. *J. f. Ornith.* **83**, 137–213, 289–413.

Lorenz, K. (1950) Ganzheit und Teil in der tierischen und menschlichen Gemeinschaft. *Studium Generale, 1950, 3/9*.

Lorenz, K. (1966) *On Aggression*. London: Methuen.

Lumsden, C. J. & Wilson, E. O. (1981) *Genes, Mind & Culture*. Cambridge, Mass: Harvard Univ. Press.

Lund, M. (1985) The development of investment and commitment scales for predicting continuity of personal relationships. *J. Social Personal Relationships*, **2**, 3–23.

Maccoby, E. E. & Jacklin, C. N. (1974) *The Psychology of Sex Differences*. Stanford: Stanford University Press.

Maccoby, E. E. & Martin, J. A. (1983) Socialization in the context of the family: parent–child interaction. In Hetherington, M. (ed.) Mussen: *Handbook of child Psychology*, IV. 1–103. New York: Wiley.

MacDonald, K. (1984) An ethological-social learning theory of the development of altruism: implications for human sociobiology. *Ethology and Sociobiology*, **5**, 97–109.

Mackintosh, N. J. (1983) *Conditioning and Associative Learning*. Oxford: Clarendon Press.

Magnusson, D. & Olåh, A. (1981) Situation-outcome contingencies. *Reports from the Department of Psychology*. Stockholm: University of Stockholm.

Mainardi, D. (1980) Tradition and the social transmission of behavior in animals. In Barlow, G. W. & Silverberg, J. (eds) *Sociobiology: Beyond Nature/Nurture*. Boulder, Colorado: Westview.

Main, M. & Stadtman, J. (1981) Infant response to rejection of physical contact by the mother. *J. Amer. Acad. Child Psychiatry*, **20**, 292–307.

Main, M. & Weston, D. (1981) The quality of the toddler's relationship to mother and father: related to conflict behaviour and the readiness to establish new relationships. *Child Development*, **52**, 932–40.

Main, M. & Weston, D. R. (1982) Avoidance of the attachment figure in infancy. In Parkes, C. M. & Stevenson-Hinde, J. (eds.) *The Place of Attachment in Human Behaviour*. London: Tavistock.

Malinowski, B (1929) *The Sexual Life of Savages*. New York: Harcourt, Brace & World.

Marks, I. M. (1969) *Fears and Phobias*. New York: Acad. Press.

Marler, P. (1979) Development of auditory perception in relation to vocal behaviour. In Cranach, M. von, Foppa, K. Lepenies, W. & Ploog, D. (eds.) *Human Ethology*. Cambridge: Cambridge University Press.

Marler, P. (1984) Song learning: innate species differences in the learning process. In P. Marler & H. S. Terrace (eds.) *The Biology of Learning*. Berlin: Springer-Verlag.

Martin, J. A. (1981) A longitudinal study of the consequences of early mother–infant interaction. *Monogr. Society Research in Child Development*, **46**, 3.

Marx, K. & Engels, F. (1976) *Collected Works*. Moscow: Progress Publishers.

Maynard Smith, J. (1977) Parental investment: a prospective analysis. *Anim. Behav.* **25**, 1–9.

Maynard Smith, J. (1978) In defence of models. *Anim Behav.* **26**, 632–3.

Maynard Smith, J. (1979) Game theory and the evolution of behaviour. *Proc. Roy. Soc. B.*, **205**, 475–88.

Maynard Smith, J. & Warren, N. (1982) Models of cultural and genetic change. *Evolution*, **36**, 620–7.

McCall, G. J. (1974) A symbolic interactionist approach to attraction. In Huston, T. L. (ed.) *Foundations of Interpersonal Attraction*. New York: Acad. Press.

McCall, R. B. (1981) Nature–nurture and the two realms of development: a proposed integration with respect to mental development. *Child Development*, **52**, 1–12.

McGarrigle, J. & Donaldson, M. (1974) Conservation accidents. *Cognition*, **3**, 341–50.

McGrew, W. C. (1985) The chimpanzee and the oil palm: patterns of culture. *Social Biology and Human Affairs*. **50**, No. 1. 7–25.

McKenna, J. J. (in press) An anthropological perspective on the sudden infant death syndrome. *J. Medical Anthropology*.

Mead, G. H. (1934) *Mind, Self and Society*. Chicago: University of Chicago Press.

Mead, M. (1950) *Male and Female*. Harmondsworth: Penguin.

Mellen, S. L. W. (1981) *The Evolution of Love*. Oxford: Freeman.

Meyer-Bahlburg, H. F. L., Feldman, J. F., Ehrhardt, A. A. & Cohen, P. (1984). Effects of prenatal hormone exposure versus pregnancy complications on sex-dimorphic behavior. *Arch. Sexual Behavior*, **13**, 479–95.

Minuchin, P. (1985) Families and individual development: provocations from the field of family therapy. *Child Dev.*, **56**, 289–302.

Minuchin, S. (1974) *Families and Family Therapy*. Cambridge, Mass: Harvard Univ. Press.

Mischel, W. (1973) Towards a cognitive social learning reconceptualization of personality. *Psychol. Rev.*, **80**, 252–83.

Money, J. W. & Ehrhardt, A. A. (1972) *Man & Woman, Boy & Girl*. Baltimore: John Hopkins Univ. Press.

Moore, B. R. (1973) The role of directed Pavlovian reactions in simple instrumental learning in the pigeon. In Hinde, R. A. & Stevenson-Hinde, J. (eds.) *Constraints on Learning*. London: Acad Press.

Moore, J. (1984) The evolution of reciprocal sharing. *Ethology & Sociobiology*, **5**, 5–14.

Morgan, C. J. (1985) Natural selection for altruism in structural populations. *Ethology and Sociobiology*, **6**, 211–18.

Morris, D. (1967) *The Naked Ape*. London: Cape.

Moyer, K. E. (1968) Kinds of aggression and their physiological basis. *Commun. Behav. Biol*. **2**, 65–87.

Murdock, G. P. (1949) *Social Structure*. New York: MacMillan.

Murdock, G. P. (1967) *Ethnographic Atlas*. Pittsburgh, Penn: Pittsburgh Univ. Press.

Murdock, G. P (1972) Anthropology's mythology. *Proc. Roy. Anthrop. Inst. Gt. Britain & Ireland*. (1971), 17–24.

Murstein, B. I. (1979) Qualities of desired spouse. In G. Kurian (ed.) *Cross-cultural Perspectives of Mate Selection and Marriage*. Westport, Conn.: Greenwood Press.

Mussen, P. & Eisenberg-Berg, N. (1977) *Roots of Caring, Sharing & Helping*. San Francisco: Freeman.

Mussen, P., Eichorn, D. H., Honzik, M. P., Bieber, S. L. & Meredith, W. M. (1980) Continuity and change in women's characteristics over four decades. *International Journal of Behavioural Development*, **3**, 333–47.

Newcomb, T. M. (1961) *The Acquaintance Process*. New York: Holt, Rinehart & Winston.

Noller, P. (1980) Misunderstandings in marital communication: a study of couples' non-verbal communication. *Journal of Personality and Social Psychology*, **39**, 1135–48.

Nottebohm, F. & Nottebohm, M. (1971) Vocalization and breeding behaviour of surgically deafened ring doves. *Anim. Behav.* **19**, 313–28.

Orians, G. H. (1969) On the evolution of mating systems in birds and mammals. *Amer. Nat.*, **103**, 589–603.

Ortner, S. B. & Whitehead, H. (1981) *Sexual Meanings*. Cambridge: Cambridge University Press.

Oyama, S. (1985) *The Ontogeny of Information*. Cambridge: Cambridge Univ. Press.

Packer, C. (1977) Reciprocal altruism in *Papio anubis. Nature*, **265**, 441–2.

Passingham, R. E. (1982) *The Human Primate*. Oxford: Freeman.

Patterson, I. J. (1965) Timing and spacing of broods in the black-headed gull. (*Larus ridibundus*) *Ibis*, **107**, 433–59.

Peabody, D. (1985) *National Characteristics*. Cambridge: Cambridge Univ. Press.

Peplau, L. A. (1976) Impact of fear of success and sex-role attitudes on women's competitive achievement. *Journal of Personality and Social Psychology*, **34**, 561–8.

Peplau, L. A. (1983) Roles and gender. In H. H. Kelley, et al (eds.) *Close Relationships*. New York, Freeman.

Peplau, L. A. & Gordon, S. L. (1983) *Women and men in love: sex differences in close heterosexual relationships*. Unpublished manuscript, University of California, Los Angeles.

Peplau, L. A., Rubin, Z. & Hill, C. T. (1977) Sexual intimacy in dating relationships. *J. Social Issues*, **33**, 86–109.

Perret-Clermont, A.-N. (1985) Contribution to editorials in Hinde, R. A., Perret-Clermont A.-N. & Stevenson-Hinde, J. (eds.) *Social Relationships & Cognitive Development*. Oxford: Oxford Univ. Press.

Perret-Clermont, A.-N. & Brossard, A. (1985) On the interdigitation of social and cognitive processes. In Hinde, R. A., Perret-Clermont, A.-N. & Stevenson-Hinde, J. (eds.). *Social Relationships and Cognitive Development*. Oxford: Oxford University Press.

Pettigrew, J. D. (1982) Pharmacologic control of cortical plasticity. *Retina*, **2**, 360–72.

Piaget, J. (1929) *The Child's Conception of the World*. New York: Harcourt Brace.

Plomin, R. & de Fries, B. C. (1983) The Colorado adoption project. *Child Development*, **54**, 276–89.

Pound, A. (1982) Attachment and maternal depression. In Parkes, C. M. & Stevenson-Hinde, J. (eds.) *The Place of Attachment in Human Behavior*. London: Tavistock.

Prechtl, H. F. R. (1950) Das Verhalten von Kleinkindern gegenüber Schlangen. *Wiener Zeitz. f. Philosophie, Psychologie und Paedagogie*, **2**, 68–70.

Prechtl, H. F. R. & Beintema, D. J. (1964) *The Neurological Examination of the Full Term Newborn Infant*. London: Heinemann.

Premack, D. (1978) Chimpanzee theory of mind. II The evidence for symbols in Chimpanzee. *Behav. Brain Sci.*, **1**, 625–9.

Quinton, D. & Rutter, M. (1976) Early hospital admissions and later disturbances of behaviour: an attempted replication of Douglas's findings. *Devel. Med. Child Neurol.*, **18**, 447–59.

Quinton, D. & Rutter,M. (1986) *Parenting Breakdown: Making and Breaking Intergenerational Cycles*. Aldershot, Hants: Gower.

Radcliffe-Brown, A. R. (1922) *The Andaman Islands*. Cambridge: Cambridge Univ. Press.

Radke-Yarrow, M. & Sherman, T. (1985) Interaction of cognition and emotions in development. In Hinde, R. A., Perret-Clermont, A.-N. & Stevenson-Hinde, J. *Social Relationships and Cognitive Development*. Oxford: Oxford Univ. Press.

Rainer, J. D. (1979) Heredity and character disorders. *American Journal of Psychotherapy*, **33**, 6–16.

Rappaport, R. A. (1968) *Pigs for the Ancestors: Ritual in the Ecology of a New Guinea People*. New Haven: Yale University Press.

Rappaport, R. A. (1971) The sacred in human evolution. *Ann. Rev. Ecology & Systematics*, **2**, 23–44.

Revusky, S. & Garcia, J. (1970) Learned associations over long delays. In Bower G. W. (ed.) *Psychology of Learning & Motivation*. **4**, 1–83. New York: Acad. Press.

Richerson, P. J. & Boyd, R. (1978) A dual inheritance model of the human evolutionary process. *J. Social Biol. Structures*. **1**, 127–54.

Richman, N., Stevenson, J. & Graham, P. J. (1982) *Preschool to School: A behavioural Study*. London: Academic Press.

Rivers, W. H. R. (1901) Vision. In A. C. Haddon (ed.) *Reports of the Cambridge Anthropological Expedition to the Torres Straits*, **2**:1. Cambridge: Cambridge Univ. Press.

Robertson, J. (1970) *Young Children in Hospital*. London: Tavistock.

Rogers, S. C. (1978) Women's place: a critical review of anthropological history. *Comp. Studies in Society and History*, **20**, 123–62.

Rogosa, D. (1980) A critique of cross-lagged correlation. *Psychol Bull*. **88**, 245–58.

Rolls, E. T. (1987) Visual information processing in the primate temporal lobe. In M. Imbert (ed.) *Models of visual perception from natural to artificial*. Oxford: Oxford University Press.

Rosenthal, T. & Zimmerman, B. (1978) *Social Learning & Cognition*. New York: Acad. Press.

Rowell, T. E. (1962) Agonistic noises of the rhesus monkey. *Proc. Zool. Soc. London.*, **8**, 91–6.

Rowland, W. J. & Sevenster, P. (1985) Sign stimuli in the three-spined stickleback. *Behaviour*, **93**, 241–57.

Royal Society. (1986) *Girls and Mathematics*.

Rubin, Z., Peplau, L. A. & Hill, C. T. (1981) Loving and leaving: sex differences in romantic attachments. *Sex Role*, **7**, 821–35.

Rumbaugh, D. M. (1977) *Language Learning by a Chimpanzee*. New York: Acad. Press.

Rushton, J. P., Brainard, C. J. & Pressley, M. (1983) Behavioural development and construct validity: the principle of aggregation. *Psychol. Bull.* **84**, 18–38.

Rushton, J. P. Russell, R. J. H. & Wells, P. A. (1984) Genetic similarity theory: beyond kin selection. *Behavior Genetics*, **14**, 179–93.

Rutter, M. (1972) *Maternal Deprivation Reassessed.* Harmondsworth: Penguin.

Rutter, M. (in press) Continuities and discontinuities from infancy. In J. Osofsky (ed.) *Handbook of Infant Development.* New York: Wiley.

Rutter, M., Quinton, D. & Liddle, C. (1983) Parenting in two generations. In Madge, N. (ed.) *Families at Risk.* London: Heineman.

Ryden, O. (1978) The significance of antecedent auditory experiences on later reactions to the 'seet' alarm call in Great Tit nestlings. *Zeit.f. Tierpsychologie,* **47**, 369–409.

Safilios-Rothschild, C. (1977) *Love, Sex and Sex Roles.* New Jersey: Prentice-Hall.

Sahlins, M. D. (1964) Culture & environment: the study of cultural anthropology. In S. Tax. (ed.) *Horizons of Anthropology.* Chicago: Aldine.

Sahlins, M. D. (1976) *The Use and Abuse of Biology: an Anthropological Critique of Sociobiology.* Ann Arbor: Univ. of Michigan Press.

Samuel, J. & Bryant, P. E. (1984) Asking only one question in the conservation experiment. *J. Child Psychol. Psychiatry,* **25**, 315–18.

Sanday, P. R. (1981) *Female Power and Male Dominance.* Cambridge: Cambridge University Press.

Sanders. W. T. & Price, B. (1969) *Mesoamerica: the Evolution of a Civilization.* New York: Random House.

Sargant, W. (1957) *Battle for the Mind.* London: Heineman.

Scarr, S. & Kidd, K. K. (1983) Developmental Behavior Genetics. In Campos J. J. & Haith, M. M. (eds.) *Mussen, Handbook of Child Psychology.* II. New York: Wiley.

Scarr, S. & McCartney, K. (1983) How people make their own environments. *Child Development,* **54**, 424–35.

Schiller, P. H. (1957) Manipulative patterns in the chimpanzee. In P. H. Schiller (ed.) *Instinctive Behavior.* London: Methuen.

Schlegel, A. (1972) *Male Dominance and Female Autonomy.* New Haven: Human Relations Area Press.

Segall, M. H. (1979) *Cross-cultural Psychology: Human Behavior in Global Perspective.* Monterey, CA.: Brooks/Cole.

Segall, M. H., Campbell, D. T. & Herskovitz, M. J. (1966) *The Influence of Culture on Visual Perception.* Indianapolis: Bobbs-Merrill.

Seligman, M. E. P. & Hager J. L. (eds.) (1972) *Biological Boundaries of Learning.* New York: Appleton Century Crofts.

Seyfarth, R. M. & Cheney, D. L. (1986) Vocal development in vervet monkeys. *Anim. Behav.,* **34**, 1640–58.

Shepher, J. (1971) Mate selection among second generation Kibbutz adolescents and adults. *Arch. sexual Behav.,* **1**, 293–307.

Shepher, J. & Reisman, J. (1985) Pornography: a sociobiological attempt at understanding. *Ethology & Sociobiology,* **6**, 103–14.

Shettleworth, S. J. (1983) Food reinforcement and the organization of behaviour in golden hamsters. In Hinde, R. A. & Stevenson-Hinde, J. (eds.) *Constraints on Learning: Limitations and Predispositions.* London: Acad. Press.

Shields, J. (1962) Twins reared apart are more similar than those reared together. *Monozygotic Twins Brought Up Together and Apart.* Oxford: Oxford University Press.

Short, R. (1979) Sexual selection and its component parts, somatic & genital selection, as illustrated by man and the great apes. *Adv. Study Behaviour*, **9**, 131–58.

Simpson, M. J. A. (1968) The display of the Siamese fighting fish, *Betta splendens. Animal Behaviour Monograph*, **1**, No. 1.

Smith, P. K. (1986). Exploration, play & development in boys & girls. In Hargreaves, D. J. & Colley, A. M. (eds.) *The Psychology of Sex Roles*. London: Harper & Row.

Smith, W. J. (1977). *The Behavior of Communicating*. Cambridge, Mass: Harvard Univ. Press.

Sroufe, L. A. (1979) The coherence of individual development. *Amer. Psychologist*, **34**, 834–41.

Sroufe, L. A. & Waters,E. (1976) The ontogenesis of smiling and laughter. *Psychol. Rev.*, **83**, 173–89.

Sroufe, L. A., Jacobvitz, D., Mangelsdorf, S., De Angelo, E & Ward, M. J. (1985). Generational boundary dissolution between mothers and their pre-school children: a relationship systems approach. *Child Development*, **56**, 317–25.

Steele, D. G. & Walker, C. E. (1974) Male and female differences in reaction to erotic stimuli as related to sexual adjustment. *Archives of Sexual Behavior*, **3**, 459–70.

Sternglanz, S. H., Gray, J. L. & Murakami, M. (1977) Adult preferences for infantile facial features. *Anim. Behav.* **25**, 108–15.

Stern, D. (1977) *The First Relationship: infant and mother*. London: Fontana.

Stern, D. (1985) *The Interpersonal World of the Infant*. New York: Basic Books.

Stevenson-Hinde, J. (1972) Effects of early experience and testosterone on song as a reinforcer. *Anim Behav.*, **20**, 430–5.

Stevenson-Hinde, J. (1983) Constraints on reinforcement. In Hinde, R. A. & Stevenson-Hinde, J. (eds.) *Constraints on Learning: Limitations and Predispositions*. London: Acad. Press.

Stevenson-Hinde, J. (1987) Towards a more open construct. In D. Kohnstamm (ed.) *Temperament discussed*. Lisse: Swets and Zeitlinger.

Stevenson-Hinde, J. & Hinde, R. A. (1986) Changes in associations between characteristics & interactions. In Plomin, R. & Dunn, J. (eds.) *The Study of Temperament*. Hillsdale, N. J.: Erlbaum.

Stevenson-Hinde, J., Hinde, R. A. & Simpson, A. E. (1986) Behavior at home & freindly or hostile behavior in preschool. In Olweus, D., Block, J. & Radke-Yarrow, M. (eds.) *Development of Antisocial & Prosocial behavior*. Orlando: Acad. Press.

Steward, J. (1949) Cultural causality & law. *Amer. Anthropologist*, **51**, 1–27.

Steward, J. H. (1968) Cultural Ecology. *In International Encyclopaedia of the Social Sciences*, **4**, 337–44.

Stokes, A. W. (1962) Agonistic behaviour among Blue Tits at a winter feeding station. *Behaviour*, **19**, 118–38.

Strathern, M. (1972) *Women in Between*. London: Seminar.

Strathern, M. (1976) An anthropological perspective. In Lloyd, B. B. & Archer, J. (eds.) *Exploring Sex Differences*. New York: Acad. Press.

Sullivan, H. S. (1938) The data of psychiatry. *Psychiatry*, **1**, 121–34.

Sullivan, H. S. (1953) *Conceptions of Modern Psychiatry*. New York: Norton.

Symons, D. (1979) *The Evolution of Human Sexuality*. Oxford: Oxford Univ. Press.

Tajfel, H. (1978) Contributions to Tajfel, H. (ed.) *Differentiation between Social Groups*. London: Acad. Press.

Tambiah, S. J. (1969) Animals are good to think and good to prohibit. *Ethology*, **8**, 423–59.

Teleki, G. (1973) *The Predatory Behavior of Wild Chimpanzees*. Lewisburg: Bucknell University Press.

Terrace, H. S. (1979) *Nim*. New York: Knopf.

Thomas, A. & Chess, S. (1980) *The Dynamics of Psychological Development*. New York: Brunner/Mazel.

Thomas, A. & Chess, S. (1982) Temperament and follow-up to adulthood. In *Temperamental Differences in Infants and Young Children*. Ciba Foundation Symposium **89**, 168–73. London: Pitman.

Thorpe, W. H. (1961) *Bird Song*. Cambridge: Cambridge Univ. Press.

Thorpe, W. H. & Jones, F. G. W. (1937) Olfactory conditioning and its relation to the problem of host selection. *Proc. Roy. Soc. B 124*, 56–81.

Tinbergen, N. (1963) On the aims and methods of ethology. *Z. Tierpsychol.*, **20**, 410–33.

Tinbergen, N., Impekoven, M. & Franck, D. (1967) An experiment on spacing-out as a defence against predation. *Behaviour*, **28**, 307–21.

Tinklenberg, J. R. & Ochberg, F. M. (1981) Patterns of adolescent violence. In Hamburg D. A. and Trudeau, M. B. (eds.) *Biobehavioral Aspects of Aggression*. New York: Liss.

Tizard, B. (1985) Social relationships between adults and young children, & their impact on intellectual functioning. In Hinde, R. A., Perret-Clermont, A.-N. & Stevenson-Hinde, J. (eds.) *Social Relationships & Cognitive Development*. Oxford: Oxford Univ. Press.

Touhey, J. C. (1972) Comparison of two dimensions of attitude similarity on heterosexual attraction. *Journal of Personality and Social Psychology*, **23**, 8–10.

Trivers, R. L. (1971) The evolution of reciprocal altruism. *Quart. Rev. Biol.*, **46**, 35–57.

Trivers, R. L. (1972) Parental investment and sexual selection. In B. Campbell (ed.) *Sexual Selection and the Descent of Man, 1871–1971*. Chicago: Aldine.

Trivers, R. L. (1974) Parent-offspring conflict. *Amer. Zool.*, **14**, 249–64.

Trivers, R. L. (1985) *Social Evolution*. Menlo Park, Calif.: Benjamin/Cummings.

Turke, P. W. & Betzig, L. L. (1985) Those who can do: wealth, status and reproductive success on Ifaluk. *Ethology and Sociobiology*, **6**, 79–87.

Ursin, H., Baade, E. & Levine, S. (1978) *Psychobiology of Stress*. New York: Acad. Press.

Vandenberg, S. G. (1967) Heredity factors in normal personality traits. *Adv. Biol. Psychiatry*, **9**, 65–104.

Vaughan, B. E., Egeland, B., Sroufe, L. A. & Waters, E. (1979) Individual differences in infant–mother attachment at 12 and 18 months: stability and change in families under stress. *Child Development*. **50**, 971–5.

Vayda, A. P. (1969) *Environment & Cultural Behavior*. New York: Natural History Press.

Vining, D. R. (1986) Social vs. reproductive success. *Behavioral and Brain Sciences*, **9**, 167–216.

Vygotsky, L. S. (1934) *Thought and Language*. Cambridge, Mass: M.I.T. Press.

Walster, E. H., Walster, G. W., Piliavin, J. & Schmidt, L. (1973). Playing hard to get: understanding an elusive phenomenon. *Journal of Personality and Social Psychology*, **26**, 113–21.

Watson, J. B. (1916) The place of the conditioned reflex in psychology. *Psychol. Rev.*, **23**, 89–116.

Wattenwyl, A. von & Zollinger, H. (1979) Color-term salience and neurophysiology of color vision. *Amer. Anthrop.* **81**, 279–88.

Weiss, L. & Lowenthal, M. F. (1975) Life-course perspective on friendship. In M. F. Lowenthal, M. Thurnher & D. Chirobag (eds.) *Four Stages of Life*. San Francisco: Jossey-Bass.

Westermarck, E. (1891) *The History of Human Marriage*. London: MacMillan.

Whiting, B. B. & Whiting, J. W. M. (1975) *Children of Six Cultures*. Cambridge, Mass: Harvard Univ. Press.

Williams, G. C. (1966) *Adaptation and Natural Selection*. Princeton, N. J.: Princeton Univ. Press.

Williams, J. E. & Best, D. L. (1982) *Measuring Sex Stereotypes*. Beverley Hills: Sage.

Williams, J. & Giles, H. (1978). The changing status of women in society. In M. Tajfel (ed.) *Differentiation between Social Groups*. London: Acad. Press.

Williams, K. B., Woodmansee, D. B. & Williams, J. E. (1977) Sex stereotypes and transactional analysis theory. *Transactional Analysis Journal*, **7**, 266–74.

Willner, L. A. & Martin, R. D. (1985) Some basic principles of mammalian sexual dimorphism. In J. Glesquiere, R. D. Martin & F. Newcombe (eds.) *Human Sexual Dimorphism. Sym. Soc. Study Human Biology*, **24**, 1–42.

Wilson, D. S. (1977) Structural demes and the evolution of group-advantageous traits. *Amer. Nat.*, **111**, 157–85.

Wilson, E. O. (1975) *Sociobiology*. Cambridge Mass: Harvard Univ. Press.

Wilson, E. O. (1978) *On Human Nature*. Cambridge, Mass: Harvard Univ. Press.

Wilson, E. O. (1984) *Biophilia*. Cambridge, Mass: Harvard Univ. Press.

Wilson, M. & Daly, M. (1985) Competitiveness, risk-taking & violence: the young male syndrome. *Ethology and Sociobiology*, **6**, 59–73.

Wittenberger, J. F. (1983) Tactics of mate choice. In P. Bateson (ed.) *Mate Choice*. Cambridge: Cambridge University Press.

Wolf, A. P. (1966) Childhood association, sexual attraction & the incest taboo. *Amer. Anthropologist*, **68**, 883–98.

Wolkind, S. N. (1974) The components of affectionless psychopathology in institutionalized children. *Journal of Child Psychology and Psychiatry*, **15**, 215–20.

Youniss, J. (1980) *Parents & Peers in Social Development*. Chicago: Univ. of Chicago Press.

Zahn-Waxler, C., Cummings, E. M., McKnew, D. H. & Radke-Yarrow, M. (1984) Altruism, aggression and social interactions in young children with a manic-depressive parent. *Child Dev.*, **55**, 112–22.

Subject index

Subject index

Name index

Name index